INFANT BAPTISM
AND THE
COVENANT OF GRACE

By the same author:

The Lord's Day
Man as Male and Female

INFANT BAPTISM
AND THE
COVENANT OF GRACE

an appraisal of the argument that
as infants were once circumcised,
so they should now be baptized

by
Paul K. Jewett

Professor of Systematic Theology,
Fuller Theological Seminary
and
The Young Life Summer Institute of Theology

William B. Eerdmans Publishing Company
Grand Rapids, Michigan

To My Friend William Starr
President of the Young Life Foundation
A Man and an Organization Dedicated to Bringing
Young People to that Decision for Christ
Confessed in Christian Baptism

Copyright © 1978 by Wm. B. Eerdmans Publishing Co.
255 Jefferson Ave. S.E., Grand Rapids, Mich. 49503

Reprinted December, 1980

Library of Congress Cataloging in Publication Data

Jewett, Paul King.
  Infant baptism and the covenant of grace.

  Includes bibliographical references.
  1. Infant baptism. I. Title.
BV813.2.J44   234'.1612   77-28329
ISBN 0-8028-1713-0

The quotation from Søren Kierkegaard, *The Point of View* (trans. by W. Lowrie, Oxford University Press, 1950) is reprinted by permission of the Oxford University Press.

The quotation from Søren Kierkegaard, *Attack Upon "Christendom"* (1854-1855), trans. with introduction by Walter Lowrie (copyright 1944 © 1974; rev. edn. 1968, Princeton Paperback) is reprinted by permission of Princeton University Press.

The quotation from Karl Barth, *Kirkliche Dogmatik*, IV, 4 (Zürich: TVZ Verlag, 1967) is reprinted by permission of TVZ Verlag, Zürich.

No doubt, I conceive, can now remain in the mind of any sober man, that those who raise controversies and contentions on the subject of infant baptism are presumptuous disturbers of the church of Christ.

— John Calvin, *Institutes of the Christian Religion*

If I thought it wrong to be a Baptist, I should give it up and become what I believed to be right. . . . If we could find infant baptism in the world of God, we would adopt it. It would help us out of a great difficulty, for it would take away from us that reproach which is attached to us—that we are odd and do not as other people do. But we have looked well through the Bible and cannot find it, and do not believe it is there; nor do we believe that others can find infant baptism in the Scriptures, unless they themselves first put it there.

—Charles Spurgeon, *Autobiography*

I venture the affirmation: the confusion into which Luther and Calvin and their respective disciples have tumbled head-long in this matter [infant baptism] is hopeless. One must concede to them that unlike the moderns they at least made a serious effort to find an answer to the burning dogmatic question. Yet one can only affirm that the relevant information which one obtains from them, and that in the decisive points, is as implausible as their exegesis is unsatisfying. Let anyone read chapters fifteen and sixteen of Book Four of the *Institutio* in order to convince himself where the great Calvin is sure of his subject and where he is not sure of it, but is patently nervous, involved in an exceedingly unperspicuous train of thought, scolding; where he lectures when he would convince, seeks a way in the fog which can lead him to no goal because he has none.

—Karl Barth, *Die Taufe*

The way in which Karl Barth slurs over this question [infant circumcision] is indeed the weakest point in his teaching on baptism. Even though it be conceded that the Reformers' grounds of proof in favor of infant baptism did not all hold water, yet at least this Reformation argument deserved greater attention. . . . For my part, I simply cannot see how Karl Barth can admit that baptism is the fulfillment of circumcision, yet on the decisive point, can deny the inner connection of the two and assert that circumcision is different, so that the fact that children were circumcised is without significance for the Christian practice of baptism.

—Oscar Cullmann, *Die Tauflehre*

CONTENTS

Part Three: BELIEVER BAPTISM DEFENDED AND EXPOUNDED IN TERMS OF COVENANT THEOLOGY

PREFACE

The subject of infant baptism is one about which it is easier to write voluminously than significantly. In the *Institutes of the Christian Religion*, John Calvin allotted twenty pages to the discussion of baptism in general, followed by thirty-eight pages defending infant baptism in particular as "perfectly consistent with the institution of Christ and the nature of the sign." How often his example has been imitated! As a result, the centuries have been flooded with books and the world with words on both sides of the question. Just to read this literature is a great chore, and much of it deserves to molder in oblivion. Yet theologians of the first rank have wrestled with the problem; and if their thoughts are not always edifying, they are nonetheless worthy of consideration.

This is true particularly because the debate over infant baptism is one out of which come implications involving the whole range of theology. Hence books concerned with the most basic theological questions sometimes touch on infant baptism. Emil Brunner's *Die Wahrheit als Begegnung*, for example, a book that probes the fundamental nature of theological truth in the light of the personal dimension, raises searching questions concerning the practice of infant baptism. In fact, these Uppsala lectures, delivered in 1938, signal the beginning of the contemporary challenge to the baptizing of infants, a challenge that could not be ignored when Karl Barth subsequently took up the argument in an address delivered in May 1943 to a group of theological students at a Swiss Alpine retreat on the lake of Thun.[1] One cannot, then, contain the discussion of infant baptism in a denominational corner sealed off from the universe of theological discourse; one can only strive to keep the complexity of the discussion from becoming, like Saul's armor to David, cumbersome and unwieldy.

The complexity of the discussion, in other words, is not altogether the fault of the theologians, the result of their supposed propensity for convoluted arguments. The question of whether the church should baptize infants is *intrinsically* complex, for it is impossible to do justice to it without bringing into the discussion the larger question of one's view of the sacraments in general. And one's view of the sacraments, their nature and efficacy, involves one's view of the whole matter of salvation, understood as God's gracious act of pardon and reconciliation mediated to the sinner in and through the community of the redeemed, the Christian church.

In the game of billiards, to use a mundane illustration, when all the balls are clustered together, even the experts may differ as to how they should be broken open; and the angle from which the player makes the crucial initial shot will determine how the game is played from then on. So it is with the discussion of infant baptism. The question, Should the church baptize infants? is really a cluster of questions. Therefore, the answer one gives to it can never be determined apart from the answer he gives to the several related questions mentioned above. To be specific, if one believes that baptism washes away the guilt of original sin, so that anyone departing this life without it is in danger of eternal damnation, he will have good reason to conclude that infants should be baptized. In fact, the question of infant baptism can hardly be raised within such a sacramental theology, since an affirmative answer is a foregone conclusion. All that

[1] *Die Kirchliche Lehre von der Taufe* (hereafter cited as *Die Taufe*). The reader will find complete publication documentation for each footnote citation in the bibliography at the end of the book.

can be seriously discussed is the abuse — never the use — of the institution.[2]

This is true not only for the Eastern Orthodox and Roman Catholics, but to a lesser extent for Anglicans (Episcopalians) and Lutherans as well. While contemporary spokesmen for these communions, especially Anglicans and Lutherans, eschew all "magical" formulations that echo a medieval doctrine of baptismal efficacy, there remains the deep and significant conviction that baptism is God's redemptive act, having a causative significance for the salvation of the one receiving the rite. Therefore, the question of the recipient's response of faith to the spoken word of grace can never be crucial in determining who is to be baptized.[3]

However, as one's theology of the sacraments moves toward the evangelical end of the spectrum, where hearing the gospel and responding by faith in Christ are essential prerequisites to baptism, the question of infant baptism becomes a real issue. According to evangelical thought, God does not save the child through baptism nor condemn the child who dies without baptism. If this much is granted, then the question can be seriously asked: Why should infants, who are incapable of either hearing or believing the gospel, yet receive the sacrament of baptism? Hence theologians in the Reformed, Presbyterian, and Free Church traditions, with an evangelical view of baptismal efficacy, are the ones who have given the most attention to this question. It was first in Switzerland, in the early days of the Reformation, that infant baptism was both challenged by the so-called Anabaptists

[2]In speaking of "sacramental" theology, I mean the view that regards the sacraments as inherently efficacious to mediate the inward grace (blessing) of which they are the outward sign. In the case of baptism, this view is known as "baptismal regeneration." Baptismal regeneration may be contrasted with the "evangelical" view of baptismal efficacy, according to which baptism "signifies and seals," but does not effect, the blessing of cleansing and renewal in Christ.

[3]See E. Schlink, *Die Lehre von der Taufe:* "The understanding of baptism as God's act or as man's act, that is, as the sign of man's own engagement before God, is the basic difference in baptismal theology which must finally determine one's answer to the question of infant baptism" (p. 140). This affirmation enjoys a much wider consensus than the Lutheran tradition for which Schlink speaks.

and defended by the leaders of the Reformed party. And in modern times it is within the Reformed communions that one finds both the most penetrating critique and the most vigorous defense of infant baptism.[4]

In the interest, therefore, of limiting the scope of the discussion, I have assumed a great deal at the outset, namely, that the evangelical view of baptismal efficacy is the more biblical view. Not that I believe baptism to be man's act in contrast to God's; but that God acts in baptism in such a manner as to *engage* the one baptized. In other words, the outward rite is best understood, in my judgment, as a cognitive-symbolic one rather than a causative-sacramental one. To some this may appear to be too simplistic — an attempt to be rid of the Gordian knot of infant baptism by arbitrarily cutting it. Actually, it is an effort to define how I understand the knot to be tied. In any case, given this assumption, I shall be principally concerned in this study with the argument for infant baptism in the Reformed and Calvinistic tradition, where the theological issues have been most radically joined. I shall pay less attention to Lutheran and Anglican writers and virtually none to Roman Catholics and Eastern Orthodox.[5] Compensation for this loss of breadth in the discussion will, I trust, be made in its depth.

Having charted my location on the spectrum of theological discourse, it remains only to note problems of a more practical sort. I refer to the polemical character of the ensuing discussion. Not to take sides on the question of infant baptism reduces baptism to the indifferent level of a pious custom, without even the necessity of precept. But if one does take sides, he devotes himself to an effort more palatable to former ages of controversy than to the present age of ecumenical tolerance. And if one argues for the baptism of

---

[4]The four authors quoted above — Calvin, Spurgeon, Barth, Cullmann — are all in the Reformed tradition.

[5]For a careful and comprehensive overview of the whole contemporary discussion of infant baptism, not only in the Reformed and Free Church traditions but in the Roman Catholic, Lutheran, and Anglican traditions as well, see Dale Moody, *Baptism: Foundation for Christian Unity.*

believers only, one finds himself in a special way on a cleft stick. Taking such a position, he must not only attack what the majority defends and negate what the majority affirms, but the very invoking of the negation pits him against centuries of ecclesiastical usage and, seemingly, against children themselves. He becomes a kind of misanthrope — though charity does not often press this point in our day. (Witness, however, the continuing complaint in the literature that those who argue for believer baptism allow no place for children in the church.) Time and the majority have never made any affirmation true, but they can make it *seem* true, especially when it is as pleasing as the affirmation that children should be embraced with their parents in the church by means of baptism.

Finally, I have personally found the task of framing an answer to the question of infant baptism difficult because I cannot persuade myself that the truth is all on the Baptist side. Not only has the Baptist argument against infant baptism sometimes been plagued with quackery and puffery, but Baptist practice is sometimes marred by a narrow exclusivism. Though the traditional Baptist usage of closed communion, first challenged so eloquently by Robert Hall,[6] has given way in our day to the more ultimate demands of Christian charity and unity, the practice of closed membership is still widely insisted on in Baptist circles. This, to me, is very unfortunate; for though the defense of infant baptism may not be a good cause, it does not follow that the people who make this defense are not good Christians and worthy members of the Christian church. To have the conviction that baptism should not be administered to infants is quite different from the intolerance that excludes all dissent from the fellowship of the church. Polemical theology that would serve a good purpose must be irenic, not divisive.

To probe the depth of the Paedobaptist argument, therefore, should make the Baptist, if not less a Baptist, yet more tolerant of his brethren. And if this is true for the Baptist, it is surely no less true for the Paedobaptist. It is with this convic-

[6]"On Communion and Baptism," *Miscellaneous Writings.*

AN ABSTRACT OF THE ARGUMENT

The consent of the Fathers, which has played a significant part in the traditional Paedobaptist apologetic as well as in the contemporary literature, marks the point of departure in this study. Beginning with Augustine and moving back to New Testament times, I have evaluated each relevant passage from ancient Christian sources and have reached the conclusion that the practice of infant baptism appears in the Western Church about the time of Irenaeus (A.D. 180) and in the Eastern Church somewhat later, but prior to Origen (A.D. 233). Items that are not always considered by Paedobaptists, such as the distinction between infants and children, the silence of certain crucial witnesses, the practice of infant communion, and the rise of the catechumenate, conclude this phase of the discussion.

Turning to the apostolic age, I touch on the biblical concept of solidarity in sin and grace, so essential for the understanding of salvation history; and I consider household baptisms in the New Testament for their bearing on the question. Having reviewed and questioned the evidence that the Christian rite of initiation was originally administered to whole families, I then give attention to Jesus' blessing the children who were brought to him, together with other allusions to children in the New Testament that have been thought to imply an early practice of infant baptism.

Finally, the discussion turns to the thesis that early Christian and Johannine baptism were modeled after the

Jewish custom of baptizing proselytes with their children. I have urged both the difficult question of dating the beginning of this Jewish usage and, more especially, significant differences between Jewish proselyte baptism and Johannine-Christian baptism against the conclusions commonly drawn by Paedobaptists. This historical portion of the study concludes with comments on the methodology employed and the results claimed by Paedobaptists.

The theological question, anticipated in the historical section, constitutes the second and major portion of the study. Taking leave of those arguments for the baptism of infants which are theologically grounded in a sacramentalist view of baptismal efficacy, I then give close attention to the so-called argument from the covenant, according to which baptism takes the place of circumcision as the covenant sign and is therefore to be administered to infants. Having reviewed the statement of the argument in the classical confessions, and having elaborated its content, I then make the claim that this argument involves the fundamental error of failing to recognize the historical character of revelation. The untenable result of this error, wherein the New Testament is read as though it were the Old and the Old as though it were the New, is illustrated by a review of the theocratic approach to church and state, the "halfway covenant" experiment in New England, and the Paedobaptist exposition of certain pivotal New Testament passages.

Having charged the Paedobaptist argument with an error in biblical theology, I then turn to two problems of dogmatic theology which result from this error and which further perplex the Paedobaptist position. The first is the contradiction between the definition of baptism as the sacrament of repentance and faith and the insistence that it pertains to infants who do not and cannot repent and believe the gospel. I discuss efforts to solve this problem in the various Paedobaptist traditions, with special attention to the view that one's baptism is complete only when one ratifies personally the faith confessed for him by his proxies at the time of his baptism. The second problem of a dogmatic sort to be confronted concerns the withholding of the Lord's Supper from those who have received the covenant sign of baptism in infancy until such time as they shall make a personal confession of faith. I argue that such a procedure is palpably inconsistent: one should espouse either believer baptism or infant communion. Paedobaptists, to the contrary, both Roman Catholic and Protestant, espouse neither. I close this theological section with strictures on certain aspects of the Paedobaptist argument which I deem unworthy, especially the diversity, prolixity, and sentimentalism with which it is sometimes compromised.

The entire discussion concludes with an apology for the position of believer baptism. I review the various weaknesses — real and alleged — to which this position is susceptible, and make an effort to frame a theological structure that will do justice to the profound truths contained in both the Paedobaptist understanding of the covenant (so-called covenant theology, to which the author is committed) and the Baptist practice of giving baptism to those, and those only, who personally confess faith in Christ as Lord and Savior.

Part One:
A CONSIDERATION
OF THE
HISTORICAL QUESTION

INFANT BAPTISM
AND THE PRACTICE
OF THE ANCIENT CHURCH

A. INTRODUCTION

On Thursday, January 29, 1523, six hundred people gathered in the town hall at Zurich, Switzerland, to hear Huldreich Zwingli and the Roman Catholic authorities debate the nature of the Christian religion. Seated at a table innocent of the woodcarver's art, with the Latin, Greek, and Hebrew Bibles open before him, Zwingli defended his views by appealing to the text of Scripture. The vicar of the bishop of Constance, with judicious modesty, declined to return the argument, and the city council resolved that no heresy had been demonstrated against the defendant. He was, therefore, "to continue to preach the holy gospel as hithertofore . . . until he was better informed."

This striking victory in debate inspired Zwingli's followers to action. Priests took wives from the Oetenback nunnery, administered baptism in the vernacular, and condemned the mass as a superstition. A group of enthusiasts toppled a great wooden crucifix in Stadelhofen; and radicalism, which Zwingli feared as emphatically as he despised the superstition which provoked it, reared its ugly, amorphous head.

The result was a second disputation (October 26, 1523) in which 350 clergymen and doctors of theology debated the issues. As the spectrum of opinion became clear, Zwingli found himself opposed by both the moderates, who wanted to step softly, and the radicals, who wanted to blast the trumpet of judgment until the walls of popery came tumbling down. In the resulting compromise, a commission was set up to enlighten the people until they should be ready for further reform. The "idol-stormers" were banished from the canton for their pains.

Disappointed that the Reformer had not taken more drastic action, about fifteen of Zwingli's followers separated themselves from the established church under the leadership of Conrad Grebel, scion of one of the first families of Zurich. They conducted their own services of worship as "brethren" in the house of "Mother Manz" and in other private dwellings in the environs of Zurich. Though they dissented from the consensus on several matters, it was their opposition to infant baptism that provoked the greatest scandal. At a public disputation in January of 1525, Zwingli, who had previously doubted the expediency of the practice, committed himself to it with arguments which we will consider in due course. The city council ordered Grebel and his followers (called Anabaptists)[1] to cease holding separate meetings and declared that parents should present their children for baptism or leave the canton permanently. The Anabaptists refused to submit, and thereby hangs our tale.

Zwingli — and those agreeing with him — argued for infant baptism principally from Scripture. But they also appealed to history as testifying to the usage from apostolic times. Even Calvin, who of all the Reformers tended to sweep away with the heaviest broom what time had built upon the apostolic foundations, fulminated thus:

> What the Anabaptists circulate among the uninformed multitude, that after the resurrection of Christ a long series of years passed, in which infant baptism was unknown, is shamefully contrary to the truth, for there is no ancient writer who does not refer its origin, as a matter of certainty, to the age of the apostles.[2]

The older directories of Reformed discipline specify that

---

[1] From the Greek, ἀναβαπτίζω, to "baptize again," since those Swiss who first received baptism as believers had already been baptized as infants.

[2] *The Institutes of the Christian Religion*, IV, vii, 16 (hereafter cited as *Institutes*).

whenever proselytes from Anabaptism are received into communion, they shall be made to acknowledge the baptism of infants as founded not only on Scripture but also on the perpetual practice of the church.

As time went on, this "argument from history" began to wane, especially with the rise of critical, historical research into the source documents of early Christianity. Adolf von Harnack declared that there is no evidence for the practice of infant baptism before the end of the second century, an opinion which many scholars have ventured since his monumental researches were first published.[3] In more recent times, however, Joachim Jeremias has adorned the argument from the *consensus Patrum* with such erudite and judicious learning as to infuse Paedobaptist ranks with a new confidence in the old claim that infant baptism may be traced back through Christian history to the apostles themselves. "The whole of the early church," proclaimed the members of the Special Commission on Baptism of the Presbyterian Church of Scotland in 1955 (Professor T. F. Torrance, convener), "was unanimous about infant baptism in the church. ... The unanimous view of the ancient Catholic church predisposes us to regard infant baptism as the unchallenged practice of the Christian church from the very beginning."[4]

Confronted with this argument from ancient custom, early Baptists used to remind their Paedobaptist brethren that subjects of the triple crown are fond of tradition, and that it ill becomes a Protestant to cry, "The Fathers, the Fathers." Yet no one wants to admit that the church has *always* practiced otherwise than he does in a matter as important as baptism. If, then, there is good evidence that Christians have baptized their children "from the beginning," no affirmation

---

[3]*Die Mission und Ausbreitung des Christentums in den ersten drei Jahrhunderten*, p. 399. Barth complains that the Liberals, who have remained Paedobaptists from Schleiermacher on, have done so by abandoning that liberty of mind which they display freely enough regarding the rest of the tradition of the church (*Die Taufe*, p. 36).

[4]As quoted by R.G. Bratcher, "Church of Scotland Report on Baptism," *Review and Expositor*, April 1957, p. 206. The original report, written in 1955, was revised and published under the title *The Biblical Doctrine of Baptism*.

of the "sufficiency of Scripture" over against ecclesiastical tradition will ever alter this stubborn fact. To admit that infant baptism has been practiced *ever since* the apostles lived, while insisting that it was not *while* they lived, is a highly implausible hypothesis, to say the least. Knowing as we do the occasional character of the New Testament documents, if it can be shown that "infant baptism was the unanimous view of the ancient Catholic church," this creates a strong probability that it is at least *implicit* in the teaching of the New Testament itself; and this is all that Paedobaptists have argued, for admittedly there is no *explicit* instance of infant baptism recorded there.

But should a candid evaluation of the evidence create doubts about the ancient pedigree of infant baptism, then, by the same token, a stone has fallen from the arch of the Paedobaptist argument; a tremor has shaken the edifice. If the Baptist may not contemn the argument from history, neither may the Paedobaptists ignore the loss of it. As the adage has it, what is sauce for the goose is sauce for the gander.

B. INFANT BAPTISM IN THE WESTERN CHURCH

1. Augustine, A.D. 400

The stream of evidence for infant baptism, like the waters of Ezekiel — first to the ankles, then to the knees, then to the loins — becomes, by the age of Augustine, "waters to swim in, a river that cannot be passed over." Though the good bishop was not himself baptized until after his conversion, by his day the practice of baptizing infants could fairly claim the universal suffrage of the church catholic. Entering the stream at this point, we shall seek to trace it back to its fountainhead.

Although the testimony of Augustine in favor of infant baptism would fill several pages of fine print, for our present purpose we need only consider his claim that the usage rests on apostolic authority.

If anyone should ask for divine authority in this matter, though that which the whole church practices and which has not been instituted by councils — but was ever in use — is very reasonably believed to be no other than a thing delivered by authority of the apostles, yet we may besides take a true estimate, how much the sacrament of baptism does avail infants, by the circumcision which God's former people received.[5]

There are other passages like this in Augustine, but the language is generally reined and the evidence wanting when it comes to giving infant baptism apostolic sanction. Though it is a usage which is "from the beginning"; though it is "what the church always taught"; though it is, therefore, a "reasonable belief" that it came from the apostles — he never cites by name anyone who teaches it earlier than Cyprian (A.D. 251). It is also worthy of note that Augustine makes similar claims for apostolic authority for the practice of infant communion.

The Christians of Africa do well to call baptism itself, one's salvation, and the sacrament of Christ's body, one's life. From whence is this, but, as I suppose, from that *ancient and apostolical tradition,* by which the churches of Christ do naturally hold that without baptism and partaking of the Lord's table, none can come either to the kingdom of God, or to salvation and eternal life . . . ? If then, as so many divine testimonies do agree, neither salvation nor eternal life is to be hoped for by any, without baptism and the body and blood of

[5] *De baptismo, contra Donatistas* (A.D. 400), IV, xxii-xxiv, as quoted in W. Wall, *The History of Infant Baptism,* I, 159. Wall's *History* first appeared in 1705. It is a prodigious monument to patient labor containing virtually all the relevant passages on infant baptism found in the writings of the first four centuries. The original texts are given in context, with a translation and copious notes furnished by the author. We are genuinely grateful to the good vicar — pastor of one parish for fifty-three years! — who pioneered the way through the jungle of Greek and Latin syntax confronting every student of patristics. We shall follow him in it, taking the liberty to modernize his translation in a very minor way in the interest of readability. We shall use either the London edition of Griffth or, as above, the Oxford edition of 1862. The latter contains the *Reflections on Wall* by Dr. John Gale, a precocious young Baptist scholar whose zeal was not without knowledge, though sometimes without restraint. The most exhaustive list of patristic sources ever published, to our knowledge, including some items not found in Wall, is provided by the more recent study of Joachim Jeremias, *Die Kindertaufe in den Ersten vier Jahrhunderten.* The dating of sources given in the present study conforms to that of Jeremias.

our Lord, *it is in vain promised to infants without them.*[6]

Unless one is willing to accept as apostolic the Eastern usage of communicating infants, statements such as this must be discounted, a concession which considerably abates, if it does not destroy, the force of Augustine's appeal to apostolic authority for infant baptism.

2. *Cyprian*, A.D. *251-253*

Moving up the stream of Christian history toward its source, we take for our next witness Cyprian, the bishop of Carthage. Cyprian asked the delegates at a church council (A.D. 251 or 253) whether or not they felt infant baptism should be delayed until the eighth day. The discussion of this detail was occasioned by a letter from a rural bishop, Fidus, who was of the opinion that such a delay was to be observed after the analogy of circumcision in the Old Testament (Gen. 17:12). The judgment of the council is rendered in a letter from Cyprian to Fidus, charming in its simplicity if not convincing in its theological profoundness. In this first defense of infant baptism ever written, Cyprian argues that the growth of the body in aging may make a difference to the world but not to God, who bestows his heavenly grace equally upon all, infants as well as adults. Therefore, we should grant the grace of baptism to one at birth, not delaying even for so brief a time as eight days, lest in so doing we expose the soul of the child to the risk of eternal perdition.

Since our present task is to appraise the historical pedigree of, rather than evaluate the theological arguments for, infant baptism, we need not tarry over the contents of this epistle. Suffice to say that it comes from the middle of the third century and represents the consensus of sixty-six bishops in North Africa. Because they sat in council only one hundred fifty years after the apostles, it might seem there could be no accounting for their unanimity were the usage of infant baptism not apostolic in its origins.

[6]*De peccatorum meritis*, I, xxxiv, as quoted by Wall, *History*, I, 633 (italics mine).

It must not be forgotten, however, that the earliest ages of Christian history are marked not only by rapid expansion, but also by rapid change. For example, the very episcopal office these bishops held was unknown in the year A.D. 100: in the apostolic age there were no monarchical bishops; yet in the year A.D. 251 sixty-six of them were convened in North Africa. If the office of bishop was unknown to the apostles, it is surely possible that the practice of baptizing infants, which these bishops approved, was also unknown in apostolic times. Furthermore, though we may consider Fidus' inquiry about the delay of baptism a reflection of a rural parson's ignorance, it is puzzling that someone as informed as Cyprian should have discussed the matter at such length in a council of church bishops. If infant baptism were indeed practiced from apostolic times, would the question of *when* it should be given require so much deliberation after nearly two hundred years? Nor should one overlook the fact that the bishops not only decided *when* infants should be baptized but also elaborated at length on the reasons *why*. And in setting forth these reasons they made no appeal to an earlier tradition; rather their epistle has the aura of a pioneering endeavor on the part of men who were thinking their way through a subject for the first time.[7]

One may suppose, then, that this Carthaginian council constituted the first official effort of the church to give a theological basis to a practice widely accepted though not of ancient pedigree. One is fortified in this surmise by Cyprian's reference to infant communion as the custom in Carthage, in a document (*De lapis*, 9, 25) written in the same year the council was convened. If we can be sure that the bishop had no authority from the apostles to *communicate* infants — and it is the consensus of scholarship that he did not — we may suspect that he had no more authority from them to *baptize* infants either, though he and his fellow bishops defended the custom as the received usage of the church.

[7]To feel the force of this last observation, one should read the entire text, omitted here in the interest of brevity. See Wall, *History*, I, 63-64. The original is Cyprian, *Epist.* 64 (Panelii ed. 59), *ad Fidum*.

3. *Tertullian*, A.D. *200-206*

Christianity was probably established in proconsular Africa by the year A.D. 100. The most plausible theory is that it spread, by a kind of mitosis, from Italy, for there was constant intercourse between North Africa and the Italian mainland. The first great figure to emerge in this distinctively Western church was Tertullian. With him we are close to the headwaters of the stream of African Christianity, and the writings of this fiery father of Latin theology are our earliest documents for ascertaining the belief and practice of the church in this land of sand and sun. Indeed, it is perhaps not too much to say that Tertullian is the star witness in the infant baptism debate, so far as the patristic evidence is concerned. What he says about infant baptism would hardly fill a page, but the comments stimulated by these remarks would fill a book.

In a treatise on baptism, written between A.D. 200 and 206, Tertullian questions the wisdom of giving baptism to infants. We quote his remarks *in extenso*:

> But they whose duty it is to administer baptism, are to know that it must not be given rashly. 'Give to everyone that asks you' has its proper subject, and relates to almsgiving. But that command is rather here to be considered, 'Give not that which is holy to dogs, neither cast your pearls before swine'; or again, 'Lay hands suddenly on no man, neither be partaker of other men's faults. . . .' Therefore, according to everyone's condition and disposition, and also his age, the delaying of baptism is more profitable, especially in the case of little children. For why is it necessary — if [baptism itself] is not necessary — that the sponsors should be thrust into danger. For they may either fail of their promise by death, or they may be mistaken by a child's proving of wicked disposition.
>
> Our Lord says, indeed, 'Do not forbid them to come to me.' Therefore, let them come when they are grown up; let them come when they understand, when they are instructed whither it is that they come; let them be made Christians when they can know Christ. What need their guiltless age make such haste to the forgiveness of sins? Men will proceed more warily in worldly things. And he that should not have earthly goods committed to him, yet shall have heavenly? Let them know how to desire this salvation, that you may appear to have given to one that asks. . . .
>
> For no less reason unmarried persons ought to be kept off,

who are likely to come into temptation; those as well that never were married, upon account of their coming to ripeness, as those in widowhood, for the miss of their partner; until they either marry or be confirmed in continence. They that understand the weight of baptism will rather dread the receiving of it, than the delaying of it. An entire faith is secure of salvation! *(Fides integra secura est de salute!)*[8]

There can be no doubt that this passage is significant for our inquiry, for it constitutes the earliest express mention of infant baptism in the history of the church. That it should be mentioned by way of opposition, and by no less an authority than Tertullian, has understandably caused Paedobaptists no little concern. They prefer to say that Tertullian, two hundred years after Christ, is the first to speak *against* infant baptism, as though his were the only nay in two centuries of ayes! Some have even implied that as a heretical innovator, a man of singular opinions "who fell into great and monstrous errors of the faith" (Wall), he is in this passage raising his voice against a practice which he knew to be prevalent and commonly accepted by the church at large.[9] But the noble African's reputation as a Christian and theologian scarcely needs defense against such beggarly invective.

Others have suggested that Tertullian's reservations concerning infant baptism grew out of a fear that the baptized infant would have no more laver of cleansing for postbaptismal transgressions. This, it is further suggested, was due to the superstitious idea that baptism is accompanied by the remission of all past sins.[10] Such a superstition may indeed by found in the Fathers, but it is most clearly seen in those who *defend* infant baptism (witness the letter to Fidus noted above), not in Tertullian, who opposes it. In fact, Tertullian roundly repudiates the thought that remission of sin is effected by baptism as such in Chapter Six of his *De paenitentis*. Still others have even gone so far as to suggest that

[8]*De baptismo*, ch. xviii.

[9]Against this older Paedobaptist polemic it may be observed that critical opinion regards Tertullian's treatise on baptism (the first ever written) to be an early, ante-Montanist piece, in which he speaks as a Catholic not only in theology, but also by affiliation.

[10]See B.B. Warfield, "The Polemics of Infant Baptism," *Studies in Theology*, p. 403.

Tertullian really approves infant baptism and that his scruples against it, expressed in the passage quoted, apply only to the infants of heathen converts.[11]

Tertullian's fundamental point is clear enough: it is better to wait until one is ready to live what he professes in baptism than to repudiate that profession by subsequent wickedness of life. In our baptism we renounce "the devil, his pomp and his angels"; it behooves us, then, to stop and think before we receive the rite. Hence the advice is given that one postpone his baptism until the season of youthful temptation be passed. Though such advice may be censured as a pious extreme, it can hardly be condemned as a pernicious superstition. While Tertullian's ascetic tendencies undoubtedly reveal an indefensible rigor in matters pertaining to sex, those solemn words at the close of his *De baptismo* (18), ". . . they that understand the weight of baptism will rather dread the receiving of it than the delaying of it," are a wholesome antidote to the practice, all too common in subsequent ages of Christian history, of administering baptism indiscriminately to infants and minor children.

To summarize the evidence in the African church, Augustine, about A.D. 400, assumes infant baptism as an apostolic usage; Cyprian, about A.D. 250, assumes it as a proper usage; while Tertullian, about A.D. 200, challenges the usage as of doubtful consequence. These items are the joints and marrow of our matter so far.

4. *Hippolytus*, A.D. 215-217

Leaving Africa, we turn next to Italy, where there is considerable testimony to infant baptism dating from the late third and fourth centuries. However, since infant baptism is clearly witnessed in North Africa at the beginning of the third century, there appears little to be gained for our pur-

[11]See Joachim Jeremias, *Die Kindertaufe in den Ersten vier Jahrhunderten*. Jeremias subsequently relaxed this conviction, however, under the searching criticism of Kurt Aland. See the latter's *Die Säuglingstaufe im Neuen Testament und in der Alten Kirche*. For a brief summary of this aspect of the debate, especially as it bears on the interpretation of Tertullian's *De Anima*, chs. xxxvii-xl, see Dale Moody, *Baptism*, pp. 150-151.

poses from this later testimony. But there is one document over which we must pause. It bears the significant name *The Apostolic Tradition*. Written by the schismatic bishop Hippolytus after he had left the established church to be consecrated bishop of the "true church" of Rome, *The Apostolic Tradition* is a handbook of rules for the organization of the church, the ordination of the clergy, the conduct of worship, and the administration of the sacraments. If the church of Rome understandably showed little respect for Hippolytus' work, the Eastern churches accepted it as having high authority, though the many Oriental versions are inflated with subsequent additions. In the Latin and Sahidic versions there is a rubric concerning the order in which the candidates shall be baptized, which reads as follows:

> And first baptize the little ones; and if they can speak for themselves, they shall do so; if not, their parents or other relatives shall speak for them. Then baptize the men, and last of all the women; they must first loosen their hair and put aside any gold or silver ornaments that they are wearing: let no one take any alien thing down to the water with them.[12]

The complexity of the historical setting has evoked a variety of opinions on the value of this datum. No one, of course, supposes that this "Apostolic Tradition" literally inscribes the teaching of the apostles, and some would dispute the certainty with which we may attribute this particular portion of the liturgy even to the time of Hippolytus. All that precedes and follows contemplates responsible persons as the only proper subjects of baptism. Each candidate must be a catechumen of three years' instruction, exemplary in life; he must prepare himself by bathing, fasting, and prayer; submit himself to exorcism and sealing; spend his last night in vigil, listening to reading and instruction; and he must bring with him to the "baptismal tank" his offering for his first Eucharist. On this backdrop, the reference to the baptism of little ones who cannot speak for themselves — that is, confess their faith — is so unexpected that some scholars

---

[12]*The Apostolic Tradition of Hippolytus*, p. 45. "... last of all the women," to whom the risen Lord appeared *first*, the same Lord who reminded us that many who are first shall be last and the last first (Mt. 19:30).

suspect a later interpolation, which is indeed pausible.[13]

This possibility would be heightened to probability, almost to certainty, if the reference to infants were found solely in the tertiary tradition of the Ethiopic version. The present text, however, seems secure; and indeed, if Tertullian knows of the sponsoring of infants in baptism as early as A.D. 205 in Africa, one should not be surprised that the practice is allowed in Rome about A.D. 217, when Hippolytus composed his *Apostolic Tradition*.

Granting the authenticity of this rubric, more difficult to decide is the question, How long had this baptism of little ones been the custom in Rome when Hippolytus wrote? Jeremias, anxious to close with the apostles, assures us that Hippolytus here assumes infant baptism as an undisputed usage that required no justification; all the rules and regulations for adults to qualify for baptism are simply waived. Therefore, it must have been a long-established practice in the Roman church when Hippolytus composed his treatise. Jeremias further presses the point that Hippolytus, as the title of his work implies, is concerned not with introducing new rules but preserving the old, the "apostolic" tradition, which makes his witness to infant baptism as significant in the West as is Origen's in the East.[14] Kurt Aland, on the other hand, underscores the countertruth that ancient church orders were contemporary documents, basically concerned to fix for the future the usage prevailing at the time of their composition by appealing to past tradition. Hence their witness has little merit in retrospect.[15]

Probably the truth in this instance is to be found somewhere between confidence and skepticism regarding Hippolytus' testimony. It must be remembered that he was the learned and obstinate champion of tradition against Callistus, Rome's innovative bishop, and that his purpose in recording these rules was to preserve his own flock in Rome, and all the true church throughout the world, from "lapse or error"

[13] See K. Aland, *Die Säuglingstaufe im Neuen Testament und in der Alten Kirche*, pp. 25-26.
[14] *Die Kindertaufe*, pp. 86, 88.
[15] *Die Säuglingstaufe*, p. 26.

which had "recently occurred" (1:4). Much of what he writes must reflect the practice of the church during his early tenure in the presbytery of Rome (he was made a presbyter under Zephrinus sometime before A.D. 200) and may therefore reflect the practice of thirty to fifty years prior to his writing. In other words, infant baptism may have been known in Rome even before A.D. 200. It is in this period of Hippolytus' youth — A.D. 180 to 200 — that the mists close in on the witness to infant baptism in the ancient church generally; but to fill out this picture we must look to Irenaeus of Gaul.

5. Irenaeus, after A.D. 180

Turning to the church in Gaul, we find in Irenaeus, bishop of Lyons and mentor of Hippolytus, a crucial witness. The first theologian of the church — if not in eminence, surely in time — Irenaeus was born in Smyrna and acquainted with Polycarp, a disciple of John the Apostle. Obviously, then, a clear statement from his pen as to the apostolic origin of infant baptism would be most helpful. Unfortunately, we have no such. Toward the end of his life, Irenaeus produced his *magnum opus,* a five-volume tome written to help a friend refute the doctrines of Valentinus, the Gnostic heretic. Before it was finished, the work had grown under his nervous hand to a full-orbed system of Christian theology. In this mine of information about the early Catholic faith, there is one passage that is usually thought to reflect the practice of infant baptism. Observing that Jesus passed through all the stages of human development in the course of his life, Irenaeus says:

> he came to save all persons by himself; all, I mean, who by him are regenerated unto God: infants and little ones and children and youths and older persons. Therefore, he went through the several ages; to little ones he was made a little one, sanctifying those of that age . . . to youths he was a youth, becoming an example to youths and thus sanctifying them to the Lord. . . .[16]

By the fourth century, the phrase "regenerated unto

---

[16]*Adv. Haer.,* III, xxii, 4, *The Ante-Nicene Fathers,* 1885-96, I, 455.

God" (*renascunter in Deum*), which Irenaeus uses here of infants and others, was rather commonly employed of baptism. Whether or not Irenaeus so uses it is difficult to say. There are places where he speaks of "baptism" as the "laver of regeneration," yet he always associates it with faith. In the above passage, however, there is no mention of either faith or baptism. It is a singular confidence, therefore, which Paedobaptists have shown in affirming, without qualification, that Irenaeus is speaking here of infant baptism.

If it is true that when Irenaeus speaks of Christ's "regenerating unto God" he always has baptism in view, then he entertained some extraordinary conceits. He believed — on this hypothesis — that Christ baptized all the patriarchs from Adam down (*Adv. Haer.*, III, xxii, 4); that the Virgin Mary administers baptism through faith (IV, xxxiii, 4); and that her pure womb baptizes men unto God (IV, xxxiii, 11). Such absurdities show that simply to equate "regeneration to God" with "baptism" in the vocabulary of Irenaeus is too facile and thus unconvincing.

When Irenaeus uses the formula "regenerated unto God," he seems to include what happens at baptism; but baptism does not include everything he means by "regenerated unto God." The two cannot simply be equated. Were we to venture a general interpretation, it appears that for Irenaeus Christ regenerates us unto God in that he is born into our race and thus brings our humanity into a new relationship with God. Restoring it to communion with God, summing it up anew in himself as the second Adam, Christ becomes the regenerator of mankind. This is true for all — infants, children, and adults — since he himself, by birth of the Virgin, became an infant, a child, and an adult. It is true even of the ancient Fathers who lived before his advent, for he descended to them after his crucifixion to proclaim his triumph in the realm of the dead. In some instances this renewal is mediated through baptism; but there is no compelling reason to suppose in a given passage where Irenaeus employs the phrase "regenerated unto God," that he is thinking of baptism, unless he says so. The most that can be supposed is that he *may* have had baptism in mind when he speaks of Christ's regenerating little children and infants.

We have lingered over a line in Irenaeus, not that we might arraign the ordinary Paedobaptist interpretation as unthinkable, nor applaud the anti-Paedobaptist interpretation as incontrovertible, but rather to demonstrate with what caution one must appraise such testimony. The year A.D. 180 brings us, then, to the verge of our quest for infant baptism in the Western church; and the evidence is illusive. Perhaps we have here the first "allusion" to infant baptism in any Christian writer, or at least an expression of certain ideas "out of which infant baptism arose and which procured for it at length a universal recognition."[17] But such evidence is far from conclusive.

6. *Aristides*, A.D. *117-138*

The historical pedigree of infant baptism, threatened by ambiguity in the text of Irenaeus, has been timidly divined by some Paedobaptists in a passing remark of the Athenian apologist Aristides, who wrote during the reign of the emperor Hadrian (A.D. 117-138). Noting that Aristides disclaims the purpose of elaborating the doctrine in order that he may enlarge on the ethics of the Christian community, Jeremias sees a tacit allusion to baptism in his use of the phrase "to thank God." Such a conclusion, here as in the case of Irenaeus, depends on whether or not a given expression is construed to betray an underlying meaning. "To thank God," it is suggested, may be a liturgical usage associated with baptism. In his *Apology* (XVII, 4), Aristides says:

> And when it happens that one of them [a heathen] is converted, he abases himself before the Christians because of the things he has done and *thanks God*, in that he says, I have committed them in ignorance. And he cleanses his heart and his sins are forgiven him.[18]

---

[17] See A. Neander, *General History of the Christian Religion and Church*, I, 311.

[18] Jeremias, *Die Kindertaufe*, p. 82, from Aristides, *Apologia*, 15, 11 (Jeremias' italics).

Since in all the early Christian writers the grace of cleansing and pardon is joined with the outward rite of a bath in water, in this passage we may — possibly — trace the image of baptism. But if we see "baptism" when a heathen convert "thanks God" and is cleansed and forgiven, may we not, reasons Jeremias, see *infant* baptism when Aristides puts the same phrase in the mouth of Christians at the birth of a child?

> However, when a child is born to them, they [the Christians] thank God; but if it should die at a very early age, they thank him exceedingly, because it has departed this world without sin.[19]

Having descried a possible allusion to baptism in this passage, Jeremias supposes that the sinless departure of the dying infant, for which these early Christians uttered a double thanksgiving, was secured not by the native innocence of the child but by the gift of forgiveness in its baptism. But how likely is such a suggestion? Since Aristides is writing long before the debate between Augustine and Pelagius over original sin, Jeremias' argument seems more ingenious than substantial. Forsaking the assurance with which Irenaeus' phrase "regenerate unto God" is claimed exclusively for baptism, he admits that Aristides' fondness for the expression "to thank God" leads the apologist to use it in situations which can having nothing to do with baptism, as when he employs it to characterize morning prayers and grace at meals (XV, 10). Since it is Aristides' favorite expression to describe how people regularly act after they become Christians and forsake their former sins — when they rise in the morning, gather at table, rejoice in the birth of a child, hope in the sorrow of death — one may style the phrase "to thank God" as "liturgical" if he will; but clearly baptism claims no exclusive property in this "liturgy of thanksgiving" in the mind of Aristides.

[19]*Ibid.*, p. 83.

C. INFANT BAPTISM IN THE EASTERN CHURCH

1. Introduction

One might expect that tradition would preserve the evidence for infant baptism in the Eastern church — if the usage is indeed apostolic — with an aspect of plausibility corresponding to the fact that the apostles principally lived and labored there. Thus one cannot but register surprise that the witness to infant baptism boasts a less ancient pedigree in the East than in the West. Tertullian, as we have seen, alludes to the liturgy of sponsorship as early as A.D. 205 in North Africa; whereas Gregory Nazianzen, in a sermon on baptism (delivered at Constantinople as late as A.D. 381), expresses a preference for baptizing children at the age of about three years, that they might hear and answer the questions for *themselves* and so have no need of a sponsor.[20]

A similar contrast is noticeable between Eastern and Western church orders prescribing the baptism of infants. Whereas Hippolytus, it would seem, includes instruction for the baptism of infants and small children at Rome in a manual dating from A.D. 217, the first such rubric in the East is found in the seventh book of the *Apostolic Constitutions*, dated around A.D. 370-380. History has bequeathed us not a word from Basil the Great (ca. A.D. 329-379) or Cyril of Jerusalem regarding the subject of infant baptism, though the *Catechetical Lectures*, delivered by the latter in A.D. 348 at the Church of the Resurrection, contain the most complete and full account of baptism in the fourth century!

However, Asterius the Sophist, a native of Cappadocia and an Arian pupil of Lucian, in his recently discovered *Homilies on the Psalms* (no. XII, dating sometime after A.D. 341) counterpoints the silence of Cyril by expressly teaching the baptism of infants.[21] Before Asterius, there is a lacuna in the Eastern sources of almost a century, which brings us

---

[20]*Oratio XL*, in *Sanctum baptisma;* see sections 17 (p. 367), 28 (p. 370), in *The Nicene and Post-Nicene Fathers*, Second Series, Vol. VII (New York, 1894).

[21]See under "Asterius," *RGG*, I, 3 Auflage; also Jeremias, *Die Kindertaufe*, p. 109.

directly to Origen, whose significant testimony we must now consider.

2. *Origen*, A.D. 233-244

The precocious and scholarly Origen, whose indefatigable labors are well known to every student of church history, traveled widely throughout the Christian world, settling toward the end of his life in Palestine. Here he enjoyed unquestioned fame as a teacher, and his intrepid zeal to expound the Scriptures produced the homilies and commentaries where we first hear of infant baptism as the practice of the Eastern church. The passages are few in number and brief in extent.

The first occurs in his *Homily on Luke* (14), where he addresses himself to a question frequently asked by the brethren: why infants should be baptized when they have not sinned. To this he answers that none is free from pollution though he has lived but a day on earth. "And it is for this reason, that by the sacrament of baptism the pollution of our birth is taken away, that infants are baptized."

In his *Commentary on Romans,* we read:

> It is also due to this [hereditary sin] that the church has a tradition from the apostles to give baptism even to infants. For they, to whom the divine mysteries were committed, knew that there is in all persons the natural pollution of sin, which must be done away by water and the Spirit, by reason of which the body itself is also called the body of sin.[22]

Finally, in his *Homily on Leviticus* (8), speaking of the psalmist's confession that he was conceived in sin and shaped in iniquity (Ps. 51:5), Origen affirms the sin existing in infants and the necessity for their baptism; for if there were nothing in them wanting forgiveness, then the grace of baptism would be needless in their case.

In evaluating this evidence, the first point to be noted is that Origen wrote in Greek; but time and change have exacted their toll so that we have two of the above passages

---

[22]Origen, *Commentary on Romans,* as cited in Wall, *History* (Griffith), p. 51.

(*Romans* and *Leviticus*) only in the Latin of Rufinus. The latter's unscrupulous retrenchments and additions as a translator have perplexed and annoyed researchers for centuries. Mindful of the unpopular status of Origen's views in the West, Rufinus apparently studied to avoid the odious reputation of being the translator of heretical treatises by altering the original text so that it would better harmonize with the views of the Latin church.[23]

This problem especially gives one pause in evaluating Origen's appeal in the *Commentary on Romans* to an *apostolic* tradition for baptizing infants. "It is due to this fact [that we are born sinners] that the church has a tradition from the apostles to give baptism even to infants" is a statement so typical of those with which Augustine and Jerome sought to confute Pelagius that it may well be a gloss of Rufinus. Even those scholars who accept the text as genuine often display an illiberal contempt for its significance. "When Origen," observes Windisch, "grounds infant baptism in an 'apostolic tradition,' this is pure fiction."[24] In other words, a claim to apostolicity can hardly be regarded as of great weight in an age when the inclination was so strong to trace back to the apostles every institution that was considered of special importance, and when so many walls of separation, hindering the freedom of prospect, had already been set up between those making the claim and the apostles themselves.[25]

Those Paedobaptists who are concerned to give the witness from history for infant baptism as plausible an aspect as possible have understandably demurred at this ungenerous depreciation of Origen's appeal to apostolicity. They affirm not only that Origen made the appeal, but that in doing so he implied that he himself was baptized as a little child.[26] Since

---

[23]Erasmus once quipped, disgustedly, that the reader is uncertain, in the Latin Origen, whether he is reading Origen or Rufinus.

[24]"Zum Problem der Kindertaufe in Urchristentum," *ZNW*, 1929, p. 142.

[25]See Neander, *History*, I, 314.

[26]See Jeremias, *Die Kindertaufe*, p. 76. The statement that Origen was himself baptized in infancy is the common property of Paedobaptist apologists. Cf. B.B. Warfield, *Polemics*, p. 402. No direct evidence, however, is adduced by way of support — because there is none.

his parents were Christians, it is indeed possible to infer his own baptism in infancy if one feels that Origen's published statements mirror his private experience. If such was the case, his own baptism as an infant may have occurred as early as A.D. 185 and would constitute evidence of the practice in Egypt dating between that of Tertullian in Africa and Irenaeus in Gaul. In any event, Origen does testify to infant baptism as known in the Eastern church in the third decade of the third century. The statement in his *Homily on Luke,* composed about A.D. 233, is preserved in the original Greek and is therefore beyond all reasonable doubt. The question is, How old was the practice when Origen first mentioned it?

In the course of seeking to answer this question, some have detected in Origen's manner of speaking of infant baptism a defensive stance that would betray the recent appearance of the practice, as when he says that "it is a thing causing frequent inquiries among the brethren." Why should this be so? Why would people question infant baptism if it was received from the apostles? It is difficult to know how great a weight of merit this reasoning deserves, for what practice of the church has not provoked "inquires among the brethren"? Jeremias at least is confident that the question in Origen's day concerned not the practice itself but the theology of the practice. As the original eschatological significance of baptism waned, the innocence of a newborn child disputed a need for his purgation from the defilement of sin. And it is to this question, in the judgment of Jeremias, that Origen addresses himself.[27] Thus we are left with two possible interpretations of Origen's witness, the convictions of the one subduing the confidence of the other to a kind of neutrality.

3. Clement of Alexandria, A.D. 195

Concerned neither to condemn Origen's witness to the "apostolic tradition" of infant baptism as valueless, nor to

---

[27]*Nochmals: Die Anfange der Kindertaufe,* p. 62.

betray an uncritical enthusiasm for a mode of expression often indulged by the Fathers and seldom authenticated, we have suggested that such a manner of speaking may imply his own baptism as a little child in Egypt. This timid hypothesis invokes a vivid interest in the witness of his predecessor, who was the head of the school of Pantaenus in Alexandria.

Titus Flavius Clemens, commonly called Clement of Alexandria, came from Greece, probably Athens, and adorned his written Greek with duals and optatives. Having embraced the Christian faith as a mature man, like Origen he traveled extensively in both the East and the West to learn from the most distinguished teachers, "who preserved the tradition of pure saving doctrine and implanted the genuine apostolic seed in the hearts of their pupils." In his *Paedagogos*, written about A.D. 195, he makes one remark that might possibly allude to the practice of infant baptism. Speaking of rings and ornaments which were the fashion of the day, he warns Christians that they should never use anything which might be idolatrous or lascivious. Advising that which is innocent and useful, he continues, ". . . let our seals be a dove or a fish or a ship running with the wind or a musical harp . . . and if anyone is a fisherman, let him remember the apostle and the children drawn out of the water."[28]

If Clement is thinking of the baptism of infants by one of the apostles, he cannot have reference to any incident mentioned in the New Testament, though he may be alluding to some tradition deriving from extrabiblical sources which he assumes to be reliable. But since there is no evidence anywhere of such tradition, and since Clement speaks as of something generally known to his readers, he is most likely referring to the place in the Gospels where Jesus calls his disciples "fishers of men" (Matt. 4:19; Mark 1:17). The references to drawing out of the water could conceivably echo baptism (since he conceived it as the laver of regeneration);

---

[28]*Paedagogos*, Bk. III, ch. xxiv, as quoted by Wall, *History*, I, 51-52. Wall apologized for having overlooked, in previous editions, this place where Clement so speaks "as to suppose and take for granted that the apostles did baptize infants or little children."

but probably he is simply carrying through Jesus' figure of speech and saying that the apostles, as "fishers of men," drew men and women (by their preaching) out of the water, that is, saved them. This is a most natural way to construe the phrase, since linguistic usage, wherever the outward form of the baptismal act is treated, favors "going down into" water or "dipping in" water rather than "lifting out of" water, as in this passage.

Substantiating this interpretation is the fact that Clement concludes chapter 10 (a few paragraphs before this passage) with the observation that fishing is a legitimate sport, but it is better for the Christian to do as the Lord instructed Peter when he taught him to "catch men as fishes in the water." Those who are thus fished out of the water are called "children" by Clement, not because he is thinking of physical children but because his subject is the Divine Pedagogue. A pedagogue (παιδαγωγός) was a trusted slave who acted as a guide, guardian, and teacher of children; and Clement is thinking of the Christian's relationship to God after the analogy of a child's relationship to a pedagogue. Throughout the book he speaks of Christians as God's spiritual children; the one figure inspires the other. There is, then, no particular reason to suppose that he is here thinking of infant baptism. "Beyond doubt," observes Neander, "the writer is speaking in this passage, directly of conversion and regeneration, in reference to all men."[29]

Aside from this passage, the writings of Clement are virgin so far as infant baptism is concerned, a circumstance which could readily be ascribed to fortuity were it not that he so frequently speaks both of baptism and of children, yet always in the allegorical sense of children in spirit, those whose hearts and minds have been brought into subjection unto Christ. Never does he speak of literal children, even

[29]*History*, I, 312, n. 1. Barker, *Duty and Benefits of Baptism*, pp. 73-75, gives a score of instances from Clement's *Pedagogue* where he calls all Christians "children" or "little ones" in a figure. Though Jeremias does not deem it "beyond doubt," he also is inclined to see in Clement's mode of expression the color of allegory. See his *Die Kindertaufe*, p. 74. The same could be said of the appeal, sometimes made by Paedobaptists, to the use of the expression "children" by John in his first epistle (cf. I John 2:12; 5:18).

when expounding those familiar New Testament passages which Paedobaptists have viewed as clearly implying infant baptism in New Testament times. As Aland has observed, even when one unavoidably expects it, there is nothing in Clement about the baptism of infants. Commenting, for example, on Jesus' receiving children (Matt. 19:14), Clement expounds the passage without so much as a word about baptism. This argument from silence is perhaps not conclusive; but the thought of a contemporary Paedobaptist preaching on Clement's text, yet making no reference to the baptism of infants, is highly implausible to say the least.

D. CHILDREN IN THE ANCIENT CHURCH

Paedobaptists frequently appeal to other passages in the literature of the early church in which they see infant baptism by implication. Polycrates of Ephesus and Polycarp of Smyrna, for example, both confess a lifelong commitment to Christ. The former declares in a letter to Rome (ca. A.D. 190) that he had lived for sixty-five years "in the Lord," and the latter sealed his doom before the proconsul of Smyrna (A.D. 167-168) by testifying that he had "served the Christ for eighty-six years." Assuming that both men were describing the entire span of their lives, it is inferred that they must have been born of Christian parents and baptized in infancy. In Polycarp's case this would date his baptism about A.D. 80, a date falling well within the New Testament era.

One cannot deny such a possibility; yet probably the meaning of both witnesses is simply that they had served Christ all their lives. Such a common way of speaking does not necessarily imply baptism at birth. In fact, the passive notion of being "numbered among the saints by baptism" is hardly compatible with the active mode of Polycarp's expression, that is, his accent on "serving Christ." How could one "serve Christ" as an infant through baptism? When Justin Martyr refers in his *Apology* to men and women of sixty and seventy years who had been "made disciples" from their youth, Paedobaptists are confident that the passive voice of the Greek verb signifies discipleship by baptism rather than by choice. But in Polycarp's case the verb is in the active voice; yet they see infant baptism here also. One sometimes gets the impression that all voices, active and passive, speak to the Paedobaptists of the baptismal font.

But this whole method of argumentation is really more subtle than appears at first glance. Over and beyond the obvious uncertainty involved in such reasoning, one needs to be aware of a semantic imprecision arising from the fact that all infants are children, but not all children are infants.[30] Paedobaptists exploit this ambiguity by equating the "Baptist position" with "adult" baptism and their own with "child" baptism. If one assumes that Baptists forbid baptism to all but adults, and if one uses the same word (as the Germans do) for the baptism of both infants and children (*Kindertaufe*), certain data in the historical record which are really quite compatible with the Baptist point of view appear to favor the Paedobaptist. The frequent appeal by Paedobaptists to passages in the literature which speak of those who have been "Christians from their youth" is a case in point. Consider the following:

> [Justin speaks of] many men and women of sixty and seventy years of age, who became disciples of Christ from their childhood. . . . The most natural interpretation of the passage seems to involve the baptism of these people as infants. Sixty or seventy years from the date of the *First Apology* takes us back to *circa* A.D. 80 or 90.[31]

The screw that is loose in this argument is the assumption that since these children were not *adults* when they became Christ's disciples, they must have been *infants*. Once this assumption is granted, it is at least possible to suppose that their discipleship was by baptism apart from a personal confession of faith. But if Justin is talking about children, not infants, it is a commonplace that children are capable of a devout and godly faith which sometimes puts to shame that of adults. (For example, Robert Hall, son of a Baptist minister,

---

[30]The same is true of Greek usage: the infant is ὁ βρέφος; the child, ὁ παῖς.

[31]W. F. Flemington, *The New Testament Doctrine of Baptism*, p. 132.

"was given to secret prayer before he could speak plain," read and re-read Edwards' *Treatise on the Will* and Butler's *Analogy* before he was nine years old.)[32] Inasmuch as Baptists as well as Paedobaptists embrace such children as Christians in grateful acknowledgment of God's grace in their lives, and baptize them, the evidence that there were such children in the ancient church is irrelevant so far as the pros and cons of *infant* baptism are concerned.

One suspects that such evidence of *child* baptism is used because there is no witness to *infant* baptism at the time of Justin. One is fortified in this suspicion by noting that Paedobaptists never refer to the careful account that Justin gives of the Christian rite of baptism in sections LXI and LXV of his *Apology*. To ascertain the baptismal practice of the church between A.D. 150-155, they have bestowed extravagant attention on a passing allusion which he makes to those who "became disciples in early youth," contained in a chapter which has nothing to do with baptism as such. By contrast, they display a singular taciturnity with reference to those portions of the same work which treat baptism expressly. The reason for this anomaly seems quite clear. When discoursing on baptism, Justin not only mentions the prerequisite of faith but underlines it with a heavy pencil. Baptism is for "as many as are persuaded and believe that what we teach and say is true. . . ." Nothing that he has to say about baptism favors the Paedobaptist view. May this not be the reason why Paedobaptists, when they claim that Justin favored infant baptism, cite passages in which he obviously is not talking about baptism at all?

In response to this observation, Paedobaptists are quick to affirm that when Justin speaks of those who are baptized as being "persuaded that what we teach and say is true," he is thinking of converts from heathenism. He has in mind people like himself who, "being born without their knowledge or choice, were brought up in bad habits and wicked training," but have now become no more "children of necessity and ignorance," but "children of choice and knowledge,"

---

[32]*Encyclopedia Britannica, loc. cit.*

obtaining in the waters of baptism the remission of their sins.[33] Therefore, say the Paedobaptists, since Justin speaks of baptism from the point of view of his own experience as an adult convert, it did not so much as occur to him to speak of infants when discoursing on baptism as such. This reasoning will exorcise all doubt from the minds of those only who have no doubts to begin with.

Dedicating his *Apology* to the emperor with the intent that it should serve as an antidote to the opprobrious charges brought against Christians, Justin is at pains to provide his sovereign with a full and uncensored account of all that the Christians believe and practice. He introduces baptism with the protestation that he will relate "the manner in which we dedicate ourselves to God . . . lest, if we omit this, we seem to be unfair in the explanation we are making."[34] Supposing, as Paedobaptists do, that infant baptism was practiced by the year A.D. 150, surely the Roman church was sufficiently large that the baptism of converts from paganism would not have completely overshadowed the baptism of infants born to believers. Why, then, should it not occur to Justin to speak of the baptism of infants? Why should he treat exclusively the baptism of adult converts, leaving the baptism of infants to a tacit assumption? In Chapter 27 he expressly says that Christians have been taught not to expose infants lest they injure the creature and offend the Creator. What a telling contrast he could have drawn between the pagan practice of infanticide and the Christian practice of infant baptism! What an excellent opportunity for introducing the "solidarity of the Christian family in the dispensations of grace" and the "inclusion of infants in the bosom of the church by their baptism"! But Justin does not use the opportunity.

Speaking of the "solidarity of the family" and the inclusion of infants in the church, the "family of God," by baptism (matters on which we shall have more to say later), we must pause at this point to make one final observation about the testimony of Justin. If it is true that in his *Apology* his account of baptism reflects only the baptism of heathen con-

---

[33]*Apologia*, ch. lxi.
[34]*Ibid.*

verts like himself — that form of baptism which Jeremias calls "missionary baptism" — then his language is singularly individualistic to describe a rite that all Paedobaptists suppose to have been administered to *households* converted from heathenism after the analogy of Jewish proselyte baptism. "After we have thus washed *him*," says Justin, describing the baptismal service ("and his house, including infants," understands the Paedobaptist), "we bring *him* to the place where those who are called brethren are assembled" ("together with his house, including infants," understands the Paedobaptist) "in order that we may offer hearty prayers in common for ourselves and the baptized *person*" ("and the baptized persons," understands the Paedobaptist). Although this Paedobaptist "understanding" escapes the charge of being a mere arbitrary affirmation by appeal to the Jewish custom of baptizing the families of proselytes from heathenism, along with the proselyte himself, such an explanation will satisfy only those who bring to the discussion a mind already convinced. Obviously Justin's account of baptism is most easily understood as describing what is called in our day "believer baptism."

E. CONCLUSION

1. Introduction

As one traces the stream of evidence for infant baptism back through the centuries beyond Tertullian, it becomes a feeble trickle. With Irenaeus it dwindles to the vanishing point, and we are limited to inference for the rest of the second century, an inference which Jeremias is pleased to call "indirect evidence." The meager character of all literary sources of the early Christian era might seem to Lilliputianize this fact. There are many details, one could argue, about the practice of the ancient church that must be filled in between the few lines that we have, especially in the age immediately after the apostles and before the first theologians of the church. This is granted; therefore, any argument from silence against infant baptism would have little force if there were nothing but an occasional allusion to baptism in the subapostolic age. The lack of all mention of infant participation in the rite could then be ascribed to the accidents of history.

However, the plausibility of this reasoning is diminished by the character of the allusions to baptism in the sources of the second century. Barnabas, for example, in his so-called *Epistle* (ca. A.D. 120-130), devotes a brief chapter to the subject of baptism, but reflects only the baptism of believers: "We go down into the water full of sins and foulness and we come up bearing fruit in our hearts, fear and hope in Jesus in the Spirit."[35] Hermas, of *Shepherd* fame (ca. A.D. 150), makes repentance the condition of baptism.[36] Still more striking in this regard is the *Didache* (A.D. 100-110), the most ancient handbook of Christian baptism extant. This document, which may have been produced in the Syrian church, is even more detailed than Justin in its account of baptism. It contains careful instructions for the candidate's moral conduct and directs that he shall fast one or two days before he is baptized. It specifies even such minutiae as that the water should be running water; if not available, then standing water; if cold water is out of the question, then warm water may be used. And if there is not enough water of any kind for immersion, then water may be poured thrice upon the head of the candidate in the name of the Father, and of the Son, and of the Holy Spirit.

How shall we account for the omission of all reference to infant baptism in this primitive manual of proper baptismal usage? It is hard to imagine such an omission occurring under Roman Catholic, Anglican, Lutheran, or even Presbyterian, Methodist, or Congregational auspices. Some Paedobaptists not only adorn the rite of infant baptism with rubrics for clerical guidance but even include in the back of their hymnals special instructions on the baptism of infants for lay use in the event of emergency. Is it not, then, highly implausible that the *Didache* was produced by a community

[35]See the *Ante-Nicene Christian Library, Apostolic Fathers,* I, 121.
[36]See "Vision" III; "Mandates" ("Commandments") IV, *The Ante-Nicene Fathers,* II, 1ff.

of early Paedobaptists who just happened to say nothing about infant baptism? Jeremias, following A. Oepke, scents the air of this primitive Christian time and suggests that the minute regulations in the *Didache* concerning water may reflect technical problems encountered in the baptism of infants.[37] But the more obvious explanation is that they reflect problems encountered in administering baptism by immersion after the analogy of Jesus' baptism in the river Jordan.

To be sure, one may somewhat avert the force of this argument from the silence of the *Didache* with the observation that antique baptismal orders were written with adults in view, yet without intending to exclude infants and little ones. However, this is only a possible, not a necessary — perhaps not even a probable — reading of the evidence. If early Christian baptismal orders were framed with adults in view and only tacitly included infants, why, it may be asked, have present-day Paedobaptists found it necessary to distend their manuals of instruction for the baptism of infants until they all but eclipse those prepared for the baptism of adults? The answer may be given that the situation has changed from what it then was: the early Christian community, being in a missionary situation, was primarily concerned with the baptism of adults converted from heathenism, not infants born to believing parents. But even this salvo will hardly satisfy the doubts which a careful reflection on the nature of the evidence begets. So far as the historical argument for infant baptism is concerned, the silence of the crucial witnesses of the second century is a crucial silence indeed.

2. *Infant communion*

Doubts about the historical argument for infant baptism are due not only to the silence of the earliest witnesses but also to the way in which the evidence for infant baptism is related to the evidence for infant communion. Early Christian sources from the *Didache* onward reflect the unity of the

[37]*Hat die Urkirche die Kindertaufe geübt?*, p. 29.

sacraments; they were always celebrated together. Hence the first act of the baptized, following his baptism, was to partake of the Eucharist. If, then, evidence for infant communion appears only a short time after the first clear evidence for infant baptism, to repudiate the former as a post-apostolic superstition, as most Paedobaptists do, is to threaten the latter with the same odious pedigree.

To see that this is the case, one need only recall that the earliest express mention of infant baptism is found in Tertullian's *De baptismo* (A.D. 200-206), a document in which the author entertains reservations about giving baptism to infants. But Cyprian, on whose shoulders his mantle fell, speaks not only of infant *baptism* but also of infant *communion* as a custom which provoked no scruples. Barely fifty years separates these two witnesses. Obviously, therefore, the initial evidence for infant baptism and infant communion shows a proximity in time (A.D. 205-250) and place (North Africa) which makes it difficult to see why the former usage should be accepted while the latter is rejected.

These two practices, moreover, share a democratic exegetical pedigree. Understanding John 3:5, "Except a man be born of water and the Spirit, he cannot enter into the kingdom of God," to make baptism essential to salvation, the Fathers concluded — naturally — that it should be given to infants. In like manner, understanding John 6:53, "Except you eat the flesh of the Son of Man and drink his blood, you have no life in yourselves," to make the Eucharist essential, they argued, in a similar vein, that it should be given to infants (so Augustine against Pelagius, A.D. 412). It is true that Augustine is the first expressly to conjoin an argument from John 3 for infant baptism with a similar one from John 6 for infant communion; however, Cyprian argued for infant baptism in a similar manner in his *Letter to Fidus* (A.D. 251-253) and likewise approved the communication of infants in his admonition against apostasy. It seems difficult, therefore, to suppose that infant communion stems from a later misunderstanding of Scripture, while infant baptism altogether escapes this difficulty.

Nor did it ever occur to anyone in the ancient church to

question the right of infants to the Eucharist once the right to embrace them in the church by baptism had been established. The theory that infants are to be baptized but not given communion rests on medieval dogmatic developments in the Western church that had nothing to do with an evangelical view of the sacraments. This has given some Paedobaptists pause, and in the past there have been those who have questioned the propriety of withholding communion from infants. Wall, for example, considering the antiquity of infant communion — that it was recognized by the church universal for six hundred years and that it is still practiced by Eastern Orthodox Christendom — questioned whether it was an error or a duty to bring infants to the communion table.[38] Other Paedobaptists have been outspoken in favor of the practice. But the great majority have been inclined to remand infant communion to the limbo of pious abuse, or, more frequently, to pass over the matter in discreet silence.

3. The catechumenate and sponsorship

When time had silenced the living voice of the apostles and swelled the ranks of Christian converts, many inevitably were enlisted among the number of the faithful who neither understood nor genuinely sympathized with the faith as it had been "once for all delivered to the saints." Gathering converts from "all sorts of curious moral highways and hedges" (Easton), the church needed to be discerning and to dissuade the incipient heretic, as well as to build a bridge from the world to the church for the novitiate. It increasingly became the custom, therefore, to require of candidates for baptism not only that they give evidence of integrity of purpose but also that they submit to a period of instruction in the Christian faith. Since this instruction was given orally, by asking questions to which the convert gave answers, those receiving such instruction were called catechumens. Participating in all the acts of worship except the sacraments, these catechumens came from every stratum of society, from

---

[38]See Abraham Booth, *Paedobaptism Examined*, II, 445-446.

the mean to the mighty. To guard against the vagaries of the Docetists, Gnostics, and others, the church by the early third century required all new converts to spend a period of time in instruction before being admitted to baptism. As we have noted, the rigorous *Apostolic Tradition* (ca. A.D. 215) suggested a three-year probation for all catechumens who desired baptism.

One cannot but note the contrast between this antique usage and that of contemporary Paedobaptist communions, where catechetical instruction is given not *before* but *following* baptism to children who are preparing for confirmation. The disparity between the ancient sequence of catechism, baptism, confirmation, and communion, and the present-day sequence of baptism, catechism, confirmation, and communion cannot be denied and should not be ignored. One may, indeed, suppose that the original catechumenate looked both to the instruction of adult converts from paganism before baptism and to the teaching of their children after baptism. But if so, the sources that plainly testify to the former are strangely silent about the latter. The original catechesis *always* anticipated rather than followed baptism.

Apparently around A.D. 200, when the custom of baptizing small children and infants began to be established, especially in the West, the catechists, who had formerly taught the baptismal candidates and vouched for their candidacy, now began to "sponsor" children by guaranteeing a *post factum* candidacy. This candidacy was to be achieved through instruction in the Christian life after the sacrament had been administered. Tertullian, who first mentions the baptism of infants, in the same passage refers for the first time to these *sponsores*. They are endangered, he argues, by the rash promise that the infant who is baptized will prove a Christian in later life. Why the danger? Because no one can be sure in such matters.

To cover this situation, some scholars have suggested that Tertullian was thinking of a custom whereby children of heathen converts (as distinguished from those born to Christian believers) were presented for baptism with their parents after the analogy of Jewish proselyte baptism. But this theory does not explain why the office of sponsor is first mentioned at the same time infant baptism is first mentioned. If converts from paganism had, from the time of the apostles, presented their children for baptism on the strength of their own confession as parents, the emergence of sponsorship at the beginning of the third century, though clear in its purpose, remains obscure in its cause. Why should Christians "sponsor" the children of heathen converts in Tertullian's time when there had been heathen converts with children from the beginning? But if the baptism of infants and small children is established *after* the institution of the catechumenate, then the emergence of sponsors can be easily explained. It is a usage born of the necessity to adjust the older practice to the new requirements. When baptism came to anticipate rather than complete one's catechetical instruction, responsible adults (sponsors) were asked to guarantee that the necessary instruction would subsequently be given the child in order to insure his confession of faith in later life.

> After infant baptism became established, instruction hitherto-fore given before baptism became impossible; it was then made the responsibility of parents. . . .[39]

The appearance of sponsors, then, is one more reason to doubt the alleged evidence for the practice of infant baptism in early antiquity.

[39]H. W. Surkau, "Katechetic," Sec. 2, *RGG*, III, 3 Auflage.

INFANT BAPTISM
AND THE PRACTICE
OF THE APOSTLES

A. HOUSEHOLD BAPTISMS

Turning to the documents of the New Testament, we shall ask the same question concerning the apostles that we have asked concerning the Fathers: Did they baptize infants? Due to their complexity, the data will at times chafe under the severity of the method, yet insofar as possible we shall defer the theological question until we may have the benefit of answering it in the light of the historical one. It will, of course, prove impossible to avoid theology altogether in dealing with the basic source documents of the Christian faith, for the two strata of biblical revelation — event and meaning — cannot ultimately be separated.

That there is no instance of infant baptism recorded in the New Testament is accepted by all. This, however, is as far as the agreement extends. Traditionally, Baptists have capitalized this point and their opponents have minimized it, with all the conviction that theological debate is wont to engender. How strange, say the Baptists, that of all the thousands baptized in Jerusalem, Samaria, and the cities of the Gentile mission, there should be no instance of anyone bringing his children with him to be baptized. But Paedobaptists, scanning the same sources, have felt no strain upon their credulity. Surely, they urge, when the record swells the converts at Pentecost to three thousand, the very size of the number is pregnant with suggestion. It must have included several hundred families; thus infant baptism is as old as the church itself.

Both of these approaches appear to us extreme. To argue, as some Baptists do, that thousands were baptized in New Testament times, but — so far as the record shows — no infants received baptism, is misleading; for the relevant datum is not the number of baptisms that *occurred* but the number of occurrences that were *recorded*. Excluding the baptism of John and of Jesus' disciples, this latter count is a modest twelve. That three or perhaps four of these involved "households" shows that the practice of baptizing households must have been rather frequent in apostolic times; and it is indeed true that many of those households must have included children and infants. To argue, however, that this shows that apostolic baptism "went by households," as some Paedobaptists do, so that we need not so much as stop to ask if there were infants in those families specifically mentioned, reflects a cavalier indifference to the scrupulous, persevering quest for accuracy which is the humble guide to all truth. Before we come to any conclusions in this matter, then, we need to look once more at the household baptisms recorded in Acts.

The first instance of such household baptism is that of Cornelius (Acts 10). The account of this happy event stresses the preaching of the word to all those "present in the sight of God to hear all things that have been commanded by the Lord" (10:33). While Peter was still speaking, "the Holy Spirit fell on all who heard the word" (10:44). Peter appealed to the fact that they "had received the Holy Spirit as well as we" as constituting legitimate ground for their baptism. Everything in the narrative commends the conclusion that those who were baptized were those who heard the word and received the Spirit in his charismatic endowment. It is perhaps for this reason that the case of Cornelius' house is seldom urged, sometimes not even mentioned, in the literature defending infant baptism.

The second instance of household baptism in the New Testament involves Lydia, a seller of purple from Thyatira, who responded to Paul's preaching in Philippi and was baptized with all her household (Acts 16:15). Here Paedobaptists, with a minimum of detail from the text to encumber the discussion, have enlarged their commentary. Inasmuch as the baptism of all the house is mentioned, but Lydia only is said to have been converted, this merging of the whole house under her single name forces one to conclude — it is supposed — that either adults were baptized without conversion, or children, too young to believe, were baptized in the faith of the mother. But such a conclusion is by no means necessary. Nothing in the passage implies that Lydia was a married woman with nursing children, for she traveled on business some 300 miles from her native city and felt the liberty, as head of the house, to invite men into her home. Since Luke speaks of *her* household being baptized, and of the importunity with which she constrained the apostles to abide in *her* house, no mention being made of her husband, the most likely hypothesis is that she had no husband. In any event, there must have been other adults in her household — domestics, friends, business associates — who were led by her example to confess their faith with her in baptism. That infants may also have been involved can neither be affirmed nor denied from the evidence as it stands.

The third instance of household baptism in the New Testament concerns the Philippian jailor (Acts 16:25-34). Paul, it will be remembered, exorcised a "python spirit" (πνεῦμα πύθωνα) from the maid who cried out after him in the streets of the city. Threatened by economic loss, her master haled him before the magistrates. Stripped and beaten, he and his companion Silas were imprisoned under maximum security measures. But before the night was out the jailor and all his house were baptized amid much rejoicing and a lively faith in God (16:33). Literally, the Greek text says that the jailor "rejoiced, with all his house, himself believing" (16:34). From this it has been concluded that in this case infants were baptized "in and because of the supposed faith of the parent," which would constitute "positive proof of infant baptism, in apostolic times."[40]

[40] See H. Bushnell, *Christian Nurture*, pp. 153-154.

But there is no reason to put the Greek under such rigorous contribution. We are told that the word was preached to the jailor and *all* his house, that they *all* rejoiced in the Lord. Can we suppose that they all heard and rejoiced but that only he believed? And while there may have been infants and small children in the home, is it plausible that the word was proclaimed to babes in arms or that they rejoiced in the Lord? Why then suppose that they were baptized, unless we know for reasons not found in the text that such was the case? Taken at its face value, the account in Acts sets before us a hearing, believing, rejoicing household that received baptism. The universe of discourse is household salvation, not infant baptism. As Calvin observes,

> Luke commends the pious zeal of the jailor because he dedicated his whole house to the Lord, in which also the grace of God illustriously appeared, because it suddenly brought the whole family to a pious consent.[41]

The fourth and last instance of household baptism in the New Testament concerns Stephanas, mentioned in I Corinthians 1:16; 16:15. "And I baptized also the household of Stephanas," writes Paul; "besides I know not whether I baptized any other." At the close of this same letter, the apostle observes that this family enjoyed a double honor: they were his first converts in Achaia, and they had proven genuinely faithful, setting themselves to minister to the saints. When Paul declares, "I baptized the house of Stephanas," and later adds that they "set themselves to minister to the saints," the same question confronts us that does in the case of the Philippian jailor and his house: How plausible is it to make the circle of his meaning larger in the one instance than in the other? "I baptized *all* the house of Stephanas, of which *some* have ministered to the saints" is the way we should have to understand the apostle if we are to see clear evidence for infant baptism in this passage. Such an interpretation is possible, but it is a rather thin thread on which to hang the practice of bringing infants to baptism. Paedobaptists seem to sense this, for though they cite this

[41]*Commentary on Acts*, II, 86-87.

text, they frequently leave it without comment.

The long and short of the matter is that the issue of infant baptism cannot be resolved from such passages. In fact, the traditional use of these verses as proof texts by Paedobaptists has complicated matters by posing the question, What about infants? This is the wrong question to ask, since these texts have to do, not with infants, but with the conversion and baptism of families to whom the gospel was proclaimed. For Baptists to deny, as for Paedobaptists to affirm, that there were infants in these homes is a kind of theological impertinence.[42] When we read that Jesus healed the nobleman's son and his *whole* house believed (John 4:53); that Cornelius was a man who feared God with *all* his house (Acts 10:2); or that certain unruly persons subvert *whole* houses with their teaching (Titus 1:11), who will quibble about infants? We all know infants cannot "believe in the Lord," "fear God," nor be "subverted" in their minds by heretics; therefore, we read such texts without so much as thinking to ask if there were infants in these houses. Why then insist, when we read that "he and all his were baptized" or that "she was baptized and her household," that these homes were or were not blessed with infants, according to our theological proclivities? Why not rather see in these passages a testimony to the illustrious displays of grace that marked the way along which Christianity marched in splendid triumph over the paganism of Greece and Rome?

Tacitly admitting as much, the more recent Paedobaptist literature is not given to citing these texts as positive "proofs" for the apostolic practice of infant baptism. Rather, it is argued that the record of household baptisms in Acts reflects an Old Testament "ritual formula," according to which the expression "the whole house" included — perhaps even principally referred to — children along with their parents.[43] Since the formula occurs in the New Testament documents, which originated in a time when many of the members of the

---

[42]See Markus Barth, *Die Taufe, ein Sacrament?* pp. 163-164.

[43]On the οἶκος formula, see E. Stauffer, *Die Theologie des Neuen Testaments,* the section on the sacraments; also Jeremias, *Kindertaufe,* p. 76.

Christian community were also members of the synagogue, the inference is drawn that small children must have been embraced in the baptismal practice of the early church, since household baptisms are mentioned. Not that there were infants and small children in each case of recorded household baptism; but under no circumstance could Luke have used the "household formula" had he wished to say that only adults were baptized.

However, many scholars, including Paedobaptists, have doubted that there is evidence for such a "household formula" in the usage of the New Testament. In the author's opinion, this contemporary debate has really contributed little — except more pages — to the discussion, for all the erudition brought to the study. Not only may the evidence for a "household formula" in the New Testament be questioned, but the statements in the Old Testament concerning "corporate personality" and family solidarity, to which the argument also appeals, do not show that the expression "all his house" always included every individual in the household. I Samuel 1:21-22, for example, uses the phrase "all his house," but immediately excludes important individual members.

> The man Elkanah, and *all his house*, went up to offer unto the Lord the yearly sacrifice.... But Hannah went not up, for she said unto her husband, I will not go up until the child is weaned.

Furthermore, Old Testament usage frequently takes particular note of children when they are involved: an enemy is destroyed, "both men and women, children and sucklings" (I Sam. 22:19); there is a solemn assembly to hear the reading of the law and it includes "the women and the little ones" (Josh. 8:35; cf. II Chr. 20:13); the king of Babylon, having made Gedaliah governor, commits to him "men and women and children" (Jer. 40:7).

In the New Testament we have the same mode of expression. In Matthew 14:21 we read: "And they that did eat were about 5,000 men, besides women and children" (see also Matt. 15:38). Luke tells us, as a careful historian, that when Paul journeyed from Tyre to Jerusalem, the Christians, "with wives and children, brought us on our way, till we were out of the city" (Acts 21:5). Yet in Acts 8:12, when recounting the results of Philip's ministry in Samaria, he says, "But when they believed Philip . . . they were baptized, both men and women" — with no reference to children. How can Paedobaptists be confident that the very author who in one instance expressly mentions three groups — men, women, children — as having a part in the events recorded, in another instance mentions only two — men and women — and leaves the third to a tacit assumption? At least one should not suppose that the Baptist is tyrannized by his system when he raises such a question.

One further matter should be mentioned at this juncture. The entire discussion of the so-called "household formula" has been limited in the contemporary literature to the question of baptism; nothing has been said about the Lord's Supper. But if there is any aspect of Old Testament history that confirms Stauffer's contention that "the whole house" is a "ritual formula" which "demonstrably includes small children,"[44] surely it is the institution of the Passover feast (Exod. 12:3-4), which is the Old Testament equivalent of the Lord's Supper. Otto Michel, in a pregnant study of the word "house" as it bears on the New Testament idea of the church, observes that the fellowship of the early Christians in the breaking of bread (Acts 2:42, 46) was "householdwide."[45] Since we know that the Old Testament Passover feast embraced the whole house, including the children, and since we are told that the early Christians broke bread in households, why have the Paedobaptists not suggested infant communion on the basis of this particular use of the "household formula"? Michel notes that the weighty significance of "house" and "family" for the structuring of the early church seems not to have been sufficiently recognized.[46] When it has been recognized, however, the conclusions reached have not always enhanced the Paedobaptist cause. Dom Gregory Dix, for example, argues that since primitive eucharistic worship was domestic and private, one could not be deemed of the

[44]*Die Theologie des N.T.*, p. 140.
[45]G. Kittel, V, 132-133.
[46]*Ibid.*, V, 133, n. 42.

"household of faith" (whose domestic worship was the Eucharist) until he expressly stated his personal faith.[47] Here a Paedobaptist uses the "household formula" to *exclude* infants from the Eucharist, which is the reverse of the way other Paedobaptists have used it to *include* them in baptism. Whichever is the valid use of the argument, it would seem that both cannot be equally valid.

B. CHILDREN IN THE NEW TESTAMENT CHURCH

Paedobaptists have appealed not only to the household baptisms in Acts as evidence for the apostolic practice of infant baptism, but also to the place of children in the New Testament church generally. Paul, it is noted, addresses a letter to the Colossian "saints and faithful brethren in Christ" (Col. 1:2), in which he speaks directly to children, admonishing them to obey their parents in the Lord (Col. 3:20). We make no quarrel with those who insist that these children who were young enough to be the subjects of parental nurture were at the same time reckoned among the number of the saints and faithful brethren. But it is hardly clear that the apostolic admonition to filial obedience implies the apostolic approval of infant baptism. At least one Paedobaptist (Windisch) has observed that the admonition to reverence parents implies, not infant baptism, but the new obedience of faith on the part of these children, a faith which delivers from the bondage of sin (Rom. 6:17).[48]

Be that as it may, in Baptist as well as Paedobaptist churches, there are many children — "sober, submissive, growing up in the Christian way" (Bushnell) — who surely do not need to be baptized before their mentors can impress upon them such basic obligations as preserving the honor and performing the duty belonging to their parents and superiors in the Lord. The fifth commandment is in the Decalogue for Baptists as well as Paedobaptists. When such children come to the age of discretion — sooner in some

[47] *The Shape of the Liturgy*, pp. 16-19.
[48] Windisch, "Zum Problem . . . ," p. 128, n. 2.

instances, later in others — if they give credible evidence of obeying the gospel from the heart, they may be baptized into the fellowship of the saints and numbered among the faithful. It would seem that such a position fulfills every reasonable implication of the several apostolic admonitions to children contained in the New Testament.

C. JESUS BLESSES LITTLE CHILDREN

1. Introduction

Eclipsing all other references to children in the New Testament — so far as the argument for infant baptism is concerned — is the gospel pericope in which Jesus blesses little children, lays his hands on them, and assures his hearers of their interest in his kingdom (Matt. 19:13-15; Mark 10: 13-16; Luke 18:15-17). Thus, before he ever gave the charge to his disciples to baptize in his name, he bequeathed to children an indefeasible title to his kingdom. With this prospect indelibly imprinted in their memories (as is evidenced by the preservation of the incident in the three-fold Synoptic tradition), the disciples, it is argued, could hardly have refused baptism to children and infants. Hence this beautiful scene, associated as it is with the most pleasing sentiments — a scene that has inspired artists and hymnists — has become dearer to Paedobaptists than any other in Scripture. There is no question about what Jesus said and did on this occasion; the historical facts are plain. But the implication of what he said and did is another matter. In this respect the text has often been probed in depth and sometimes pressed to extremes; and it is to these scholarly endeavors that we must now give attention.

It appears that as early as A.D. 200, some appealed to Jesus' act of blessing the children as constituting a basis for infant baptism (see the remarks above on Tertullian). In any case, such an appeal is frequently made in the subsequent centuries of ancient and medieval church history. With the advent of Anabaptism at the time of the Protestant Reformation, appropriation of this Scripture passage in the interest of infant baptism in no way diminished, but rather increased. Zwingli, in his treatise on baptism, alludes to the incident; and Calvin devotes a page and a half in the *Institutes* to Jesus' receiving and blessing children. In Richard Baxter's celebrated treatise, *Plain Scripture Proof of Infant Church-Membership and Baptism*,[49] the words "Suffer the little children to come unto me" are the very first which meet the eye. These words have been quoted or summarized in virtually every order of worship for the giving of baptism to infants ever prepared under Lutheran, Anglican, Presbyterian, Reformed, Congregational, or Methodist auspices, and they have been intoned as frequently as the triune name of God himself in the administration of the sacrament to infants.

Charles Spurgeon once preached a sermon on Jesus' blessing the children (Mark 10:13-16) entitled "Children Brought to Christ, Not to the Font."[50] He testifies that he chose this text because, of all the passages cited against him for his views on infant baptism, none occurred more frequently than this one. In more recent times, Oscar Cullmann and Joachim Jeremias have made these verses the object of a penetrating critical analysis in the interest of reinstating them in the arsenal of Paedobaptist defenses, from which contemporary critical studies have tended to dislodge them. And the Scottish Commissioners, in their *Interim Report* (May 1955), relying upon this contemporary German research, affirmed once again that Jesus' blessing of the children authenticates the practice of baptizing them.

2. The contemporary discussion

It should be acknowledged from the beginning that the task of ascertaining exactly what Jesus intended on this occasion, and the relevance of his act for the church today, is a difficult one. Thus no writer can make claims to oracular finality. In Spurgeon's sermon mentioned above, he said:

See that you read the word [about blessing the children] as it is

---

[49]London, 1651.
[50]*Metropolitan Tabernacle Pulpit*, Lord's Day Morning, July 24, 1846.

written, and you will find no water in it, but Jesus only. Are the
water and Christ the same thing? Nay, here is a wide difference, as wide as between Rome and Jerusalem ... between
false doctrine and the gospel of our Lord Jesus Christ.

Responding to this challenge, Cullmann and Jeremias have
squeezed the pumice stone of this passage once more in the
confidence of finding — with the help of form criticism —
some water in it after all.[51]

This contemporary effort to link Jesus' act of blessing
the children to infant baptism is twofold. First of all, attention has been given to the verb "to hinder" (κωλύω),
employed by all three of the evangelists who report the incident. When Jesus says, "Suffer the little children ... and
hinder them not," the Greek word is the same as that used in
other New Testament passages having to do with baptism.
"What," asks the Ethiopian eunuch, "*hinders* me to be baptized?" (Acts 8:36); "who can *hinder* water that these should
not be baptized?" asks Peter, referring to the members of
Cornelius' household (Acts 10:47); "who was I that I should
hinder God?" he asks, recounting that experience in
Jerusalem (Acts 11:17). When Jesus came to John to be
baptized, John *hindered* him (Matt. 3:14). Cullmann detects
in this usage a suspicious regularity and a formality of expression that suggests a primitive baptismal formula already
in use when the New Testament was written. Just as we
commonly say before solemnizing a marriage, "If anyone
can show just cause why these two may not be joined in holy
wedlock, let him now speak or forever hold his peace" (or
words to this effect), so, it is argued, the question, "What
hinders this man/this woman from being baptized?" very
early came to have the status of a *terminus technicus* in the
baptismal liturgy, and shines through the tissue of the language in these passages. If this assumption be allowed, then
we may conclude, Cullmann argues, that although Jesus did
not baptize the children brought to him, what he said and did
at that time had a significant bearing on infant baptism *in the
opinion of the evangelists reporting the incident.* Hence they

[51]For a brief review of the more quixotic efforts to find baptism in
Jesus' blessing the children, see R.E.O. White, *The Biblical Doctrine of
Initiation*, pp. 331-334.

reported it in the later language of the baptismal liturgy of the church.[52]

In evaluating this hypothesis, we must remember that the verb κωλύω ("to hinder") is such a common one and its occurrence so natural in those passages where it occurs in the Gospels and in Acts that it is hardly possible to be sure it was used for any special reason. This obvious consideration weakens the argument that seeks to close the gap between Jesus' blessing the children and the Christian rite of baptism as administered by the apostles in the book of Acts. Since the former contains no reference to baptism and the latter no reference to children, the only common ground between them is the word itself, a mode of expression so obvious that it raises no questions and poses no problems as to why the evangelists employed it in reporting what Jesus said. That Tertullian, somewhere around A.D. 200, reflects the use of Mark 10:13-16 as bearing upon the question of infant baptism proves only that this passage was, by that date, interpreted as implying infant baptism. But such an interpretation, venerable though it may be for its antiquity, does not come to us with the authority of Jesus himself.

A second effort to find in Jesus' blessing of the children the implication that they should be baptized has been made by Joachim Jeremias. He observes an affinity of structure between the Synoptic report of Jesus' word about children in the kingdom (Matt. 18:3; Mark 10:15; Luke 18:17) and the Johannine saying that one must be born of water and the Spirit to enter the kingdom (John 3:5). By associating a saying that may involve baptism in the way John reports it with one in the Synoptics involving children and their place in the kingdom, Jeremias and others find the conclusion likely that the incident of Christ's receiving and blessing little children was preserved in the ancient church as a justification of infant baptism.

It seems almost a pity not to be convinced by so ingenious an effort. Yet the analysis is uncertain inasmuch as the report in John of Jesus' conversation with Nicodemus is

---

[52]See his "Les traces d'une Formule Baptismale dans le Nouveau Testament," *Revue d'Histoire et Philosophie Religieuses* (1937), pp. 424ff.

sufficiently different from the Synoptic account of his blessing the children that it seems highly implausible that the
same logion lay behind them both. Such scholarly conjec-
ture, though capable of brilliant turns, seldom coincides with
the assured results of the historical, critical method. There
is water in John and there are children in the Synoptics, but
to bring the two together in infant baptism is to conscript the
text in a cause for which it will not volunteer.[53]

3. Conclusion

However uncertain contemporary Paedobaptist expositions of this text may be, that fact in no way lessens the
obligation to face the implications of Jesus' statement about
children for a "theology" of children and their place in the
church. What did he mean when he said that children should
be brought to him, because "of such is the kingdom of
heaven"? When early Anabaptists pointed out that Jesus did
not say, "Suffer the children to come unto me for *of these*
(τούτων) is the kingdom," but rather "*of such as these*
(τοιούτων) is the kingdom," Calvin dismissed the point "as a
cavil by which our opponents endeavor to elude the force of
this passage, but only betray their ignorance."[54] The Anabaptist argument, however, did not die, and down to the present
day a vast array of scholarly opinion can be marshaled for the
view that Jesus meant to secure the blessings of the kingdom
to those who evidence a childlike faith, those who are not
held fast by adult skepticism and misgivings.[55]

Though correct as far as it goes, can we say that this
interpretation exhausts the meaning of the text? Does it not
seem forced and arbitrary to understand that Jesus meant,
"Let the little children come to me, for the kingdom belongs
to people who are like them, people who resemble them in

[53]The stubborn disjunction between the children in the Synoptics and
the water in John is only illustrated, not removed, in Jeremias' subsequent
analysis, in which he adds alongside the Gospels two columns from Justin's
Apology, I, 61, 4, and the *Apostolic Constitution*, VI, 15, 5. See his *Die
Kindertaufe*, p. 64.

[54]*Institutes*, IV, xvi, 7.

[55]See F.C. Grant, *The Interpreter's Bible*, Mark 10:15.

spirit"? The Greek (τοιούτων) by no means implies the exclusion, but rather the inclusion, of the ones mentioned. When the Jews cried out against Paul (Acts 22:22), "Away with such a one (τοιοῦτον)!" they could hardly have meant, Away with someone *like* this man Paul. Rather, they meant, Away with Paul and every one of his kind! By the same rule, when Jesus bade little children to come to him, "for of such is the kingdom of heaven," he most likely meant, "The kingdom belongs to these children and all others who are like them in that they have a childlike faith." The truth that the kingdom belongs to the childlike should not prejudice the affirmation that it also belongs to children.

Now the charge of Paedobaptists is that Baptists fall short of what is written at this point. If the kingdom belongs to children, and if the church is a manifestation of Christ's kingdom — which Baptists as well as others affirm — how can anyone exclude children from the church by refusing them baptism? By so doing, Baptists reflect, it is alleged, an entirely different spirit from that of Jesus, who took little children into his arms and blessed them, assuring his disciples that theirs was the kingdom of heaven.

Such reasoning has a sweet rhetoric about it which seems to leave those who advocate believer baptism on the horns of a dilemma. Either they must admit the validity of this argument or assume the despicable role of the disciples, whose treatment of the little ones exposed them to a deserved rebuke by Jesus. By a kind of intuition the Paedobaptists have grasped this situation and exploited it fully. Their panegyrical oratory about Christ's "dear little lambs" has been exceeded only by the exuberance with which they have spelled out the melancholy implications of the Baptist position.

> If it is reasonable for children to be brought to Christ, why [asks Calvin] is it not allowable to admit them to baptism, the symbol of our communion and fellowship with Christ? ... How unjust shall we be if we drive away from Christ those whom he invites to him; if we deprive them of the gifts with which he adorns them; if we exclude those whom he freely admits![56]

[56]*Institutes*, IV, xvi, 7.

Richard Baxter, the champion of tolerance and brotherly kindness, apparently exasperated by the needling of a Mr. Tombes (and others), took up the jawbone of this argument and thrashed the Baptists thoroughly as those who

> do plainly play the devil's part in accusing their own children and disputing them out of the church and house of God, and out of his promises and covenant, and the privileges that accompany them, and most ungratefully deny, reject and plead against the mercies that Christ hath purchased for their children and made over to them.[57]

In a similar vein Bushnell expresses wonder that anyone could suppose that Christianity, which spreads its arms to embrace the world in God's love (John 3:16), should have in it no place for children. Such a clumsy preparation gives to little children the heritage of Cain, requiring them to be driven from the presence of the Lord to grow up outside the church as aliens and enemies.[58] *The Interim Report* on baptism of the Church of Scotland even goes so far as to declare,

> Surely it were better for a man to have a millstone hung around his neck and to be drowned in the depth of the sea than to hinder [as Baptists do] one of these "holy" ones from being received into the name of the Lord Jesus Christ.[59]

The validity of such reasoning hangs on the assumption that bringing children to Jesus involves bringing them to baptism; and therefore, since Jesus was displeased with his disciples for keeping children from him, he must be displeased with Baptists for keeping them from the font. But can such an argument be made good? That is the question.

It should be clearly understood, as we face this question, that even those who reject the rite of infant baptism emphatically approve of much that is said and done when infants are

[57]*Plain Scripture Proof*, pp. 12-13.

[58]*Christian Nurture*, pp. 142f.

[59]P. 27. A good indication that an apologist for infant baptism is secure in his argument, observes Barth, is his ability to argue calmly. When he loses his aplomb, Barth continues, it is a sign that he feels himself wounded in a vulnerable spot, that he has no good conscience respecting his cause, and consequently slashes out in every direction vehemently (*Kirchliche Dogmatik*, IV, 4, pp. 187-188). One is reminded of this observation when he reads the above passages, though Barth had others in mind than those we have quoted.

brought to the font. Surely if parents brought their children to Jesus when he was in the flesh, we may bring them to the house of prayer where he meets with his people in the Spirit. And if Jesus blessed children, laying hands on them, there is every propriety in those who minister in his name doing the same. Prayer for our children, whereby we acknowledge that they are an inheritance from the Lord and that their nurture is our trust as parents and as members of the congregation, prayer in which we confess our weakness and plead his assistance — this is a catholic, not a sectarian act. Therefore, one may say that in *all* Christian churches the children of confessing parents belong to the congregation and that the congregation should pray for them and provide for their instruction in the Christian faith.

Hence the solemn pledge on the part of Paedobaptist parents who present their children for baptism, that by precept and example they will instruct them in the truths of the Christian faith and seek by all the means in their power to persuade them in years of discretion freely to commit themselves to the Savior, is gladly made by Baptist parents as well. With such a pledge (though not with the subsequent baptism of the child) Baptists are in hearty agreement. Services of "infant dedication," as they are sometimes called, in which parents dedicate their children to Christ in the presence of the congregation and promise to bring them up in the nurture and admonition of the Lord, have been practiced by Baptists for centuries. As Barth once observed,

> Why may not parental obligation if it needs a ritual expression — but does it? — really be just as well expressed in some other way [than baptism]; perhaps, by some sort of public presentation and blessing of the new born child.[60]

Paedobaptists may be inclined to smile at such a suggestion as a kind of infant baptism in the dry; yet, may it not be argued that often their baptism is simply infant dedication

---

[60]*Die Taufe*, p. 37. Barth's mode of expression reflects the usual continental ignorance of Baptists and their ways. "Quite recently a prominent German theologian of the Faith and Order Movement addressed a question to me on the assumption that Baptists deny the Trinity!" (Beasley-Murray, *Baptism in the New Testament*, p. 306, n. 3).

with water?[61] But is dedication the meaning of baptism? Neither in the New Testament nor in the classic Paedobaptist confessions is this unique theology of the sacrament to be found. One might rather say, in the light of the New Testament, that bringing children to Jesus is the first step in a Christian nurture which the parents hope will result in their confessing him in baptism. To practice believer baptism, then, is not to keep children from Christ, unchurch and disfranchise them. In order to bring their children up in the nurture and admonition of the Lord, parents need not start by bringing them to baptism. As we shall argue later, according to the New Testament, baptism is not something to which a person is *brought,* but to which he *comes;* it is the goal, not the presupposition, of Christian nurture. This distinction must be maintained if we are to have a biblical view of the sacraments.

D. THE BAPTISM OF JEWISH PROSELYTES

We have traced the stream of historical evidence for infant baptism back to Jesus himself; and surely, it would seem, this brings us to its fountainhead. But many Paedobaptists do not think so. Even before Jesus commissioned his disciples to baptize, indeed before John the Baptist came preaching the baptism of repentance, Jewish proselytes and their children — so many scholars believe — were commonly admitted into the Jewish church by baptism as well as by circumcision. Therefore we must assume, there being no evidence to the contrary, that when John administered the rite of baptism he also baptized infants. And since it cannot be doubted that the baptism with which Jesus commissioned his disciples was patterned after John's, we may fairly say that Jesus commanded infant baptism — since he did not forbid it — when he sent forth his disciples to baptize in his name.

---

[61]The Constitution of the United Presbyterian Church in the U.S.A., 1960-62, affirms that children born within the pale of the visible church are *dedicated* to God in baptism. See the office, "Of the Admission to Full Communion of Baptized Persons."

Obviously a pre-Christian dating of Jewish proselyte baptism is essential to this argument. Sparing the reader the technical aspects of the debate, we need only observe that there is no incontrovertible evidence for such a date. All clearly pre-Christian sources pertaining to proselytes and their admission to Judaism are notably silent on the subject of their baptism. But the "notable silence" of the sources does not disprove an early date for proselyte baptism; and for the present, at least, the majority of scholars suppose a pre-Christian origin of the practice. This current consensus, since it is not due to direct evidence (which remains as tenuous and indecisive as ever), is generally based on the many apparent affinities between the baptism of Jewish proselytes and the baptism which John and the early Christians practiced.

In spelling out these affinities, the following considerations have been urged. The baptism of John and the disciples of Jesus, like that given to Jewish proselytes, was once for all; it was by immersion, preferably in running water; it had sacramental significance; and it imposed ethical obligations. These similarities, it is argued, are too close to be assigned to fortuity. Either Christian baptism derives its historical pedigree, via John, from Jewish proselyte baptism, or the Jews borrowed their baptism from the Christians. Since the polemic that developed between Christians and Jews is prejudicial of the latter hypothesis, the former, it is alleged, must be true. Therefore, Christian baptism must have derived historically from the baptism of Jewish proselytes.

This reasoning is not without force. What is often overlooked, though, especially by Paedobaptists, is the fact that, however proselyte baptism and Johannine-Christian baptism may have been related to each other historically, there were some obvious differences that are significant for our discussion. For one, Jewish proselyte baptism differed from Christian baptism in that it was tentative as far as children were concerned. "If an offspring of a proselyte baptized in infancy later resolved to turn his back again on Judaism, he was not treated like a renegade Jew, but was looked upon as one who had lived all his life as a non-Israelite."[62] This gives to the baptism of the infants of proselytes a provisional character which the baptism of infants by the Christian church has never had. Paedobaptists do not say that he who repudiates his infant baptism by an adult skepticism is to be looked upon as one who has never been baptized. Rather, they frequently stress the dire consequences for the one who allows his baptismal covenant to lapse. Cullmann, for example, says it is "infinitely worse" for such a person than if he had never been baptized, and darkly invokes the New Testament warnings against the unpardonable sin and incorrigible apostasy.[63]

Furthermore, proselyte baptism was exclusively for Gentiles, but John's baptism, like that of the primitive church in Jerusalem, was exclusively for Jews. This difference is so significant for Bultmann that he calls into question the whole thesis which the Paedobaptist apologetic assumes. "The analogy which prevails between primitive Christian baptism and Jewish proselyte baptism does not mean that the former arose from the latter. Otherwise it would be administered only to Gentiles."[64] That baptism was only for the Gentiles is exactly the idea John attacked. He made it very plain that his fellow Israelites, who were "holy" and proud that they did not need to be baptized like the heathen, were the ones who needed his baptism most.

For these reasons it is hardly convincing to make Jewish proselyte baptism the model for administering baptism to the children of confessing Christians; for it is in this regard that the difference between the two rites is most strikingly in evidence. The Jews did not baptize their own children, nor those born to proselytes after their baptism, because these children were not heathen but born "in holiness." The Paedobaptists, on the other hand, defend the position that the offspring of believers, in contrast to others, should be bap-

---

[62]Strack-Billerbeck, *Kommentar zum Neuen Testament aus Talmud und Midrasch*, p. 110.
[63]*Die Tauflehre*, p. 36.
[64]*Theologie des Neuen Testaments*, I, 41.

tized precisely because they are holy covenant children. Referring to this incongruity, H. H. Rowley observes: "Not seldom, indeed, modern defenders of infant baptism hold that it should be administered only to the children of Christian parents; that is, to precisely those corresponding to the children who did not receive the Jewish baptismal rite."[65] Though Rowley made this observation nearly thirty years ago, to our knowledge no one has really answered it. One can only wonder, then, at the commanding confidence with which some Paedobaptists continue to infer from Jewish proselyte baptism that John the Baptist baptized infants.

Yet, though one may wonder at the anomaly, one can understand why the analogy persists in the literature, since John's baptism is the obvious model for Christian baptism. If infants were not baptized by John, with whose baptism Jesus and his disciples (presumably) were baptized, and after whose example they also baptized others (John 3:22-4:3), it is hardly plausible to suppose that at Pentecost the disciples began to do something for which there was no precedent in John's baptism. Therefore, what the Paedobaptists need to prove is simply affirmed against the evidence, that is, that John must have included children with their parents when he baptized the penitents who came to him at the river Jordan. So Cullmann insists:

> We have not the slightest ground for assuming that John, in contrast to Jewish proselyte baptism, excluded children whom penitent parents, coming to him at Jordan, brought with them, that they might be at the same time embraced in the Messianic community.[66]

The furtive doubt, which such reasoning reveals but cannot entreat, is heightened when one reflects on the depth of the ethical requirements of John's baptism, requirements which go beyond anything the Jews expected of proselytes. We do not deny, as is often done, that proselyte baptism had moral as well as ceremonial implications. But John protested that it was not enough to be separated from heathenism and

[65]"The Origin and Meaning of Baptism," *Baptist Quarterly*, XI (1945), 310ff.
[66]*Die Tauflehre*, pp. 56-57.

to be a citizen of the holy nation. The chosen people of God are themselves in need of cleansing of the heart; and John called upon his fellow Israelites to repent and be baptized because the kingdom of God was at hand.

The theological meaning of John's baptism, then, is not oriented to the idea of legal or ceremonial cleanness, but to the prophetic vision that in the end time the reception of salvation would be marked by an inward cleansing of the people (cf. Ezra 36:25: "Then will I sprinkle clean water upon you and you shall be clean from all your filthiness. . . ."). To have a part in this eschatological kingdom which is about to break into history, to escape the axe that is laid to the root of the tree and the purging of chaff from the threshing-floor, it was not enough to say that one had Abraham for his father (Matt. 3:9). One had to be more than a Jew or a proselyte. One had to repent: to undergo a conversion that involved a clear "no" to his former life as a Jew. One might well have been circumcised as a Jew, or both circumcised and baptized as a proselyte; yet one now had to be baptized with the baptism of "repentance unto the remission of sins" (Mark 1:4; Luke 3:3).

And this radical, existential, eschatological character of the new age, an age of which John was the harbinger, is congenial to a theology that makes personal repentance before God and faith in Christ the necessary prerequisites of baptism. By contrast, it goes against the very grain of the theology of infant baptism — with its stress on the "federal holiness" of "covenant children" as "members of the visible church" by virtue of their "physical birth" to believing parents. How can one suppose that John came preaching the baptism of repentance (Mark 1:4) and at the same time baptized infants who were incapable of repentance? John warned the Pharisees not to say, "We have Abraham as our Father"; how, then, can one suppose that he baptized infants by virtue of their parental connection? Here we move to a problem that is not historical (such as the question of the date of Jewish proselyte baptism) but theological. And the fact that we are constrained to do so indicates that it is time to conclude our review of the historical argument for the practice of infant

III

CONCLUDING OBSERVATIONS ON THE HISTORICAL QUESTION

The most obvious problem with the historical argument for infant baptism is the notable silence of the witnesses the nearer they are to the apostolic age.[67] This, combined with the silence of the New Testament itself, cannot but evoke questions in the inquiring mind. Paedobaptists assure us that one need not stumble at this silence, since in the early years of the church's mission the primary concern obviously must have been with the baptism of adults. We should, then, hardly expect the historical record to reflect more than a "silent, scarcely conscious flow of transition" as children, with their parents, are reckoned in the Christian Israel. Thus all that should be necessary, it would appear, is that the early sources, especially the New Testament sources, should say nothing expressly *against* infant baptism.

Some have gone even further. They have, as it were, put the lack of explicit evidence on the rack of their argument and stretched it, until the very silence of the New Testament becomes a testimony *in favor* of infant baptism. "In the New Testament," says Cullmann, "there is . . . *no trace whatever*

---

[67]It is to focus this problem of the silence of the crucial witnesses that we have reversed the order of chronology in our treatment of the historical question. Beginning with Augustine, we have moved back to the apostles. Paedobaptists, on the contrary, always follow the order of history, which enables them to end the discussion, as Beethoven ended his symphonies, on a grand note. Going down the stream of time, the evidence for infant baptism increases until all doubt is overwhelmed by the universal witness of the fourth-century Fathers.

of any baptism of an adult who had been born and reared from the beginning by Christian parents."[68] In our judgment, this argument is hardly worthy of the italicized dignity with which it marches across the page. Obviously, there is no mention of such baptisms in the Gospels, since the evangelists are concerned with events in Jesus' lifetime, before the Christian church was established. And inasmuch as the first half of Acts treats of the history of the church up to A.D. 50, while the remainder of the book is concerned with the activity of Paul and his associates as pioneer missionaries among the Gentiles, any mention of the "baptism of an adult who had been born and reared from the beginning by Christian parents" would be a plain historical impossibility. As for Paul's epistles, they were written from two to fifteen years after the founding of the churches to which they were addressed. One would hardly expect the apostle, then, to be able to speak of the baptism of adults who had been born and reared in these nascent Christian communities. Besides Paul's epistles, the New Testament contains mostly brief letters or documents which are not concerned specifically with baptism. This is particularly true of the Apocalypse of John. Though written toward the end of the first century, when second-generation Christians had reached the age of accountability, one can hardly attribute significance to the fact that there is no mention of the "baptism of adults who had been born and reared by Christian parents" in a document of this sort. The very subject matter of the book excludes such a possibility. This oft-repeated argument, then, is really quite irrelevant.

The same may be said of Jeremias' reiterated insistence that nowhere in the earliest period of Christian history is there evidence of an age limit (*Altersgrenze*) in granting baptism, of a postponement of baptism (*Taufaufschub*), or of a renunciation of the right to have one's children baptized (*Taufverzicht*). Does not the very use of such terms betray the bias of the investigation and justify the complaint of Aland

[68]*Die Tauflehre*, p. 21 (italics his). Likewise, one hundred years ago, James Bannerman, *The Church of Christ*, II; and two hundred years before Bannerman, Richard Baxter, *Plain Scripture Proof*, ch. vii.

that the "terminology" Jeremias brings to the discussion is inimical to any interpretation but his own?[69] It is only when one is incapable of conceiving of a world without infant baptism that he can speak of the baptism of the children of Christians upon their own confession of faith as a "postponement" of their baptism or a "renunciation" by the parents of their rights. The issue is not a matter of "postponement" or "age limits" or "parental right," but of the spiritual qualifications of those baptized. "We baptize," said Justin, "those who are convinced and consent to Christian teaching."

The long and the short of the matter is that infant baptism nowhere appears in the sources until well into the second century. In the words of Erich Dinkler,

> One must learn to live with the fact that the literature of primal Christianity is silent concerning child and infant baptism and that all indications speak against the introduction of this custom before the third century. If in Ephesians 1:13f, after hearing, believing, being sealed = baptism, the gift of the Spirit is named as an earnest (compare also, for example, II Corinthians 1:19-22; Acts 2:37ff; 12:35ff), then here the theological sequence of primal Christianity finds expression: baptism seals the invariably preceding gift of faith in Christ. A baptism of infants cannot be historically grounded in the New Testament; it must be "theologically inferred."[70]

This "theological inference" of infant baptism from the New Testament, and the fundamental assumptions that have impelled it, shall occupy our attention in the ensuing pages.

---

[69]*Die Säuglingstaufe*, p. 80.
[70]*RGG*, 3 Auflage, VI, "Taufe," Sec. II, Im Urchristentum, Sec. 1.

Part Two:
A CONSIDERATION OF THE THEOLOGICAL QUESTION, WITH SPECIAL ATTENTION TO THE REFORMED TRADITION

INFANT BAPTISM
AND THE
COVENANT OF GRACE

A. INTRODUCTION

At the time of the Reformation, Lutherans and Anglicans tended to follow the medieval doctors in ascribing
"power" to the waters of baptism. Luther considered the
sacrament a means of regeneration and thanked God that it
had been preserved throughout the centuries unimpaired.
The *Augsburg Confession* (A.D. 1530) teaches that baptism is
necessary to salvation and condemns the Anabaptists, who
do not allow the baptism of children and who affirm that
children are saved without the sacrament.[1] The *Formula of
Concord* (A.D. 1576), in a long and lugubrious catalogue of
Anabaptist errors, which "can be tolerated neither in the
church, nor by the police and in the commonwealth, nor in
daily life," also charges the Anabaptists with teaching that
children may attain salvation without baptism (Art. XII, 4).

The doctrine of the Church of England concerning this
rubric is scarcely less candid than that of the German church.
Baptism is the instrument by which a child is grafted into the
church (*Thirty-Nine Articles*, Art. XXVII, A.D. 1571). According to the *Book of Common Prayer*, the water of baptism
is sanctified to the "mystical washing away of sin," and the
child is regenerated and born anew of water and the Spirit. At

---

[1]Thus the Latin text. The German text, accepted by many Lutherans
today, simply says that the Anabaptists ". . . who teach that infant baptism is
not right are rejected."

confirmation all children answer the question, "Who gave you your name?"[2] by repeating the Catechism (Q. 2): "My Godfathers and Godmothers in my baptism; wherein I was made a member of Christ, the child of God, and an inheritor of the kingdom of heaven."

Undoubtedly there is room for evangelicalism in both the Lutheran and Anglican churches, as the existence of an evangelical party in these communions demonstrates.[3] However, as far as the baptismal teaching of these churches is concerned, evangelicalism hangs on the slender thread of linguistic ambiguity. The soul of the symbols cannot be made to feel at home in evangelical raiment. The service of infant baptism begins with the fact that all men are conceived and born in sin and proceeds directly to the point that no one can enter the kingdom of God except he be born anew of water and the Spirit (John 3:5). These ideas were old friends long before the Reformation and have continued so down through the centuries. We can hardly escape the impression that before the water is applied sin is there, but after it is applied sin is not there. There is a predictable coincidence in calendar time between the application of water and the presence of cleansing, renewing grace, however mysterious the *modus operandi* may be. As Pusey, the high priest of English high churchmen, said, "We know it [regeneration] in its author, God; in its instrument, baptism; in its end, salvation. . . . We only know it not in the mode of its operation."[4]

For this reason George Whitefield, baptized and confirmed, would have made a perfectly good Anglican priest, had he never read the writings of Franke and been converted.

---

[2]This name, received in the new birth of baptism, is one's "Christian" name, in contrast to one's surname, which was received at the time of natural birth. See Shakespeare, *Romeo and Juliet*, Act II, Scene II: "I take thee at thy word;/Call me but love, and I'll be new baptized;/Henceforth I never will be Romeo." See also Laurence Stearn, *Tristram Shandy*, I, 19, for a dash of genuine humor on this "name" theme. For further comment, see below, p. 223, n. 10.

[3]In fact, when the Tractarians and Puseyites in the nineteenth century declared a full-orbed sacramentalism to be the only legitimate view in the Church of England, the Judicial Committee of the Privy Council (in the Gorham case of 1851) expressly declared that an evangelical view was also legitimate.

[4]*Scriptural Views of Holy Baptism*, p. 23.

The same may be said of John Wesley, had he never come in contact with the Moravians and experienced a warming of his heart when he met with them at Aldersgate. As the teachings of the German Pietists incur the censure of the classic Lutheran symbols in the matter of baptismal grace, so it is with the preaching of Whitefield and Wesley vis-à-vis the Anglican symbols. Their insistence on a conversion experience is indeed "enthusiasm" (as their detractors claimed), at least as far as the baptismal theology of the *Book of Common Prayer* is concerned.

The question, however, of the efficacy of the sacraments is too large for our present purpose. Being straitened by the specific question of infant baptism, we have not the leisure here to ruminate on the larger subject of the proximity of the sacramental sign to the thing signified. For the present we can only observe that to say with the *Augsburg Confession* that baptism "is necessary to salvation," or with the *Anglican Book of Common Prayer* that a child is "by baptism regenerate and grafted into the body of Christ's church," seems to us to be playing the part of Lot's wife in furtively looking back toward the medieval doctrine of sacramental efficacy (*ex opere operato*). When the ancient Fathers began seriously to frame a reason for baptizing infants, they wrote the prologue to this medieval sacramentalism by saying that baptism is the divinely appointed instrument for mediating the grace of cleansing from original sin and renewal in the image of Christ. The position of the Lutheran and Anglican confessions is but the epilogue to this same position. Though in the latter communions, as in the early Fathers, the ties between the outward sign and the inward grace are looser than in the Roman Church, yet cleansing from sin and inward renewal are still tied to the waters of baptism.

B. THE REFORMED TRADITION

At the time of the Reformation a new thing occurred. Like the river of Eden, the argument for infant baptism was parted and a genuinely evangelical defense of Paedobaptism emerged, a defense that viewed the sacrament of baptism simply as "a washing with water, signifying and sealing our engrafting into Christ and partaking of the benefits of the covenant of grace."[5] The interminable debate over infant baptism and believer baptism has tended to obscure this significant fact. It is commonly acknowledged that there were essentially two points of view on baptism at the Reformation: that of the Reformers, which was infant baptism; and that of the sectarian Anabaptists, which was adult baptism. But a closer examination reveals that the thinking of the Paedobaptists themselves, from the very beginning of the Reformation, is further split by a difference of opinion which goes far deeper than the question of whether or not infants should be baptized. This fundamental difference involves the whole theology of the sacrament of initiation. Whereas Luther could thank God that the sacrament of baptism had been preserved unimpaired, Zwingli could only conclude that ever since the apostles, all the doctors in the church had been in error in this matter. In this latter statement we have the beginning of a *radical break* with the past and the appearance of a new constellation of ideas in the theological heavens. To perceive that this is so, one has only to turn to the confessional literature of the major Reformed communions, read with a theologically critical eye, and he will at once perceive that in this area the Reformed confessions differ significantly not only from the teaching of the medieval Schoolmen but also from their Lutheran and Anglican counterparts quoted above.

In none of the Reformed confessions is there a reference to the necessity of baptizing infants in order that they may be saved. Whereas Lutherans "condemn the doctrine that children are saved without baptism,"[6] the Reformed tradition repudiates with abhorrence the thought that unbaptized children may be forever lost as a "cruel judgment against infants departing without the sacrament."[7] Furthermore, there is nothing in the Reformed confessions about being "born of

---

[5] See *Westminster Shorter Catechism*, Q. 94.
[6] *Augsburg Confession*, I, ix.
[7] *Second Scottish Confession* (A.D. 1580).

water," which is so prominent in the Lutheran and Anglican confessions. Rather, there is the express statement that baptism is a washing of regeneration only in the sense of a "divine pledge and token . . . that we are really washed from our sins spiritually. . . ."[8] It should be noted further that in the Reformed view the children presented for baptism are not regarded as needing cleansing and as outside the church prior to their baptism. Instead, it is because they are heirs of God's covenant promise and numbered by him as among his people and members of his church that they are to be baptized. "Why should they [covenant children] not be consecrated by holy baptism, who are God's peculiar people and are in the church of God?"[9]

How different is this from the prayer that God will grant to this child, being baptized with water, that he may thereby be received into Christ's holy church and made a lively member of the same! The one perspective moves in a dimension of evangelical propriety; the other echoes sacramental necessity. In Lutheran and Anglican theology, baptism is to be administered privately, even by laymen and laywomen, if death impend. By contrast, in Reformed theology, though baptism is not to be unduly delayed, "it is not to be administered in any case by any private person, but by a minister of Christ. . . . Nor is it to be administered in private places or privately, but in the place of public worship and in the face of the congregation. . . ."[10]

The whole difference that we are noting here was succinctly put in the *Saxon Visitation Articles* (A.D. 1592). Though never of ecumenical authority in Lutheran circles, these articles are nonetheless a clear statement of the orthodox Lutheran position in contrast to that of the Calvinists. In repudiating the allegedly false doctrine of the Calvinists on baptism, the *Articles* accuse the latter of teaching that baptism merely signifies inward ablution; that it does not work regeneration, faith, and grace, but only sig-

[8]*Heidelberg Catechism*, Q. and A. 73.
[9]*Second Helvetic Confession*, "Of Holy Baptism," ch. xx.
[10]*The Directory for the Public Worship of God*, agreed upon by the Assembly of Divines at Westminster, 1645.

nifies and seals them; that salvation does not depend on baptism, so that when a minister of the church is not available, the infant should be permitted to die without baptism; and that infants of Christians are already holy before baptism, being received into the covenant of life, otherwise baptism could not be conferred on them (I-VI).

Now if one views the sacraments evangelically as outward signs and seals of an inward grace secured to those who worthily receive them by the efficacious working of the Spirit, and not as guaranteeing, in themselves, the grace which they signify, then the traditional reason for baptizing infants — that they be cleansed from the guilt of original sin, regenerated, and thus made members of Christ's church — is deprived of all force. But then why should infants be baptized, if it does not secure their salvation? It was Zwingli who first pioneered the answer to this question. Caught between the sacramentalism of the Roman Catholics, who made the baptism of infants necessary for salvation, and the innovations of the Anabaptists, who refused even to allow infants to be baptized, he sought a *via media*. He decided to walk with the Fathers and contrary to the Anabaptists in retaining the *usage* of infant baptism, but at the same time to walk with the Anabaptists and contrary to the Fathers by denying the *necessity* of infant baptism.

We can thus appreciate the significance of a sentence from the opening paragraph of Zwingli's treatise on baptism. Having observed that the doctors "have erred from the time of the apostles, by ascribing a power to the waters of baptism which they do not possess," he concludes that "at many points we shall have to tread a different path from that taken either by ancient or more modern writers or by our own contemporaries."[11] This new path, says the Reformer, opens up before one when he perceives that Christ has transformed the blood of circumcision into the water of baptism. By this Zwingli meant that infant circumcision, as the mark of the covenant between God and the seed of Abraham, is the final *raison d'être* for infant baptism. As circumcision was the sign between God and the seed of Abraham, so now baptism is the

---

[11]*De Baptismo, Library of Christian Classics*, p. 130.

sign between God and the seed of Christians who are the true heirs of the covenant made with Abraham. Of course, the great Swiss Reformer marshaled many supporting arguments from the testimony of the Fathers and the practice of the apostles, but this "argument from circumcision" was destined to cast all its confreres into the shadows.

The argument, to be sure, was not absolutely new. As we have already seen, the opinion that infants should be baptized because they were circumcised is of ancient pedigree, having been mentioned by Cyprian in his letter to Fidus. Prior to Zwingli, however, it had enjoyed only an ancillary place in giving propriety to infant baptism. But with the Swiss Reformer it became a full-orbed theological principle, moving into the center of the argument, a position which the centripetal pressures of the subsequent debate — especially in the Reformed tradition — entrenched and fortified. Calvin called it, very candidly, the sum of the matter.[12] To the question, "Are infants also to be baptized?" the *Heidelberg Catechism* answers, "Yes, for since they, as well as their parents, belong to the covenant and people of God . . . they also are to be baptized as a sign of the covenant, to be ingrafted into the Christian church and distinguished from the children of unbelievers, *as was done in the Old Testament by circumcision, in place of which in the New Testament baptism is appointed.*"[13] Besides Calvin and the authors of the *Heidelberg Catechism,* many another illustrious theologian has followed Zwingli down this path, smoothing, widening, straightening the argument, until the concept of "children of the covenant" has become the main highway connecting an evangelical view of the sacraments with the practice of infant baptism.

It must be admitted from the outset that this "argument from the covenant" is a challenging synthesis. Here is a theological idea that has dominated the confessions and liturgies of all branches of the Reformed Church, as well as of the Free Church communions of both England and America. Even the Methodists, though their roots are Angli-

[12]*Institutes,* IV, xvi, 24.
[13]Q. 74 (italics mine).

can, have felt no impropriety in defending infant baptism along these lines.

The theological conception, therefore, that undergirds the argument for infant baptism at this point is too challenging and persistent to be ignored by any but those who see through the hollow eyes of predisposition. The dogmatician who slights it despises his own reputation. Cullmann's point in this regard is well taken when he complains that Barth did not pursue the theological implications of the argument from circumcision as he should have.

> The way in which Karl Barth slurs over this question is indeed the weakest point in his teaching on baptism. Even though it be conceded that the Reformers' grounds of proof in favor of infant baptism did not all hold water, yet at least *this* Reformation argument deserved greater attention. ... For my part, I simply cannot see how Karl Barth can admit that baptism is the fulfillment of circumcision, yet on the decisive point, can deny the inner connection of the two and assert that circumcision is in its essence different, so that the fact that children were circumcised is without significance for the Christian practice of infant baptism.[14]

Pierre Marcel, a leading spokesman for the orthodox party in the Reformed Church of France, published an answer to Barth in *La Revue Réformée*, the very title of which is significant: "Le Baptême, Sacrement de l'Alliance de Grace."[15]

C. THE COVENANT ARGUMENT ELABORATED

1. Introduction

Because of the significance for our study of this argument from the covenant, we must pause to amplify the covenant concept as it is used in Scripture and theology. The word "covenant" (Hebrew בְּרִית) connotes an agreement or compact between two or more parties. Drawing from the

---

[14]*Die Tauflehre*, p. 51.

[15]Translated under the title *The Biblical Doctrine of Infant Baptism: Sacrament of the Covenant of Grace*.

realm of the ancient suzerainty covenants (treaties) binding vassal to lord, the writers of the Old Testament under the inspiration of the Spirit employ this legal, political term to illuminate the unique relationship established by Jahweh with the children of Israel, in which he declares himself Israel's God and Israel engages to be his people. The mutuality of the covenant idea is seen in the condition imposed: if Israel keeps God's commandments, she will be blessed as the head of the nations (Deut. 26:16-19).

As the prophets deepen the meaning of this covenant relationship by such analogies as the Shepherd and the flock (Ezek. 34:1ff.), the Vinedresser and the vine (Isa. 5:1-7), the Father and the first-born (Jer. 31:9), the Mother and the child (Isa. 49:15), and especially the Husband and the bride (Ezek. 16:6-14), mutuality gives way to a dominant unilateralism. God's covenant love becomes an unconditional love that will not let his people go (Hos. 11). Even though Israel breaks the covenant as an unfaithful wife and is afflicted in the overthrow of Samaria (II Kgs. 17:7-23) and the captivity of Judah (II Kgs. 23:26ff.), the covenant still stands so far as God is concerned. Israel's national ruin, exile, and dispersion do not finally frustrate his gracious covenant purpose. A new covenant will be made in which the law will be written on their hearts (Jer. 31:31-34; 32:37-41).

This new covenant, mediated by the servant of the Lord (Is. 42:6), will enlarge the promises made to the fathers to embrace all nations (Is. 49:6). This is the covenant which God remembered (Luke 1:72) when he sent his Son, a light to lighten the Gentiles and the glory of his people Israel (Luke 2:32). This new covenant is sealed with the blood of the Mediator and acknowledged by the covenantees in their drinking the cup of the new covenant in his blood (Mark 14:24; Matt. 26:28; Luke 22:20). This new covenant, which is a gracious promise of salvation on God's part, is the ultimate ground of the sinner's hope. Only when the sinner perceives that there are no conditions to be met, no stipulations attached; only when he understands that his interest in Christ is simply that he is a sinner and that Christ has graciously suffered in his stead, wound for wound, stripe for

stripe, and death for death, does the covenant become to him
a covenant of free grace. The theological designation "covenant of grace," therefore, is a happy formulation to describe
this new covenant in Christ, pointing up both the divine
sovereignty on which it rests and the comfort of the sinner
who rests upon it.[16]

Along with the sovereignty of the covenant, stress
should also be laid on its unity. The covenant idea is a
fundamental concept of redemptive revelation: it unites the
entire purpose of God throughout salvation history. Though
Scripture speaks of the old and the new covenants, this
plurality is not so ultimate as to impugn a deeper singularity.
The God of Abraham, Isaac, and Jacob and of Sarah, Rebekah, and Rachel is the God and Father of our Lord Jesus
Christ, the Angel of the old covenant and Mediator of the
new.[17]

It is specifically the property of unity or oneness in
God's covenantal dealings with his people that is most relevant to our inquiry at this juncture. Since the Bible teaches
that the gracious acts of God toward man's salvation are in
fulfillment of the promises and engagements of the covenant
of grace, it follows that there is one people of God, whom he
has redeemed and who are united to him by faith; one

---

[16]This factor of divine sovereignty (unilateralism) undoubtedly bears
on the Septuagint rendering of ברית. The most plausible answer to the
question of why the Septuagint translators did not employ συνθήκη, the
common word for covenant, rather than διαθήκη (testament) is that they
wished to escape any connotation of a contract between equals. W. Bauer,
Greek-English Lexicon, significantly observes that whereas "last will and
testament is its exclusive usage in Hellenistic times, διαθήκη — as a translation of ברית — loses this sense because, as decreed by God, a διαθήκη cannot
require the death of the testator to make it operative. Nevertheless, an
essential characteristic of a testament is retained, namely, that it is the
declaration of one person's will, not the result of an agreement between two
parties, like a compact or contract. This is, without doubt, one of the main
reasons why the LXX rendered ברית by διαθήκη. In the covenants of God, it
was God alone who set the conditions; hence, *covenant* can be used to
translate διαθήκη only when this is kept in mind."

[17]As Emil Brunner well observes, the ". . . difference [between the Old
and the New Covenant] concerns the *modus administrationis;* the oneness,
the *substantia.* The different modes of administration — what we call the
form [*Gestalt*] of revelation — are a matter of the *verbi dispensatio,* which, in
its turn, is an *accommodatio* to the *diversitas temporum*" (*Offenbarung und
Vernunft,* p. 196).

Mediator of the covenant, in whom all the promises are yea and amen; and one destiny for all the saints, namely Mount Zion, the city of our God, the New Jerusalem. To all these truths, evangelicals — Baptists as well as Paedobaptists — have been unreservedly committed.

If these things are true, it further follows — and here the pincers of the argument begin to close — that the sacrament of circumcision, which was the sign and seal of the covenant as originally administered, is essentially like the sacrament of baptism, the sign and seal of the covenant as newly administered in Christ. Ursinus, co-author of the *Heidelberg Catechism*, in his *Commentary* on the same, has reduced this argument to a syllogism:

> Under the Old Testament, infants were circumcised as well as adults. Baptism occupies the place of circumcision in the New Testament and has the same use as circumcision had in the Old Testament. Therefore infants are to be baptized as well as adults.[18]

If we grant the truth of the premises, the conclusion surely does follow. Since the major premise, that children were circumcised under the old covenant, cannot be disputed, the only place we need to scrutinize the argument is in its minor premise, that circumcision equals baptism. Let us now give ourselves scrupulously to this task.

2. *The analogy of baptism to circumcision*

While it is true that the rites of circumcision and baptism do not agree in every particular (obviously baptism is not limited, as is circumcision, to males eight days old), yet the argument for the basic similarity between them will lose little of its claim to respectability from such considerations. If anyone will look a little more deeply beneath the surface, he will perceive that the Old Testament is clearly concerned

---

[18]*Commentary of Ursinus*, p. 367. The section quoted above concludes on the following less than charitable note: "Wherefore this and similar follies of the sect of the Anabaptists should be carefully avoided, since they have without doubt been hatched by the devil, and are detestable heresies which they fabricated from various errors and blasphemies."

with the theological and ethical meaning of circumcision, which, as elaborated in the New Testament, lies too close to that of baptism to be depreciated. One's circumcision signified his entry into the fellowship of God's covenant people and assured his participation in those blessings and benefits which belong to the covenantees as a whole. This privilege brings with it certain ethical demands, specifically obedience to the God of the covenant, whose sign is borne in one's body and who says to the covenantee, "Walk before me and be thou perfect" (Gen. 17:1).

Thus circumcision becomes a symbol of renewal and cleansing of heart, and the Old Testament characterizes a lack of feeling and receptivity for things divine as being "uncircumcised in heart" (Lev. 26:41; Jer. 9:26; Ezek. 44:7). By the same token, through circumcision the heart is enabled to receive spiritual things and to submit to the divine will (Deut. 10:16; 30:6; Jer. 4:4, 9:26; Ezek. 44:7). Hence, even in the Old Testament we see that circumcision, the mark of citizenship in the Jewish nation, had not only a socio-political but also an ethico-theological meaning. This ethico-theological meaning, as the New Testament interprets circumcision, is not lost but taken up in the meaning of baptism.[19] This is seen, for example, in Romans 4, where Paul sets forth the faith of Abraham as the prototype of the Christian faith and defines Abraham's circumcision as the sign and seal of the righteousness which he had by faith, while he was yet uncircumcised. Some scholars have gone so far as to affirm that the term Paul uses in Romans 4 for circumcision (σφραγίς, seal), he uses in other places for baptism. The most likely instance is found in II Corinthians 1:22: "Now he who has established us with you in Christ, and anointed us, is God, who also *sealed* us and gave us the earnest of the Spirit in our hearts." It is, indeed, plausible that in II Corinthians 1:22 Paul is referring to baptism under the figure of a "seal." In any case, baptism may be likened to

---

[19]It is for this reason that we cannot subscribe to the affirmation that circumcision in the Old Testament "had no relation to moral renewal; the prophetic call for heart circumcision is an application of the rite in symbol, not an exposition of the rite itself" (Beasley-Murray, *Baptism in the New Testament,* p. 341).

a seal because it marks, affirms, attests, and authenticates — though it does not effect — our ingrafting into Christ.

We say that baptism seals, but does not effect, a vital union with Christ because the function of a seal is to ratify something that has happened, not to bring it to pass. The seal of King Ahasuerus, for example, would have wrought nothing to deliver the Jews from Haman's hand had it not been impressed upon a document already written in the King's name declaring that fact (Esth. 8:8). So it is with baptism and the grace of cleansing and renewal which it signifies. It is the Spirit's cleansing of the inner man, his writing the law on our hearts, that makes baptism meaningful. Apart from such a work of grace in the heart, there is nothing to be sealed in baptism. But is not this just to say that Paul's definition of circumcision in Romans 4:11 could very well be applied to baptism? As circumcision was the seal of the righteousness of the faith which Abraham had, being uncircumcised, so our baptism is the seal of the righteousness of the faith which we have, being unbaptized. This conclusion appears inescapable, and it establishes the claim of the Paedobaptists that there is a fundamental affinity of meaning between circumcision in the Old Testament and baptism in the New.

When one examines Ephesians 2:11-12, where Paul refers to the pre-Christian state of his readers as "uncircumcision," one must come to the same conclusion, inasmuch as the basic thrust of the apostle in this passage can hardly be a literal one. By referring to his converts as formerly uncircumcised, he is not siding with the Jews who vainly cast this aspersion in the teeth of the Gentiles. In fact, the apostle elsewhere rebukes his Jewish brethren for not realizing that their own transgression of the law had turned their physical circumcision into uncircumcision (Rom. 2:25). Rather, Paul describes the Ephesians as uncircumcised in the spiritual sense that, prior to their conversion, they were apart from Christ. But if to be apart from Christ is to be spiritually uncircumcised, "alienated from the commonwealth of Israel and strangers from the covenants of promise," then to be in Christ must be to possess those blessings of which circumcision in the flesh was no less certainly the sign in the Old

Testament than is baptism in the New. Hence, in writing to Gentile Christians, Paul identifies with them and declares, "For we are the true circumcision" (Phil. 3:3). Such Gentile Christians, in other words, are Jews "inwardly," having the circumcision of the heart, a circumcision which is in the Spirit and not in the letter (Rom. 2:29).

Again, having declared (Gal. 3:26) that Christians are children of God by faith, Paul elaborates his thesis in a striking figure of speech by affirming (v. 27) that as many as were baptized into Christ have "put on" Christ. The verb used in verse 27—ἐνδύω—means "to clothe oneself in," "to wear." As Alexander the Great wore the holy garments of the gods so that he would appear like Hermes or Hercules, we by our baptism have clothed ourselves with Christ so that we may appear like him. That is to say, we have declared our purpose to wear the garment woven of his righteousness, fabricated of those dispositions and graces which adorned his life. But if we are Christ's, the apostle continues (v. 29), then we are also Abraham's seed and heirs according to the promise given to him. Now when one remembers that the mark of Abraham's progeny in the Old Testament, which identified them as his seed, was circumcision, one can hardly doubt that baptism has the same essential significance for Christians in the New Testament. By baptism we are identified as disciples of Christ, and as such we are Abraham's children and heirs of the promise made to the fathers.

The crucial text for this line of reasoning is Colossians 2:11-13:

> In him also you were circumcised with a circumcision made without hands, by putting off the body of flesh in the circumcision of Christ; and you were buried with him in baptism, in which you were also raised with him through faith in the working of God, who raised him from the dead. And you, who were dead in trespasses and the uncircumcision of your flesh, God made alive together with him, having forgiven us all our trespasses.

Whether or not one understands the "circumcision of Christ" in this passage objectively to include the cross, surely one cannot doubt its subjective reference. The sinner is not circumcised with Christ's circumcision until he "puts off the body of flesh" by dying to the old man and puts on the new man by faith. Paul is here arguing that those who are in Christ have experienced this heart circumcision. That it is a matter of the heart, something spiritual and inward, is made indubitably clear by its being defined — in contrast to outward circumcision — as "not made with hands." (Literal circumcision, by contrast, which is "made with hands," is worthless: "In Christ Jesus neither circumcision avails anything, nor uncircumcision, but faith working by love," Gal. 5:6.) Now the Christian is one who has received this inward circumcision of Christ, "having been buried with him in baptism, wherein he was also raised with Christ through faith in the working of God." The use of the aorist passive throughout the passage (περιετμήθητε, συνταφέντες, συνηγέρθητε) makes it evident that to experience the circumcision of Christ, in the putting off of the body of the flesh, is the same thing as being buried and raised with him in baptism through faith. If this be true, the only conclusion we can reach is that the two signs, as outward rites, symbolize the same inner reality in Paul's thinking. Thus circumcision may fairly be said to be the Old Testament counterpart of Christian baptism. So far the Reformed argument, in our judgment, is biblical. In this sense "baptism," to quote the *Heidelberg Catechism*, "occupies the place of circumcision in the New Testament."

D. A CRITICAL EVALUATION OF THE ARGUMENT FROM THE COVENANT

1. Introduction

In the above summary we have had occasion to stress the unity of redemptive revelation as that revelation unfolds in terms of God's covenant promise. The argument from infant circumcision to infant baptism patently turns on the assumption that the promise made to Abraham and his descendants is the promise ratified in Christ to all believers. The new covenant in Christ's blood is the unfolding and fruition of the covenant made with Abraham. We should never forget, however — and the time has now come to stress this point — that this *affinity* of the old with the new must be counterbalanced by a proper emphasis on the *diversity* between the two. Although the promise of salvation, then as now, had its foundation in Christ, the Old Testament obviously differs from the New in that God condescended to man's weakness by exhibiting the promise of eternal life, for the partial contemplation and enjoyment of the saints in the Old Testament, under the figures of temporal and terrestrial blessings. Since the Old Testament people of God did not enjoy the superior light of the gospel age, God stooped, as it were, to this inferior mode of instruction. Not that he signified in the covenant with Abraham no more than earthly blessings but that these earthly blessings should be a mirror in which the Israelites might contemplate heavenly things.

Nevertheless, as long as the old covenant was in force the temporal and terrestrial blessings were a part of the promise given to Abraham. In fact, the Abrahamic covenant given in the Genesis narrative was exceedingly objective and concrete. The promised land was a piece of geography which Abraham could survey with his eyes and tread upon with his feet (Gen. 13:14-15). The seed descending through Isaac and Jacob was just as empirically real as the stars in the sky and the sand on the seashore to which it was likened (Gen. 22:17). Even that aspect of the covenant which contemplated the blessing of others — "in thee shall all nations be blessed" or "bless themselves" — was not without its temporal side: Lot is said to have prospered in flocks, herds, and tents while he lived with Abraham (Gen. 13:5f.); and the petty kings of the Pentapolis were put in the patriarch's debt when he restored their captives and goods from the pillaging hand of Chedorlaomer, king of Elam (Gen. 14).

It is all very well for Paedobaptists to insist that the promise sealed by circumcision contained more than meets the earthly eye. In this vein, Calvin does well to remind us that Jacob, a fugitive from the rage of his brother; defrauded by Laban, his uncle; vexed by the violation of his daughter; duped by the bloodstained cloak of his son; and disgraced by Reuben's incest, was constrained to testify that his days on earth had been few and evil, by which he bore witness to the truth that the blessings of the covenant transcended the carnal securities of this life. Yet it is also true that when Jacob rebuked Laban, he appealed to the tangible fact of his earthly substance as evidence that the God of Abraham and the Fear of Isaac was on his side. Because of heaven's blessing he had not been forced to leave Paddan-aram empty-handed (Gen. 31:42). He celebrates the faithfulness of God in keeping his covenant promise by remarking that he had crossed the Jordan with naught but his staff and was returning with two companies (Gen. 32:10).

With the advent of Messiah — the promised seed *par excellence* — and the Pentecostal effusion of the Spirit, the salvation contained in the promise to Israel was brought nigh. No longer was it a hope on the distant horizon but rather an accomplished fact in history. Then — and for our discussion, this THEN is of capital significance — the temporal, earthly, typical elements of the old dispensation were dropped from the great house of salvation as scaffolding from the finished edifice. It is our contention that the Paedobaptists, in framing their argument from circumcision, have failed to keep this significant historical development in clear focus. Proceeding from the basically correct postulate that baptism stands in the place of circumcision, they have urged this analogy to a distortion. They have so far pressed the *unity* of the covenant as to suppress the *diversity* of its administration. They have, to be specific, Christianized the Old Testament and Judaized the New.

It is this double movement within the argument from circumcision — reading the New Testament as though it were the Old and the Old Testament as though it were the New — which makes the argument so easy to use and so difficult to criticize. The reader should be advised at the outset that Paedobaptist reasoning does not flow in one direction like the water in a brook but rather can be likened to the great currents of the sea. As the deep, heavy water is constantly flowing over the sill at the Straits of Gibraltar and out to sea, while the lighter, less saline water is flowing inward from the Atlantic to replace it, so it is with the Paedobaptist argument from circumcision. It moves in two directions at the same time, reading the Old as though it were the New and the New as though it were the Old. It is this compounded error that makes the Reformed argument for infant baptism, apparently so plausible on a superficial level, seem utterly confused when one probes it in depth. Speaking to this point, Karl Barth once commented:

> I venture the affirmation: the confusion into which Luther and Calvin and their respective disciples have tumbled headlong in this matter is hopeless. One must concede to them that unlike the moderns they at least made a serious effort to find an answer to the burning dogmatic question. Yet one can only affirm that the relevant information which one obtains from them, and that in the decisive points, is as implausible as their exegesis is unsatisfying. Let anyone read chapters XV and XVI of Book IV of the *Institutio* in order and convince himself where the great Calvin is sure of his subject and where he obviously is not sure of it, but is patently nervous, involved in an exceedingly unperspicuous train of thought, scolding; where he lectures when he should convince, seeks a way in the fog which can lead him to no goal because he has none.[20]

This is how Barth expressed himself in 1943. His final word to the church on this subject, some twenty-five years later, may properly be noted at this point as anticipating the argument we are about to elaborate:

> The force of this argument of Calvin's [from infant circumcision to infant baptism], which one cannot deny, rests on his unfolding of the correct and weighty insight that although the old and new covenants are formally different, there is an essential *unity* between them (*Institutio*, II, 9-11). According to this insight, Christ, as the Lord of both "economies" or "dispensations," is also Lord of both circumcision and baptism. It is basically this thesis . . . which Calvin has obviously made a fundamental pillar in all his thinking. But in that section [of the *Institutes*] which we mentioned above, there is also a chapter (II, 11) entitled *De differentia unius testamenti ab altero*. Even the knowledge of the unity of the covenant (because it is knowledge of the unity in its *diversity*) excludes the thought that what is to be said of Old Testament circumcision, is, without qualification, to be said of New Testament baptism, as though the definition and meaning of the two were entirely

[20]*Die Taufe*, pp. 35-36.

interchangeable. At this juncture Calvin's argument comes unglued, as, in its own way, Luther's also does.[21]

Of course, the Paedobaptists have demurred from this judgment and sometimes eliminated it with a pomposity of magnificent words. Such objections to their view, we are assured, arise from "*a priori* philosophical notions" which tend to "set the two Testaments in opposition to each other." They reflect a "non-legitimate anti-legalism" that "destroys the unity of revelation, degrades the Old Testament" and "corrupts the Scripture without leaving any part of it secure from perversion."[22] But where nothing is ventured, nothing is gained. Hence, despite all these Paedobaptist warnings, we shall now survey the landscape of the argument from the covenant for infant baptism to see how it involves, first of all, a Christianizing of the Old Testament by reading it as though it were the New, after which we shall see how it involves a Judaizing of the New Testament by reading it as though it were the Old.

2. The Old Testament read as though it were the New

a. Introduction

All Christians, of course, read the Old Testament in the *light* of the New; but it is another matter to read the Old Testament as though it *were* the New, as though the terms "old" and "new" had no theological significance. Yet this is what Paedobaptists do when they argue that circumcision, like baptism, signified and sealed spiritual blessings exclusively. So to equate the two rites, as though every time the word "circumcision" occurs in the Old Testament one might substitute "baptism" and have a perfect theological fit, is simply to impose one's theological conclusions on the evidence. It is an instance of proceeding in dogmatic theology without due respect for biblical theology. Calvin, in the famous

---

[21]*Kirchliche Dogmatik*, IV, 4, Fragment, pp. 195-196. Here is at least a brief answer to Cullmann's complaint, noted above.

[22]P. Marcel, *The Biblical Doctrine of Infant Baptism*, pp. 80ff. See also Calvin, *Institutes*, IV, xvi, 10.

sixteenth chapter of Book IV of the *Institutes,* to which Barth refers above, insists on nearly every page that what-ever the New Testament says about baptism is also true of Old Testament circumcision. Ergo, there is no reason for withholding baptism from infants which is not also a reason for withholding the rite of circumcision from them. Speaking of Colossians 2:11-12, he asks:

> What is the meaning of this language, but that the ac-complishment and truth of baptism is the *same* with the ac-complishment and truth of circumcision, since they both rep-resent the *same* thing? For Paul's design is to show that bap-tism was to the Christian the *same* that circumcision had be-fore been to the Jews. But as we have now clearly evinced that the promises of these two signs and the mysteries represented by them are *precisely the same,* we shall insist no longer on this point at present. I will only recommend believers to consider, whether that sign ought to be accounted earthly and literal, which contains *nothing but what is spiritual and heavenly.*[23]

So he concludes:

> [The Anabaptists] will always be held fast by this dilemma: Either the command of God, respecting the circumcision of infants, was legitimate and liable to no objections, or it was deserving of censure. If there was no absurdity in that com-mand, neither can any absurdity be detected in the practice of infant baptism.[24]

This is a mighty line — if one appraises its worth by the continued use Paedobaptists have made of it. It never fails to turn up, somewhere or other, in every theological disquisi-tion dedicated to infant baptism. At the heart of James Ban-nerman's defense of infant baptism, written 300 years after Calvin, are these propositions:

> *In the first place,* then, circumcision and baptism are both to be regarded as the authorized ordinances for the formal admission of members into the church.

> *In the second place,* circumcision and baptism are expressive of the same spiritual truths and are to be identified as signs and seals of the same covenant blessings.

[23]*Institutes,* IV, xvi, 11 (italics mine).
[24]*Ibid.,* IV, xvi, 20.

> *In the third place,* the oneness of circumcision and baptism is yet further established by the fact that baptism has come in the room of circumcision.[25]

Some modern Paedobaptists have stated their position a bit more cautiously, but one can still discern underneath the age-old predilection to read the Old Testament institution of circumcision rather exclusively from the New Testament perspective of baptism. Any significance which circumcision had of an ethnic or national character is not only subordinated to its religious and spiritual meaning but, for all practical purposes, submerged by it. All that is "essential" to the understanding of circumcision is continuous with the meaning of baptism. Circumcision is the sign of the covenant of grace in the "highest reaches of its meaning and in its deepest spiritual significance."[26] The promise made to Abraham was spiritual, affirms Pierre Marcel; therefore, the rite of circumcision was also spiritual in its significance.

> *All* that we have today in our sacraments, the Jews had formerly in theirs, namely, Jesus Christ and his spiritual riches. The efficacy of the sacraments of the Old Testament is *identical* with that of the sacraments of the New, because equally they are signs, seals, and confirmations of the good will of God for the salvation of men. There is, it is true, a difference between the sacraments as regards outward appearance, but they are *identical* as regards their internal and spiritual significance. The signs have changed while *faith does not change.*[27]

Cullmann makes the same point, though with more caution and skill. Referring to Romans 4:17-18 and Galatians 4:28, according to which Abraham's circumcision was a seal of the righteousness of faith, and believers are, like Isaac, Abraham's children by promise, he argues:

> If, in the New Testament view, circumcision is the seal of *this* faith of Abraham [a faith which] *from the first envisioned the inclusion of the heathen nations,* then to see nothing more in this act than an admission into Abraham's natural posterity is

[25] *The Church of Christ,* II, 84.
[26] J. Murray, "Christian Baptism," *Westminster Theological Journal* (Nov. 1951), p. 22.
[27] P. Marcel, *Infant Baptism,* pp. 86, 90 (italics his).

absolutely unreconcilable with this *New Testament* conception of circumcision.[28]

Expressed in this manner, the Paedobaptist argument contains, to be sure, a significant truth to which no Baptist can justifiably turn a deaf ear. But it is not the whole truth. It is easy to appeal, as Cullmann does, to the "*New Testament* conception of circumcision," and to intone such conventions as, "Circumcision was not *exclusively* a national sign"; "there is an *essential* unity between circumcision and baptism"; "it is a grave mistake to think circumcision was a sign *merely* of external privilege."[29] But unless one is willing to explore the *Old Testament* conception of circumcision, to ask the sense in which circumcision, unlike baptism, *was* national and external in its meaning, such pronouncements sink to the level of stock responses that manacle all progress in understanding.

We have agreed that circumcision means "essentially" what baptism means in the New Testament. What is needed is not a repetition of this point but rather a close look at the Old Testament to determine exactly what is the nature of the non-essential diversity between the signs. Paedobaptists, it would seem, are so committed to the similarity of circumcision and baptism that they care little for the task of determining wherein the two are dissimilar. Circumcision *is* baptism and baptism *is* circumcision, for all theological purposes. The difference between the signs is so incidental that no good thing, theologically speaking, could come from probing it. But if this is the case, then where is the warrant for "old" and "new" as appropriate adjectives to describe the difference between the covenants? Why is the Bible in two parts?

Therefore, we cannot approve this method that simply identifies the new with the old. We can only protest that such an emphasis on the inward and spiritual blessings sealed by baptism as the key to the interpretation of the Old Testament rite of circumcision is a faulty approach, which needs to be balanced by a recognition of the outward and external blessings that circumcision also represented to those who re-

---

[28]*Die Tauflehre*, p. 52 (italics his).
[29]*Ibid.*

ceived it. To interpret circumcision exclusively in terms of baptism is to read the New Testament back into the Old in a manner that violates the movement of holy history and denies the progressive character of revelation. We must never write systematic theology at the expense of biblical theology. We must explore the ways in which the Old Testament teaching about circumcision differs from the New Testament teaching about baptism. In so doing we shall see that the Paedobaptist argument, based on the identity of the two rites, is like a jar lid that almost fits, but never tightly, no matter how many turns it is given.

It is our contention that the covenant as administered in the Old Testament had a twofold aspect: one temporal and earthly, one eternal and heavenly. And circumcision was the sign and seal of earthly covenant blessings as well as of heavenly. To say this is not to deny that the earthly was at the service of the heavenly. Many nations have inherited a country as a piece of geography, but only to the Hebrew people was the land a type and pledge of heavenly rest. The seed of other men, besides that of Abraham, has grown into a nation, but only in Abraham's case was this mundane phenomenon a type and pledge of that "holy nation, God's own people" (I Pet. 2:9) united in the universal fellowship of faith.

Now the question is: Was participation in the temporal, earthly blessings of the covenant, given by birth into the nation of Israel, sufficient in Old Testament times to give one the right to circumcision? If Paedobaptists answer yes, then the parallel which they urge between circumcision and baptism is lost, since, by their own admission, no one in New Testament times is born with a right to baptism apart from faith, whether it be one's own faith or that of one's parents.[30]

---

[30]This is not true of all Lutherans and Anglicans, since some of them practice the indiscriminate baptism of infants without consulting the faith of the parent or sponsor. Roman Catholics will baptize even the unborn fetus of a dying mother. It should be remembered that the designation "Paedobaptist," at this particular point in the discussion, refers to those whose theology of the sacraments is evangelically oriented and who, therefore, ground the propriety of infant baptism not in the efficacy of the sacrament to regenerate but in the covenant promise graciously given to the parents and acted upon in faith, as this promise supposedly relates to the child.

But if they answer no, participation in the earthly blessings of the covenant was *not* sufficient to give a right to circumcision in the Old Testament, since a man had not only to be born of Abraham's seed to claim circumcision for his children but also had personally to walk in the steps of Abraham's faith, then they must force the evidence to fit this conclusion. Let us now see how Paedobaptists proceed at this point.

b. The institution of circumcision as a covenant sign

According to Genesis 17, circumcision, as a sign of the covenant, is to be given to all those who are Abraham's seed according to the flesh, whether born in his house or purchased with his money (vv. 10-14). The emphasis is entirely on this outward relationship, with no hint that one might be disqualified to receive the rite who did not personally share the faith of the patriarch. The thrust of the whole passage is to insist that no one born in Abraham's house should, under any circumstances, fail to receive circumcision as the covenant sign.

This insistence that every male attached to Abraham's house should be circumcised — even those who were slaves bought with his money — is markedly different from anything in the New Testament regarding baptism. While it may be supposed that the members of Abraham's household submitted to the outward forms of piety approved by the group and later prescribed by the Mosaic law, and while some no doubt shared in a personal way the faith of the patriarch, such a faith was not a requirement in Genesis 17. To suggest that all the males of Abraham's household (Gen. 14:14 indicates there were several hundred) individually volunteered a "personal profession of faith" before receiving circumcision, as did Christian converts in the New Testament who received baptism, is to indulge in a gratuitous reconstruction of history. The essential similarity between circumcision and baptism goes out of focus when we think in terms of such complete *identity*. When analyzing the ground of circumcision in Genesis 17, we must remember that the text says nothing of personal faith, but only that physical attachment to Abraham's house by birth or purchase qualifies one to receive the sign. For those who were so qualified, circumcision was in fact mandatory.

c. The circumcision of Ishmael and the sons of Keturah

The point we are making is clearly illustrated in the circumcision of Ishmael. Though given the sign of the covenent (Gen. 17:25f.), Ishmael did not inherit its promise as did Isaac. As Paul writes to the Galatians (Gal. 4:30), citing Gen. 21:10-12), the son of the bondwoman shall not inherit with the son of the free woman. Why, then, was he circumcised? If "the mysteries represented by circumcision are precisely the same" (Calvin) as those represented by baptism, it would seem that he should not have been circumcised, for no one has a right to baptism who is not an heir of the promise, as Isaac was. Paul says, "Now we, brethren, *as Isaac was*, are the children of the promise" (Gal. 4:28). In the light of Paul's reasoning in both Galatians 4 and Romans 9, one may hardly respond to this question of Ishmael's circumcision by simply dismissing his role in redemptive history as inconsequential. When defending infant baptism, however, few Paedobaptist theologians have had the hardihood to bring these texts to the light of a searching discussion and face the questions such a discussion would open up.

Calvin's commentaries on this point are simply a study in paradox. Cullmann, by saying nothing about Romans 9, escapes something of the impasse to which Calvin is reduced. Yet he uses Galatians 4 against Barth in such a way as inadvertently to show that the whole argument from circumcision for infant baptism is out of joint. Barth, in his initial comments on the subject, limits the significance of circumcision (perhaps too exclusively) to the dimension of physical descent from Abraham. In response, Cullmann appeals to Galatians 4:21ff. as a proof that the promise made to Abraham and sealed by circumcision transcended the fleshly principle of natural generation. He comes to this conclusion by observing that Isaac was born not according to the flesh, as was Ishmael, but according to promise. All Christians, then, are "descendants" of Abraham and heirs of the cove-

nant promise with Isaac. Therefore, concludes Cullmann —
and this conclusion has been drawn by Paedobaptists a
thousand times —

> ... in reality, circumcision is an embracing in the *covenant*
> which God made with Abraham and his followers ... exactly
> as Christian baptism is a taking up into the body of Christ. The
> *correctly understood* circumcision which is not only outward,
> made with men's hands (Eph. 2:11, Col. 2:11), but is "circum-
> cision of the heart" (Rom. 2:19), passes directly over into
> Christian baptism as the "circumcision of Christ" (Col.
> 2:11).[31]

The little fox which spoils the vineyard of this argument
is Ishmael. If circumcision "embraces one in the covenant
exactly as Christian baptism," if the one passes over "directly" into the other, then how is it that *both* the son born of
the flesh and the son born of the promise were circumcised?
What in baptism corresponds to *Ishmael's* circumcision? It is
as easy to go from Christian baptism back to *Isaac's* circumcision as it is difficult to go from Christian baptism back to
Ishmael's circumcision. Cullmann argues the former but does
not attempt the latter. Why? Obviously because he cannot.
All of which demonstrates how the alignment between circumcision and baptism in the Paedobaptist argument is
overdrawn. If Cullmann's reasoning against Barth were correct, then Ishmael should not have been circumcised.

Similar to the circumcision of Ishmael is that of
Keturah's sons (in the light of Gen. 17:10ff., one can hardly
deny them this covenant distinctive). By his faithful exposition of the narrative at this point, Calvin becomes involved in
a palpable incongruity.[32] The sons of Keturah, he says, bore
the sign in their flesh of the "spiritual covenant" which was
the exclusive possession of Isaac. But how could this be?
How can they have a right to the sign without a right to the
thing signified? "Covenant children" who fail to appropriate
the covenant blessing and thereby forfeit covenant status —
of this we have heard; but who has ever heard of covenant
children who were never offered the covenant? How is it that

---

[31]*Die Tauflehre*, p. 52 (italics his).
[32]*Commentary on Genesis*, I, 453ff.

a lucid thinker like Calvin should involve himself in such a cul-de-sac? Is it not because he will not admit that circumcision could signify anything less than the spiritual and lasting blessings of the covenant, lest the parallelism with baptism be questioned and thereby the practice of infant baptism jeopardized?

d. The circumcision of Israel as a nation

Aside from such specific cases of circumcising those in the Old Testament who would not qualify for baptism in the New, it should be observed that the writers of the Old Testament never dispute the right of circumcision to the nation of Israel as a whole. Though individual Jews might be as surely bent on apostasy as the sparks fly upward, circumcision belonged to the nation; and the idea, sometimes propounded by Paedobaptists, that the Israelite who failed to walk in the steps of Abraham's faith forfeited his right to the covenant sign, is without warrant in the Old Testament. To question an Israelite's right to circumcision is not possible, if we let the Old Testament speak for itself; for it plainly teaches that no one descending from Abraham had the right *not* to be circumcised.

The difference, in this respect, between circumcision and baptism is tacitly admitted even by Cullmann, though his only zeal is to establish their likeness. The postponement of circumcision in the case of those whose parents are circumcised, he admits, is never contemplated in the Old Testament.[33] But when it comes to baptism, he cannot say that its postponement, in the case of those whose parents are baptized, is never contemplated in the New Testament. At the very end of his book on baptism there is this note:

> To be sure, the word "believing" must be emphasized at this point. Where the parents themselves are baptized, yet subsequently do not *believe*, the situation is different [from circumcision], and then the postponement of baptism is not only justified, from the New Testament point of view, but commanded.[34]

[33]*Die Tauflehre*, p. 55.
[34]*Ibid.*, p. 64.

And so the parallelism between the two breaks down; baptism is not properly administered in all instances where circumcision was properly administered. In other words, New Testament baptism does not take the place of Old Testament circumcision in every respect. When Barth alludes to this fact, observing that in Israel the number of those who believed was not identical to the number of those who were circumcised,[35] it is no answer to say with Cullmann that the same is true of baptism.[36] To argue thus is to miss Barth's point, which is just this: all Israelites had a right to the sign of circumcision by virtue of their participation in the earthly blessings of the covenant community: they were citizens of the nation of Israel by birth. However, since this outward form of the covenant was done away in Christ, to baptize indiscriminately in the New Testament age is either to abuse discipline in administering the rite or to be guilty of hypocrisy in receiving it.

The only way to do justice to the data is to admit that circumcision, as a sign of the covenant made with Abraham, had a double reference corresponding to the twofold aspect of the covenant as originally administered. To him who was an Israelite indeed, who walked in the steps of Abraham's faith, circumcision was the seal of the righteousness of his faith. Yet it belonged to all the seed of Abraham according to the flesh, insofar as the covenant blessings were of an earthly sort. The right to circumcision, in Old Testament times, was grounded in one's physical attachment to the house and lineage of Abraham as the sign of a nation's separation to God from the defilement of the heathen world.

It is sometimes objected that such a distinction between the earthly and the heavenly aspects of the covenant is untenable. There was one covenant, and Old Testament Israel participated in this one covenant. There can be no such thing as a participation in the covenant from one aspect and not from the other. To this objection one may reply that while it is true that no Scripture passage speaks of an external participation in the covenant in just these words, there is no

[35]Die Taufe, p. 31.
[36]Die Tauflehre, p. 61.

other interpretation that can be reasonably imposed on the data. If the typical, external aspect of the Old Testament cannot be distinguished from the spiritual blessings signified, then how could the spiritual blessings have survived the passing of the Old Testament types? It must be supposed, therefore, that even as there was a literal Israel within which there was a true Israel (Rom. 9:6), so a man could be an Israelite in the former sense without being one in the latter sense. But in either case, he was circumcised as an Israelite.

In other words, there was a *de facto* participation in the covenant as originally given, according to which a man might be circumcised of whom no more was presupposed than that he was a member of the nation of Israel "after the flesh." In fact, it is a plausible suggestion that the covenant sign was administered to the male organ of reproduction in the Old Testament for the very reason that covenant status was passed on from generation to generation by physical birth and natural descent. Thus the term "seed" in the Old Testament framing of the covenant promise had a primary reference to the fleshly seed, the notion of a spiritual seed coming into the foreground only in the new dispensation under Christ.[37]

e. The Old Testament Jewish mission

But, it may be argued, if the primary reference in the Old Testament is to a fleshly seed, then why were proselytes, who were not descended from Abraham by natural generation, always given the sign of circumcision? Cullmann, in a rather abstruse way, puts this question to Barth. Repudiating Barth's "error" that circumcision was tied to physical descent from Abraham, he appeals to the note of universalism in the covenant made with Abraham, which was the basis of proselytism. Barth is wrong, he feels, in affirming that the covenant was first made "open to the nations" with the birth of the Messiah. Long before the Messiah was born, the heathen were commanded to embrace the covenant promise,

---

[37]In this regard, it is interesting to note that Paul (Rom. 9:7ff.) uses "seed" (σπέρμα) of Abraham's literal descendants, reserving "children" (τέκνα) for his spiritual descendants.

and this proves circumcision was not tied to the fleshly principle, as Barth declares. Though Barth does not mention proselytes, says Cullmann, the mission to the Gentiles was one of the most important phases of Judaism in Old Testament times.[38]

It is difficult to comprehend how Cullmann considers this appeal to the Old Testament mission to the Gentiles an answer to Barth's point. Gentiles did not become proselytes to Judaism in the same way they became disciples of Christ. The covenant did not "stand open to all" before the coming of the Messiah in the way it now stands open to all since the Messiah has come and has commissioned his apostles to disciple the nations. To be sure, a convert to Christianity must say with Ruth, "Your God shall be my God," for Christians worship the God of Abraham, Isaac, and Jacob — and Naomi (Ruth 1:16). But he cannot literally say, "Entreat me not to leave you," for no longer is there a particular land in which God's people dwell; nor can he literally say, "Your people shall be my people," for in Christ there is neither Jew nor Moabite. Jesus' reference to the church as a "nation bringing forth the fruits" of the kingdom (Matt. 21:43) and Peter's designation of Christians as a "holy nation" (I Pet. 2:9) are figurative expressions. No one would argue that Christians are a holy nation in the same literal sense that Israel was a holy nation. Cullmann's appeal to such a Scripture passage to establish a parallel between proselyte circumcision and Christian baptism is an unwilling argument, dragged in by the heels. It is one more instance of reading the Old Testament as though it were the New.

3. The New Testament read as though it were the Old

a. Introduction

We have argued that there is indeed an *analogy* between circumcision and baptism, but that the Paedobaptists have erred in turning this analogy into *identity*. In such a scheme Israel becomes the church and the church Israel, in an un-

---

[38]*Die Tauflehre*, pp. 54, 55.

critical, undifferentiated way that ossifies the movement of redemptive history. The sacraments of circumcision and baptism become identical in every respect — save in their outward form — to be administered for the same reasons, to the same persons.

Now when the contour of revelational land is leveled in this manner, movement in two directions is also possible. For this reason, the literature defending infant baptism on the basis of infant circumcision shows a dual aspect: not only is the Old Testament read as though it were the New, but the New Testament is read as though it were the Old. Just as circumcision is given an inward, spiritual reference exclusively, answering to that of baptism, so baptism (in the case of infants) is said to seal a merely outward, visible, external privilege, answering to that of circumcision.

Both ways of arguing are nuances of the same error, but the latter is much more overtly elaborated in Paedobaptist theory and is of more consequence in practice. The tendency in Paedobaptist literature to treat circumcision exclusively in terms of New Testament inwardness and spirituality pales to insignificance compared with the tendency in the same literature to treat baptism (so far as infants are concerned) in terms of the external covenant privilege of the Old Testament. Here we touch the very nerve center of evangelical Paedobaptist reasoning. From this supposed vantage point, Paedobaptists are confident that they have bested the anti-Paedobaptists a thousand times. We shall, therefore, take the time to move about in the currents of the argument until our minds have gotten the full measure of its breadth.

   b. The Old Testament promise of a land, the theocratic ideal of the Reformers, and Kierkegaard's "Christendom"

Let us begin with the matter of a promised land. The universal spread of the gospel is so luminously set forth in the New Testament that no propensity to reduce revelation to an even plane could ever limit the covenant community in Christ to a specific nation living in a particular geographical territory (according to the model of the Jewish people in

Canaan). The Old Testament model, so essential to the fulfillment of the covenant as originally made with Israel, is palpably dated by the movement of redemptive history. Yet the Paedobaptist mind has been reconciled to this fact only with difficulty.

To illustrate this point, we may begin with an interesting bit of theology found in chapter twelve of the *Second Helvetic*, written by Bullinger in 1566. In this passage Bullinger is at pains to establish the unity of the Old and New Testaments and to show that the worthies of the Old Testament enjoyed a heavenly inheritance in Christ, just as we do. But in his zeal to establish this thesis, Bullinger betrays himself into the error we are exposing: he draws no line whatever between the Old Testament and the New, but only between this world and the world to come.

> And we do acknowledge that the Fathers [of Israel] had two kinds of promises revealed unto them, even as we have. For some of them were of present and transitory things: such as were the promises of the land of Canaan and of victories and such as are nowadays concerning our daily bread.

In other words, we Christians have external covenant promises like the Old Testament saints: the Jews had the land of Canaan, and we have our daily bread.

Now it is true that material blessings (e.g., daily bread), as well as spiritual blessings, come from God. But the New Testament nowhere hints that such earthly blessings are peculiar to the covenant community of the redeemed. What Bullinger should have said is that the Jews of old had the land of Canaan by covenant promise, and Swiss burghers have the canton of Zurich. In fact, he does say this, for all practical purposes, a little later on in chapter twenty, where we read: "Moreover, by the sacrament of baptism God separates us from all other religions *and nations* and consecrates us a peculiar people unto himself."[39] Here we have the voice of the New Testament (I Pet. 2:9), but the hands are the hands of Moses. This sentence means that everyone living in

---

[39]*Second Helvetic Confession*, "Of Holy Baptism" (italics mine).

the canton of Zurich is separated unto God, hence everyone must be baptized at the time of his birth. The scene, to be sure, is not Canaan but Switzerland; and the people are not Jews but Swiss. But in their theological essence matters are the same. Accordingly, the first Swiss Anabaptists were told to baptize their children or *leave the canton,* just as in Old Testament times idolaters were to be purged out of the holy covenant land.

Like the Swiss, the German Paedobaptists also confessed this point of view. The *Formula of Concord* (A.D. 1576) condemns the doctrine of the Anabaptists as that which "can be tolerated neither in the church *nor by the police and in the commonwealth,* nor in daily life."[40] The situation is no different when we turn from the German to the French Protestant Church, where Calvin's influence prevailed. Calvin taught that the civil government is designed to cherish and support the external worship of God, to preserve the pure doctrine of religion, and to defend the constitution of the church.[41] The same conviction undergirded the religious establishments in the Netherlands, England, and Scotland, and was embraced by the Puritans who came to the "stern and rockbound coasts" of New England. When we remember that political philosophers from antiquity had pronounced religion to be a serious object of magisterial concern, and that the Reformers themselves were nurtured in an ecclesiastical establishment that combined church and state, we can hardly wonder that they should have espoused this theocratic point of view after the analogy of Old Testament Israel in the promised land. But these mitigating historical circumstances cannot alter the fact that their views of church and state came short of the New Testament ideal.

To their credit, present-day Paedobaptists readily concede this point, though they were not the first to make it. They have not shown the same willingness, however, to admit that the question of infant baptism may have had something to do with their lack of vision in this matter. Zealous in their

---

[40]Article XII (italics mine).
[41]*Institutes,* II, iv, 20.

execration of Anabaptists for their errors[42] — some of which, no doubt, were real and serious — they have been reluctant to commend them for their insights even where they have felt constrained to follow them. But it cannot be doubted that the Anabaptists were not only among the first Protestants to suffer from the theocratic view of church and state but were also the first to protest it in principle. The verdict of scholarship, then, is all but unanimous in attributing what we call the separation of church and state to these heretics. Roger Williams, the first champion of this cause in New England, was compelled to leave "God's colony" in the New World (Massachusetts), whence he removed to the territory of Rhode Island. Though his Baptist affiliation was of brief tenure, he had convictions concerning the relationship of church and state which were patently those of the Anabaptists.

> His most famous work, *The Bloudy Tenet*, is based section by section upon the work of a Baptist who wrote while serving a prison sentence for cause of liberty of conscience. The typical Baptist arguments of Bucher, Helwys and Murton appear in the various writings of Williams. In the main arguments of *The Bloudy Tenet* and *The Bloudy Tenet Yet More Bloudy*, it is doubtful that he presents a single new idea. The reading of *Tracts on Liberty of Conscience*, a collection of early Baptist papers on the subject, reveals how alike are Williams' arguments to the first pioneers of religious liberty.[43]

Of course, the union of church and state along theocratic lines is not necessary to Paedobaptism. But this proposition is not reversible. What a membrane is to a cell, infant baptism is to each establishment of the Christian religion.[44] Without it the edges of the theocracy would tumble like cliffs

---

[42]When Edward Wightman was burned in Litchfield, England for the heresy of Anabaptism in the year 1611, the Paedobaptists convicted him of "the wicked heresies of the Ebionites, Cerinthians, Valentinians, Arians, Macedonians, of Simon Magus, Manes, Manichees, of Photinus, and [to cap the list] Anabaptists, and of other heretical, execrable and unheard of opinions by the instinct of Satan, by him excogitated and holden" (see I. Bakus, *Works*, I, 408).

[43]Clarence Roddy, an unpublished doctoral dissertation on Roger Williams, library archives, School of Education, New York University, p. 218.

[44]Witness Wall's boast in *History* that all the *national* churches in the world are Paedobaptist churches.

of sand before the breakers of the sea. In a theocracy all citizens — at least all who wish to be respectable and a great many who do not — are "Christians." This can only mean that they are members of the visible church by baptism, a fact that did not escape the scathing criticism of Kierkegaard in his attack on the state church of Denmark. "We have a church," said he, "which has slyly done away with Christianity by the affirmation that we are all Christians," a church that has abolished Christianity by expansion, "by these millions of name Christians, the number of which is surely meant to conceal the fact that there is not one Christian." Our church talks of a Christian state or world, "notions shrewdly calculated to make God so confused in his head by all these millions that he cannot discover that he has been hoaxed, and that there is not one single — Christian." Kierkegaard observes that this assembly-line production of Christians

> makes the whole difficulty of being a Christian vanish [since] being a Christian and being a man amount to the same thing. . . . Christendom has mocked God and continues to mock him — just as if to a man who is a lover of nuts, instead of bringing him one nut with a kernel, we were to bring him tons and millions . . . of empty nuts and then make this a show of zeal to comply with his wish.[45]

We do not say that infant baptism necessarily produces this evil of Christians-by-the-carload, but we do say that infant baptism is more cordial to this evil than believer baptism ever could be. Kierkegaard, it might be countered, justly attacks the abuse, not the use, of infant baptism. Actually, he attacks both. Take, for example, *The Instant*, No. 7, Item 3, entitled "The Sort of Person They Call a Christian." Here he draws a picture of a young man of real breadth of ability, knowledge, and interests, whose religion is that he has none. It just never occurs to him to think about God, any more than it does to go to church. But this same young man, who feels no need of religion, feels the need of being *paterfamilias*. So he marries, and his wife is about to have a child. Now it turns out that he does have a religion after all. Like everyone else

---

[45]*Attack Upon Christendom*, pp. 127, 156.

in the New Testament Canaan called Denmark, he is an Evangelical Lutheran. So the priest is notified, the midwife arrives with the baby, a young lady holds the baby's bonnet coquettishly, several young men — who also have no religion — render the father the service of adopting the Evangelical Lutheran religion for the occasion and of assuming the obligation of godfathers for the Christian upbringing of this child; the silken priest, with a graceful gesture, sprinkles water three times on the dear little baby and dries his hands graciously with a towel.

Then comes the significant part of Kierkegaard's attack. He goes on to complain that men dare present this "comedy" to God under the name of Christian baptism, which originally was the sacred ceremony by which the Savior was consecrated for his life's work, as were his disciples, "men who had well reached the age of discretion and who then, dead to this life . . . , promised to be willing to die as sacrificed men in this world of falsehood and evil."

> The priests, however, these holy men, understand their business and understand too that if (as Christianity must unconditionally require of every sensible man) it were so that only when a person has reached the age of discretion, he is permitted to decide upon the religion he will have — the priests understand very well in this way their trade would not amount to much. And therefore these holy witnesses to the truth insinuate themselves into the lying-in room where the mother is weak after the suffering she has gone through and the *paterfamilias* is . . . in hot water. And then under the name of baptism they have the courage to present to God a ceremony such as that which has been described, into which a little bit of truth might be brought nevertheless, if the young lady, instead of holding the little bonnet sentimentally over the baby, were satirically to hold a nightcap over the presumptive father.[46]

[46]*The Instant,* No. 7, Item 3. Perhaps the most notorious case, at least in modern times, of the abuse which Kierkegaard here satirizes was the baptism of Heinrich Himmler's son, the godfather being the young Adolf Hitler. *The Christian Century,* Nov. 3, 1976, p. 951, reports that Bishop Hendrick Christenson dismissed pastor Ruben Joergenson from the ministry of the Danish Lutheran Church, not because he would not baptize children, but because he would not baptize children whose parents refused to take prebaptismal instruction. Joergenson said he could not baptize children unless there were a visible connection between baptism and faith. Kierkegaard, it would seem, was a prophet not without honor except in his own country.

In this paragraph, it will be noted, Kierkegaard goes beyond criticizing abuse of the institution to indict the institution itself. The problem is not simply that the father and godfather have no true Christian convictions, but that the child *cannot* have. The plague upon the whole arrangement is that the person at the center of the liturgy, the one who embarrassed the father, hurried the midwife, and required the presence of the priest, cannot render that which Christianity unconditionally requires of every sensible person, namely, a decision for Christ and against the world. Though it is true that believer baptism may — and sometimes does — degenerate into a mere form and ceremony, one important difference will always remain between it and infant baptism: when a professing believer is baptized, there is no possibility that one should have wrought upon him an act whereby he is committed, wholly apart from any choice of his own. When infants are baptized, on the other hand, it cannot be otherwise.

A hundred years after Kierkegaard's attack, his lengthened shadow moved over the field of debate, as Karl Barth, addressing a group of Swiss ministerial students at Gwatt, challenged the *Landeskirche* of Switzerland by tossing this pebble into the theological pond:

> Do I deceive myself when I suspect that the real and decisive ground for infant baptism, beginning with the Reformers and continuing to the present day, very simply is this: Men at the time would not renounce, for love or money, the existence of the Evangelical Church in the form of the Constantinian *corpus Christianum,* and they will not today under any circumstances and for any price, give up the contemporary form of the People's Church? When the church breaks with infant baptism, People's Church, in the sense of a state church or a mass church, is finished. *Hinc, hinc, illae lacrimae!* [Hence, oh hence, proceed these tears!] Is it not so that the concern which at this point disclosed itself has from time to time unconsciously taken on the very frank form to which Luther occasionally confessed: that is, that there would not be too many baptized people if a man, instead of being *brought* to baptism, had to *come* to it?
>
> We do not overlook the historical, practical and essential difficulties that are so obvious at this juncture. Nonetheless we would put the question: Are these concerns legitimate? Is it not the part of wisdom here, as always, so carefully to look at the

matter which one has in mind that one can under no circumstances get away from it? Are we so certain of the essential merits of the Constantinian system or of the present-day form of our People's Church; is our conscience in this matter so void of offense that we may and must be committed to hold to what we have for dear life — even at the price of constantly adding to the church wounds and sickness through an improper form of baptism? Does not the unmistakable disorder in our baptismal practice rather indicate that in the very sociological structure of our churches there is present an elemental disorder which, it may well be, must be put up with for a long time to come, but under no circumstances can be introduced as a serious argument against a better order in our baptismal practice?

Where does Holy Writ say that Christians may not be in the minority? Perhaps even in a very small minority? Would the church not be more useful to the world about her, if she could be a healthy church? And what does the church really get out of being a People's Church in the present-day sense of the term; of being a church *of* people rather than *for* people? Be all this as it may; from the theological point of view it is high time to announce that an urgent quest after a better form of our baptismal practice is long overdue.[47]

Barth footnoted this discussion by observing that the question of how all this can be brought about on a practical level is not the task of theology. He pleaded that the reader first give his attention to the theological problem without muddying the issue with considerations of an ecclesiastico-political character. If anything is to be done, we must begin with a new theological analysis of the doctrine of baptism. He closed by reminding those who are primarily concerned with and interested in matters of church polity that they should not try to avoid the responsibility of this theological reappraisal by appealing to the "other" responsibilities they are supposed to have.[48]

[47]*Die Taufe*, pp. 39-40. We have translated freely, sacrificing the grammatical details to preserve the animus of this bold and remarkable passage.

[48]Leonard Verduin has sought to answer Barth by granting what he says about Constantinianism, but arguing that infant baptism antedates Constantine (see "Karl Barth's Rejection of Infant Baptism," *The Reformed Journal*, Feb. 1960, 13-17). While this is true, it is hardly an answer, since Constantinianism is simply a symptom of a more fundamental theological error of which infant baptism is also a symptom, namely, a failure to see the implications of the historical character of revelation.

c. The Old Testament promise of a fleshly seed and the Paedobaptist concept of "covenant children"

1) *Introduction.* *The First Helvetic Confession* argues that children ought to be baptized because they are born to those who are God's people, a relationship which grounds their right to the fellowship of his people. This relationship also leads to the devout supposition that they are elect. Thus at the outset of the Reformed tradition we find the category "people of God" construed in a quasi-physical sense. Whereas the New Testament teaches that we become children of God (and of Abraham) by faith, the former understanding makes it a matter of one's physical birth. A century later the Westminster divines spelled any lurking ambiguities out of this position with the clarity for which they are justly celebrated. In their *Directory for the Public Worship of God* we read: "The seed and posterity of the faithful born within the church have *by their birth* an interest in the covenant and right to the seal of it and to the outward privileges of the church under the gospel, *no less than the children of Abraham in the time of the Old Testament.* . . ."[49] These "children of the covenant," then, are ascertained to be such in the same literal way that all the members of the Jewish nation were children of the covenant because they were born of Abraham according to the flesh. All a child requires to be counted among God's people is to be born of blood, of the will of the flesh, and of man, provided the man gives credible evidence of being himself a believer.

Having carefully pointed out that it is only *after* Abraham had embraced the promise by faith that he partook of the sacrament of circumcision, Calvin observes that his son Isaac received the covenant sign as an infant, *prior* to the exercise of understanding and faith. This is because the child, "by hereditary right, according to the form of the promise, is already included in the covenant from its very birth." So far, so good. But then he continues: "If the children of believers without the aid of understanding are partakers of the

[49]Under the caption "Of the Administration of the Sacraments" (italics mine).

covenant, there is no reason why they should be excluded from the sign [of baptism]. . . ."[50] Here, we contend, Calvin makes an unwarranted leap from the Old to the New Testament. We agree that Isaac had a "hereditary right" in the covenant "according to the form of the promise" as given to Abraham. But is there no difference between the "form of the promise" as administered to Abraham and as newly administered in Christ? Do our children have a "hereditary right" to salvation? Is grace tied to the blood not only of the Savior but also of the parent? Because the children of Israel inherited Canaan by birth, shall we award our children membership in the church and an inheritance in heaven by birth?

In answering these questions, Paedobaptists down to the present day think and write, as did the Reformers, in terms of external covenant privilege. Though Protestant theocracies have waned, the theocratic mind lingers on. Bushnell, for example, instinctively appeals to the child's citizenship in the state as providing a telling analogy to his membership in the church. In *Christian Nurture* he assures us that just as every infant is a citizen and requires the constabulary and military force to come to his rescue if his person be seized or his property invaded — though he can neither vote nor bear arms nor even know he is a citizen — so the child of a believer is baptized as a member of the church with all the rights and privileges compatible with his years attendant thereto.[51] The same argument is echoed by the Princeton theologian Charles Hodge.

> If the father becomes a citizen of a country, he makes his children citizens. . . . In like manner when a man becomes a Christian . . . his children are to be regarded as doing the same thing. He has a right to represent his children even as in the old dispensation. When any foreigner became a Jew, his children became Jews (Exodus 12:48). The church membership of infants of believing parents is, therefore, in accord with the analogy of all human social institutions and is sanctioned by the approbation and command of God. . . . By becoming an English citizen, a man makes his infant children the subjects of the English crown, entitled to the protection and privileges

[50]*Institutes*, IV, xvi, 24.
[51]*Christian Nurture*, p. 141.

and burdened with the obligations of English citizenship.[52]

In other words, one may be a Christian just as he is an Englishman, just as in Old Testament times he was a Jew. This is reasonable enough to the Paedobaptists, for even as the theocratic ideal harks back to the Old Testament establishment of a chosen people in a literal covenant land, so the idea that our children in the flesh are "covenant children" rests on the promise of a carnal seed as it was promulgated to Abraham in Old Testament times.

Now it is true that in the shadowy age of anticipation and type the promise of a seed was fulfilled literally as well as spiritually, so that all the children who were born to Abraham according to the flesh were born in fulfillment of the covenant promise of a numerous seed. They were all "covenant children" by birth. But now that the age of fulfillment is come, the literal seed, like the literal land — so those who advocate believer baptism would hold — is no longer covenantally significant. Even as the covenant community is no longer a theocracy combining church and state in an earthly promised land, so it no longer embraces a literal seed born after the flesh. All those in every nation who share Abraham's faith are Abraham's seed, according to the New Testament. Their parents' faith can neither secure them in this status nor their unbelief deprive them of it.

Paedobaptists, as well as others, have acknowledged this when speaking of matters not having to do with infant baptism. Yet when baptism is discussed, they are so accustomed to claiming the promise for their children, in its Old Testament form of a fleshly seed, that their commitment to the argument has become a kind of instinct seldom subjected to rational analysis. It is not difficult to show, however, that the mistake of reading the Old Testament concept of a literal seed into the New Testament (as in the case of the land) is a mistake that distorts the very structure of revelation and draws in its train a host of problems that have taxed the ingenuity of theologians and produced a tangled depth of

[52]"The Church Membership of Infants," *Princeton Review*, XXX (1958), 353-354.

dogmatic pleading. Let us now examine some of these problems.

2) *The Halfway Covenant*. Although there is no longer a literal nation chosen to be God's people, there is, according to the Paedobaptists, an "external aspect" of the covenant which is the visible church into which believers' children are born. Matthew Henry expresses it this way:

> The infants of believing parents are in covenant with God and therefore have a right to the initiating seal of that covenant. When I say they are in covenant with God, understand me of the *external* administration of the covenant of grace and not of that which is *internal*.[53]

In keeping with this approach, the Puritans in Massachusetts baptized all children of professing believers. Thus there was (as is ever the case in Paedobaptist communions) a double kind of church membership. There were some who were members by baptism only, those born of professing believers; others were members in full covenant with the right of taking communion, those born again of the Spirit of Christ (hence the distinction between "noncommunicant" and "communicant" church membership in Presbyterian and Reformed polity). As a result of such an arrangement, there naturally appeared in the second generation adult persons baptized as infants who were orthodox in creed and upright in life, although making no profession of a personal experience of God's saving grace in their hearts and never coming to communion as full members of the church. These people, understandably, did not consider themselves pagans and infidels. Were they not "in covenant," and had they not received the covenant sign of baptism? Why, then, should their children be denied the same privilege? We might put it this way: If God has children (believers) and grandchildren (believers' children), why may he not have great grandchildren (believers' children's children)?

One way to answer this question is to argue that when parents are "faithful" to their "covenant vows" to bring up

---

[53]"Treatise on Baptism," *The Complete Works of the Rev. Matthew Henry*, I, 511 (italics mine).

their children in the nurture and admonition of the Lord, then the second generation will all be true Christians and there will be no problem. A much more foolproof device is "confirmation," whereby the sacrament of infant baptism is "completed" when the child is old enough to say yes to the proper questions, but too young to say no. In this way virtually all the half members are brought to their first communion and translated into full members before they have children of their own. Thus the difficulty is solved before it arises.[54] That the Almighty has deigned to use Christian nurture and confirmation to work savingly in many lives we cannot doubt; but before we consider these matters in detail, we must see how the early New England Congregationalists tried to solve the problem along somewhat different lines.

In 1634 a full communicant member of the Dorchester Congregational Church in Massachusetts requested baptism for his grandchild, since the immediate parents did not profess a personal faith in Christ. Advice was sought of the Boston church, and the counsel of compliance was given. By 1645, Cotton Mather and other influential divines, at first dubious, began openly to favor baptism of children whose parents' membership rested, as they put it, "on birth rather than experience." Thus, permanent membership was offered to those who could testify to no conscious work of divine grace in their lives, so long as they proved neither immoral nor heretical. (Its opponents nicknamed this arrangement the "halfway covenant.") It was argued that in this way the church could retain its influence over people whom it would otherwise lose, an influence which would, it was hoped, lead to their salvation.

Eventually this settlement won its way into the great majority of New England congregations — though many opposition churches, like the "Old South" of Boston, were established. In 1657 the "halfway covenant" was adopted by a General Synod of both Massachusetts and Connecticut. At

---

[54]Evangelical and Reformed Paedobaptists emphasize the former solution, parental faithfulness; Anglicans, Episcopalians, and Lutherans emphasize the latter, confirmation. These two, of course, are not mutually exclusive.

first it was applied only to persons whose grandparents had been believers, but it soon became the custom to admit any of upright character and general Christian belief, together with their children, into the church. In short, the prerequisite of personal faith for baptism was waived for adults as well as for infants. This naturally lowered the spiritual tone of the churches, since those who might have coveted a transforming Christian experience were content with a merely intellectual assent to Christian principles. Finally, toward the close of the seventeenth century, Solomon Stoddard, pastor in Northampton, Massachusetts, argued that the Lord's Supper also was a "converting ordinance," designed for adult members of the church whose lives were not scandalous but exemplary in every respect. These he called "visible saints." And so full right to both baptism and the Eucharist was granted on the basis of external covenant privilege alone.

As ministers came to be recruited from the ranks of these "visible saints," Stoddard argued that "men who are destitute of saving grace may preach the gospel" and that "a minister who knows himself unregenerate may nevertheless lawfully administer baptism and the Lord's Supper. . . ."[55] Fashionable young coxcombs, who ridiculed experiential Christianity as "enthusiasm," began to graduate from Harvard College and to be ordained to the ministry. The tide was finally turned in 1733 — though the damage was never altogether undone — when, under the preaching of Jonathan Edwards, grandson of Stoddard, a revival broke out in the very Northampton church which Stoddard had led, a revival that lasted for two years. "Scarce a grown person in the place remained unaffected and many children were effectually called."[56] As this "Great Awakening" spread throughout New England, George Whitefield sailed up from Georgia in 1739 and preached with remarkable success. Gradually, under the impact of the revivalist movement, the halfway covenant waned. Its last abode was the Charlestown, Massachusetts

---

[55]As quoted by the Reverend David Weston in "The Baptist Movement of a Hundred Years Ago and Its Vindication" (p. 20), a discourse delivered at the 112th anniversary of the First Baptist Church, Middleborough, Massachusetts, January 16, 1868.

[56]*Works*, III, 240.

church, where it died in 1828, after a long and ignominious life of two hundred years.

Since the halfway covenant, like the theocratic state, no longer exists, it may appear to some a fatuous exercise to have exhumed these ancient bones of controversy. Inasmuch as the Paedobaptists themselves have ceased to occupy this compromising ground, is it charitable to burden their position with such abuses? To such a question we can only respond by acknowledging with all joy that out of the Paedobaptists' own ranks arose those prophets of truth who put the axe to the tree of the halfway covenant; but they did not dig the stump out of the ground, and it continues to sprout to the present day. The abandonment of the halfway covenant curbed an abuse but did not remove its cause. That cause is the inveterate propensity of the Paedobaptist mind to defend infant baptism in terms of external covenant privilege after the analogy of the Old Testament.

3) *Acts 2:39: The promise made to our children.* Evidence that Paedobaptists intuitively think in terms of Old Testament externalism is found in their traditional use of certain New Testament texts, especially Acts 2:39 and I Corinthians 7:14, texts whose original meaning has been all but drowned in a maelstrom of theological argument that time has not diminished nor discussion always enlightened.

In Acts 2:39, Peter summons his countrymen to repentance, specifically for the sin of rejecting Jesus (cf. 2:23, 36, 38), a repentance to be accomplished through baptism into his name to the remission of sins. In order to encourage his hearers in this resolution, he adds the assuring words (v. 39): "For the promise is to you and to your children, and to all who are afar off, even as many as the Lord our God shall call." This verse is frequently inscribed as a sort of Paedobaptist motto at the beginning of books and pamphlets defending infant baptism; it is also generally included in the liturgy for administering baptism to young children. When the verse is so used, the "promise" is understood as the covenant of grace confirmed in baptism to Christians who claim the promise by faith for themselves and their children. Dean Henry Alford went so far as to say that Acts 2:39

contributes a "providential recognition of infant baptism at the very founding of the Christian Church."[57]

It should be noted that the specific content of the promise Peter had in mind is the anointing of the Holy Spirit (v. 38), a promise found in Joel 2:28-32. This anointing of the Spirit bestows the gifts of visions and prophecy (Acts 2:17), which are quite beyond the ken of infants and little children. It hardly seems plausible, therefore, that Peter spoke these words with infants in mind, as do Paedobaptists when they quote him at the administration of infant baptism. Jeremias seeks to minimize this point by appealing to the eschatological context of the Pentecostal message: "Save yourselves from this perverse generation" (v. 40).[58] But this form of address still clearly presupposes an audience capable of decision and action.

Probably more important for our inquiry than the eschatological milieu of this passage is the part of the verse to which Paedobaptists have paid the least attention. We refer to the conclusion, where the promise is said to be "to all who are afar off, even as many as the Lord our God shall call." It is possible to construe the phrase "to all who are afar off" temporally, as a reference to generations yet unborn.[59] The verse would then mean: the promise of forgiveness and the gift of the Spirit is to you who hear me now and to your children and to those in turn who shall be born in years to come. But it seems much more plausible, in view of the manner in which the book of Acts traces the witness of the apostles from Jerusalem, Judea, and Samaria to the uttermost parts of the earth (Acts 1:8), to understand the "afar off" reference spatially, after the analogy of Ephesians 2:17. Thus Peter's words become the harbinger of the preaching of the gospel to remote Gentile nations, a venture in which he himself became the cautious innovator when he went to the house of Cornelius (Acts 10).

In any case, whether this text be construed as limited to Peter's Jewish hearers and their children — those living and

---

[57]*Greek Testament*, II, 28. See also Jeremias, *Die Kindertaufe*, p. 48.
[58]Cf. *Die Kindertaufe*, pp. 28, 48.
[59]See Bauer, *Lexicon*, p. 488.

those yet to be born — or whether it be understood as applying both to Jews with their children and to Gentiles as well, no adequate interpretation of the text can ignore the final phrase, "even as many as the Lord our God shall call." This phrase is equally related to all the members of the preceding triad. We pause to note this self-evident fact because Paedobaptists, with their theology of Old Testament externalism, according to which believers' children are "born in covenant," are prone to read this verse as securing the benefits of salvation (including baptism) to believers and their children *in distinction to* those who are afar off. The last group are born "out of covenant" and must be called to repentance and faith in order to be baptized. This approach, without the explicit statement of "covenant theology," is reflected in Jeremias' plea that the first two terms ("you and your children") should not be "torn apart" — as though associating the three together ("you, your children, all who are afar off") as equal members of the sentence might threaten the hermetic seal between parents and children that he is so zealous to preserve in support of infant baptism.[60]

Such a Paedobaptist interpretation violates the elemental structure of the text. Whether we think of Peter's listeners or of their children or of those far removed from the immediate scene of this first Christian kerygma, the point is that the promise is to all whom God shall *call*. This fact puts the whole matter on a rather different theological axis from that which is traditionally assumed in the interest of infant baptism. It becomes no more a question of one's natural birth, as Paedobaptists have often implied; there is nothing in this Scripture passage of "visible church membership" and "external covenant privilege." Rather, the passage is concerned with the call of God, that inner work of the Spirit who enlightens the mind and renews the heart ("they were pricked in the heart," v. 37), and with the response to that call ("what shall we do?" v. 37) on the part of those who receive it. Those who are thus called are baptized into the name of Jesus, who is freely offered in the gospel as the Savior of all

[60]See *Nochmals*, p. 22.

who in turn shall call on him. The whole account of the Pentecostal witness is couched in terms of summons and response. But no one can respond to this summons by proxy — as does the infant when presented by his parents for baptism; for when God calls a person, he calls him not by his family name but by his first name.[61]

In Acts 2:39, therefore, we have a form of statement appropriate to the occasion on which it was uttered, namely the founding of the Christian church, an occasion that marked the end of the old economy and the birth of the new. Standing on the threshold of the New Testament age, Peter's words echo the Old Testament: "To you is the promise and to your children"; but they seize the future with a forward face: "and to all who are afar off, even as many as the Lord our God shall call." The Paedobaptist ear is so attuned to the Old Testament echo in this text that it is deaf to its New Testament crescendo. It fails to perceive that the promise is no longer circumscribed by *birth* but by the call of God, by the anointing of his Spirit which secures the *new* birth, according to the covenant as newly administered in Christ. The children of this new covenant are those who, having received a new heart and a new spirit (Ezek. 36:26), become children of God (and of Abraham) by faith.

d. I Corinthians 7:14: "Holy" children

1) *The traditional Paedobaptist understanding of this text.* The same basic assumption underlying the Paedobaptists' use and understanding of Acts 2:39 informs and fortifies their conclusions concerning I Corinthians 7:14: "For the unbelieving husband is consecrated through his wife, and the unbelieving wife is consecrated through her husband. Otherwise, your children would be unclean, but as it is they are holy." With the exception of the Scripture passage where Jesus blesses little children, no passage has been laid under a more laborious contribution to serve the cause of infant baptism than this one.

[61]In evangelical theology, in other words, not baptism but effectual calling is the proper locus for understanding the meaning of one's "Christian" name. See below, p. 223, n. 10.

In some instances the exposition is so eager that it simply sets aside the obvious sequence of Paul's reasoning. J. M. Mason, for example, falls into this error by declaring that the question in the mind of the Corinthians is whether or not children of mixed marriages are members of the church with a right to baptism. Paul is writing to reassure his readers (Mason reassures us) that they are. God reckons such children in the church with the godly parent.[62] This puts the pyramid of the argument on its point, for Paul is assuming the status of the children as the one thing about which there was no question whatever.

Yet even among Paedobaptist expositors who perceive this, who acknowledge that the structure of Paul's argument is from the sanctity of the children to the sanctity of that relationship from which they sprang, it is commonly assumed as indisputable that the holiness of the children implies membership in the church with a concomitant right to baptism. However, since baptism is not so much as mentioned in the text, and since the context concerns the matter of mixed marriages (a question having no particular bearing on the sacraments or church membership), one might wonder — were he unaware of the Paedobaptist tendency to assimilate the New Testament to the Old — at the confidence with which Paedobaptists appropriate this Scripture passage. This confidence, of course, rests on the conviction brought to the text that when Paul speaks of the "holiness" of the children he refers to the external holiness of covenant status and privilege after the analogy of the Old Testament. Believers' children are "holy" because born into the covenant, as were Abraham's seed. And we know that they are born into the covenant because the apostle says they are "holy."

Admitting that the passage is difficult, we must still decide whether the presuppositions the Paedobaptists have brought to the understanding of this text are a clue to the maze or a Procrustean bed that narrows rather than liberates our understanding. If one limits himself to the creedal statements, the catechetical definitions, and the liturgical for-

[62]*Essays on the Church of God*, as quoted in Samuel Miller, *Infant Baptism, Scriptural and Reasonable*, pp. 20-21.

mularies bearing on infant baptism in which Paedobaptists cite this text, he will receive the impression of an overarching unanimity that admits of no doubt by correct-thinking and informed people. Again and again we are told that believers' children are, as Paul says, "holy," which means they are "in covenant" and therefore should receive baptism, which is the sign and seal of this covenant. Doubt begins to invade the inquiring mind only when the more detailed expositions are analyzed. Just as an apparently perfect gem reveals flaws under the microscope, so the notion that Paul is here speaking of the covenantal holiness of believers' seed is marked by theological defects when viewed under the lens of a critical appraisal.

Bushnell quotes this verse and comments:

> It is not meant here that the children are actually and inwardly holy persons, but that having only one Christian parent is enough to change their presumptive relations to God, enough to make them Christian children as distinguished from the children of unbelievers. So strong is the conviction, even in these apostolic times, of an organic unity sovereign over the faith and the religious affinities of the children, that wherever one parent believes, that faith carries presumptively the faith of the children with it. And upon this grand fact of the religious economy, baptism was from the first, and properly, applied to the children of them that believe.[63]

When Bushnell here refers to "Christian children," what does he mean? He means more than merely *Christians'* children, for this is a category even Baptists would understand. Yet he does not mean that the children are personally believing Christians, for he has just declared that they are not inwardly holy. We are forced to the conclusion that these children of believers are "Christian" just as the children of Abraham were Jews. He subsequently expounds the same passage so as to make this meaning quite beyond doubt:

> Paul did not of course use the term "sanctity" in any spiritual sense as affirming the regeneration of character in the children. But he alludes only to the church idea of clean and unclean, affirming that the unclean state of a godless father or mother is so far taken away by the clean state of a godly mother

---

[63]*Christian Nurture*, pp. 129-130.

or father, that the children are counted clean or holy — so far holy, that is, that they are of the fold and not aliens or unclean foreigners without the fold, as the Jews were accustomed to regard all the uncircumcised races. One believing parent puts the children in the church classification of believers.[64]

Here we have all the essential ideas that led Bushnell's New England forebears to set up the theocracy and the halfway covenant. The times have changed, but the theology is the same. The children of the saints are holy by natural pedigree, not by personal experience. They are holy as the circumcised Jews were holy, in contrast to uncircumcised aliens and foreigners.

In more recent times Oscar Cullmann has taken a similar position. He affirms that a child born of the marital union of baptized parents belongs, from the beginning, in the body of Christ "through his birth alone." He says that Paul's language in I Corinthians 7:14

> presupposes a *collective concept of holiness* in the sense of a *taking up into the body of Christ which is not tied to a personal decision*, but to birth of Christian parents who have received baptism. ... Hence, whether or not Paul here styles the baptism of a child as unnecessary, it is certain *that a direct line leads from the concept of holiness here represented, to child baptism, but not to a later baptism of these sons and daughters born into a Christian home, which rests on their personal decision!* So far as the *doctrine* of baptism is concerned, we can, in any event, conclude from this passage that ... *the baptismal solidarity of the family* is decisive and not the individual decision of each several member.[65]

In view of our previous discussion, it is not surprising that Paedobaptists should see in this Scripture passage a "holiness of birth, connection and privilege," nor is it difficult to anticipate the problems attaching to such an interpretation. To begin with, the word "holy" (ἅγιος) is juxtaposed in this verse to "unclean" (ἀκάθαρτος). While both terms may be used of persons in a ceremonial or ritual sense,

[64]*Ibid.*, pp. 148-149.
[65]*Die Tauflehre*, pp. 38-39 (Cullmann's italics). Cullmann, like Jeremias, is convinced that Paul's language here reflects Jewish proselyte baptism; hence the paradoxical comment about the baptism of certain children as "unnecessary." See above, pp. 63ff.

to do so is highly exceptional in the New Testament. In fact, the only instance of such usage is Acts 10:28, where Peter tells the household of Cornelius that God has taught him that he should not call any man "unclean." Now if Peter, as a New Testament Christian, no longer has a right to call a man "unclean" because of his birth, by what right do Paedobaptists conclude that Paul is calling their children "holy" because of their birth? Do not all such ceremonial distinctions rest on an Old Testament basis? Are not Paedobaptists again reading the New Testament as though it were the Old?

One is confirmed in this suspicion in noting the considerable ambivalence Paedobaptists display in explaining in what sense the unbelieving spouse, mentioned in this text, is "consecrated." The very thing they most want this passage to yield for the "holy" children, namely, the right to baptism, they must deny to the "consecrated" parent who does not believe. Thus their exposition is plunged into sibylic contortions. The holy children are "so far holy that they are in the fold, not aliens"; they are "in the church classification of believers"; theirs is a holiness "that evinces the operation of the covenant"; they are "in the body of Christ" by a kind of "collective holiness"; they enjoy the advantage of "the baptismal solidarity of the family." But all these luxuriant theological formulations drop from the discussion when the unbelieving spouse is concerned. He or she is "consecrated," but not so far as to be "in the fold": he/she is an alien; he/she is "sanctified," but not in the church classification of a "believer": he/she is an unbeliever. The covenant does not "operate" for him/her as it does for the child; the "collective holiness" that gathers in the child leaves him/her uncollected. And though he/she was in the family before the child was, he/she has no part or lot with the child in the "baptismal solidarity" of that family!

There is, however, no profound difference between the Greek verb "to make holy" (ἁγιάζω), used of the parent in this verse, and the Greek adjective "holy" (ἅγιος), used of the child. Why, then, should the meaning be so different in the one case than in the other? If the sanctifying influence of the believer on the unbelieving spouse carries with it no benefit in the church above that of hearing the gospel, how may we conclude that the sanctifying influence of the believer on the child implies the right to baptism and church membership?

Finally, the Paedobaptists' exegesis of this passage jars unbearably on the larger context. One has only to take a look at the shape of the hole into which the Paedobaptist exegetical peg has been forced to see how impossible matters are. As we have already argued, the question in the minds of the Corinthians, to which the apostle here endeavors an answer, concerns not the children but the marriage of which the children were born. In verses 10 and 11, Paul asserts, on the authority of the Lord, the perpetuity of the ordinance of matrimony. A woman is not to withdraw from her husband; yet if she does, she shall remain unmarried or be reconciled to him (and the same is true for the man). Beginning with verse 12, however, it becomes apparent that a question has arisen in the Corinthian church which Jesus never expressly entertained. Hence Paul seeks, on his own authority as an apostle, to apply Jesus' general teaching concerning the perpetual obligation of marriage to this new and specific case. ("As for the rest, I speak, not the Lord.") Then for the first time we discover exactly what the problem is. Paul declares that a brother, one of his favorite terms for a fellow Christian, should not leave his unbelieving wife if she consents to dwell with him. (Paul's remark a little later [v. 39] that a Christian widow is free to remarry "only in the Lord" would suggest that he is thinking in v. 14 of those whose marriage took place before their conversion. The church of Corinth had hardly been established long enough for marriages wittingly contracted between believers and unbelievers to have become an issue.) No doubt, from the first there were many Christians whose conversion severed them, religiously speaking, from their marriage partners in fulfillment of the Lord's word that he "came not to send peace but a sword" (Matt. 10:34). We can, then, understand how a devout Christian might wonder if separation from the defilement of his former pagan life should not include separation from his pagan spouse. Did one have a right to go on living with an unbeliever in such a situation? Would he not be defiled in some sense, made "unclean," if he did? This, then, is the question that Paul answers in the celebrated fourteenth verse of I Corinthians 7.

But how does the usual Paedobaptist exposition of I Corinthians 7:14 illuminate this matter? When we say that the children of a mixed marriage are "within the covenant," that is, that the covenant blessing of membership in the visible church descends from the believing parent to the child, what does this have to do with the question, Should the believer continue to cohabit with his unbelieving partner? Many Paedobaptists have answered that it has much to do with it. For example, Dean Henry Alford:

> This being so — they being hallowed because the children of Christians — it follows that *that union out of which* they sprang must *as such* have the same hallowed character; that is, that the *unsancitity* [sic] of the one parent is in it overborne by the *sanctity* of the other. The *fact* of the children of Christians, God's spiritual people, *being holy,* is tacitly assumed as a matter of course from the precedent of God's ancient covenant people.[66]

If what Alford says here were so, it would follow that all Jews in Old Testament times, being hallowed as children of Abraham and members of the holy nation, were born of a hallowed union — including Phares, the son of Judah by his daughter-in-law Tamar, and the firstborn of David by Uriah's wife Bathsheba. But obviously such unions were not hallowed. Here we see the *reductio ad absurdum* to which the traditional Paedobaptist understanding of this passage leads. It just does not follow that if the children are "holy" in the sense of "belonging to the church," then the union from which they sprang is hallowed in the sight of God.

Such reasoning is not followed through even by the Paedobaptists themselves. If a man or woman having illegitimate children is converted, or if, after conversion, a believer should compromise his virtue as David did, yet like David sincerely repent, the Paedobaptists will receive the children with the erring parent into the church. Yet they do not reason that since the children of such a union are re-

---

[66]*Greek Testament,* I Cor. 7:14 (Alford's italics).

garded as sanctified, that is, "within the covenant," *therefore* the union from which they were born is "sanctified." Nothing in the thought that children of a believing parent participate in the holiness of covenant privilege necessarily implies God's approval — or disapproval — of the parental relationship in and through which the children were born. But some such necessary implication is what is needed to make sense out of Paul. Whatever he meant when he said, "Otherwise, your children would be unclean, but as it is they are holy," he must have intended something which, if granted (and the Corinthians apparently did grant it), clearly implied that the marriage union of which they were born was beyond the reach of ethical dubiety. If this is so, then to inject a concern for the covenant holiness of believers' children into this text — as Paedobaptists do — is alien to Paul's argument at this point.

The same problem of irrelevance also plagues the Paedobaptist understanding of the "holiness" of the unbelieving spouse. When we are told that the unbeliever is "so far sanctified" that the children are "in covenant" despite the impediment of an unbelieving parent, just how does this sanctification-of-the-unbeliever-up-to-a-point shed light on the question, Should the believer continue to live with the unbeliever as husband or wife? As we have already observed, the Paedobaptist exegesis at this juncture is not a little perplexed. We are told that Paul does not mean that the unbeliever is made inwardly holy, for he is an unbeliever still. Then what does he mean? Well, he must mean the unbeliever is outwardly holy, but not in the sense that he is in the visible church or has a right to baptism or anything else that one can put his mental fingers on. At this point, one can at least sympathize with Barth's complaint, noted above, that "the confusion into which Luther and Calvin and their respective disciples have tumbled headlong in this matter is hopeless."

2) *The contemporary discussion of this Scripture text.* The less than satisfying results of the traditional expostion of I Corinthians 7:14, however, have in no way put an end to the Paedobaptist use of the passage. If this text cannot be shown to imply the baptism of all infants in the Corinthian church,

perhaps it can be shown to reflect Jewish proselyte baptism, whereby the children of heathen converts, at least, were baptized with their parents. Several contemporary Paedobaptist scholars have put it down as incontrovertible that Jewish proselyte baptism is the prototype of Paul's mode of expression in calling believers' children "holy."[67] Supposing that primitive Christians followed Jewish usage, it is alleged that they must have baptized children when families were converted from heathenism or Judaism. However, children born to parents already Christian would be deemed "holy" and in no need of baptism. Hence Paul does not say, "Now are your children *baptized*," but "Now are they *holy*." Says Jeremias: "Paul appears in I Corinthians 7:14c to know nothing at all of the baptism of children born to Christian parents." In fact,

> Since the apostle's inference of the sanctity of the heathen spouse from the sanctity of the child by way of analogy, is compelling, only if the child as well as the heathen spouse, is not baptized, it follows that the sanctity of the child *does not rest on baptism, but upon his descending from a Christian father or a Christian mother.*[68]

In other words, when the apostle wrote his first letter to Corinth, he assumed that children born to one who was a Christian were *not* to be baptized! Since this is just the reverse of the traditional understanding of this passage, an understanding Paedobaptists have cherished through the years as incontrovertible, it is not surprising that we are told by Jeremias that Paul did not long retain this view. He theorizes that by the time the apostle wrote Colossians 2:11, he had come to believe that baptism took the place of circumcision and should therefore be given not only to the children of heathen converts but also to those born in the covenant. This change in Paul's thinking took place, he surmises, somewhere between A.D. 60 and 70.[69]

---

[67]See above, pp. 63ff., on the baptism of Jewish proselytes. This thesis is not altogether contemporary. It is reflected in J. Lightfoot, *Horae Hebraicae et Talmudicae* on I Cor. 7:14, in his *Opera omnia*, II, 899. See also Strack-Billerbeck, *Kommentar*, III, 374.

[68]*Die Kindertaufe*, pp. 54, 57-58 (Jeremias' italics). See also Cullmann, *Die Tauflehre*, pp. 20f., 38f.

[69]*Die Kindertaufe*, p. 46.

However, contemporary Paedobaptists have seemed ill at ease with this exposition, for it involves the damaging admission that the apostle did not at first teach infant baptism as it is now commonly practiced. Even though one supposes that he changed his mind within a few years of writing I Corinthians, this construction would mean that for about a decade in the apostolic age a group of second-generation Christians ("holy" covenant children) were not baptized. During this time some may even have reached the age of accountability and been baptized as believers. Rather than allow the Baptist practice even so brief and tenuous a vogue in the apostolic age, Cullmann argues that I Corinthians 7:14 "implicitly yet completely excludes the subsequent baptism as adults of these children who are born into the covenant of the Holy One."[70] In other words, there may have been a few Christians in the apostolic age who were *never* baptized because their parents were Christians when they were born. And this whole convoluted argument is framed to make sure that all who were born of Christian parents, if they received baptism at all, received it not as believers but as infants, by virtue of their physical birth. This diverting bit of Paedobaptist theology reminds one of a similar curiosity noted by Markus Barth: ". . . were Jeremias' exposition [of I Cor. 7:14] correct, then must the heathen spouse also, should he eventually be received into the church, 'renounce' all claim to baptism!"[71]

In his final statement, Jeremias — understandably — struggles with the absurd implication of his own exegesis, whereby baptism could have been withheld from those born to a Christian parent in Corinth. Though Paul was speaking as the Jews spoke when he called the children of believers "holy," and though the Jews did not baptize such "holy" children, yet Paul, Jeremias surmises, most likely *did* baptize them. And why did he? Well, says Jeremias, the Jews always circumcised a male child born after the mother's conversion to Judaism, and in the Pauline churches baptism took the place of circumcision.[72] Therefore we may conclude that,

---

[70] *Die Tauflehre*, p. 55.
[71] *Theologische Literaturzeitung*, 1960, no. 1, p. 43.
[72] "In the Pauline churches baptism took the place of circumcision" — a clear instance of the *petitio principii* at the heart of the argument.

> ... as the Jewish community circumcised male infants even when they were born "in holiness," so the Christian community baptized children even when they were born "holy." Even the "holiness" of the heathen spouse in no way excluded his conversion and baptism.[73]

Whatever one may make of the details of Jeremias' reasoning, the main thrust is plain: the practice of infant baptism in the Pauline churches from the inception of the apostle's mission must be made secure and placed beyond all doubt, regardless of all other considerations. Hence, insofar as proselyte baptism makes *for* the baptism of infants by the church, it is to be pressed as determinative of Christian usage; insofar as it makes *against* it, it is to be set aside as inconclusive. Such a method of argument appears to be more convenient than convincing.

3) *Conclusion.* By way of conclusion, it should be observed that the Paedobaptists' attempt to make I Corinthians 7:14 their own is ill-fated from the start. Whether they use the more traditional categories of covenant theology or whether they see in this text the usage of Jewish proselyte baptism, their approach to I Corinthians 7:14 is always in terms of Old Testament covenant privilege. Paedobaptists always seek to understand the apostle according to the analogy of the Old Testament concept of outward, collective holiness. In New Testament terms this means that a decision for Christ by one member of the family somehow alters the status of the whole family: all its members now have a new status — the unbelieving spouse being "sanctified" and the children "holy." Such an interpretation can only obscure the meaning of the text, because the apostle is not speaking to a situation in which a decision for Christ, made by one member, *unites* a family; rather he is speaking to a situation in which such a decision *divides* a family. He is confronted with the problem reflected in Christ's pronouncement that he came not to bring peace but a sword (Matt. 10:34f.). Not

---

[73]*Nochmals*, p. 32. In making this change in his position, Jeremias was influenced by E. Stauffer, "Zur Kindertaufe im Urchristentum," *Deutsches Pfarrerblatt*, No. 49 (1949), pp. 152-154. W.F. Flemington argues similarly. Cf. his *New Testament Doctrine of Baptism*, p. 131.

family solidarity but Christian individualism and inwardness are at the root of the Corinthian question. It is a question that arises because in a profound sense a family has been divided: one parent has become a Christian while the other remains an unbelieving pagan. Only the propensity to read the New Testament as though it were the Old can account for the failure of the Paedobaptists to perceive this fact and to sense the fundamental disparity between their interpretation and the original historical context in which the passage was written.

But what, then, did Paul mean when he spoke as he did? Having concluded our analysis of the exposition of I Corinthians 7:14 offered by those who practice infant baptism, we may yet indulge the mind's desire to understand with a brief excursus on a possible interpretation of this much-discussed passage.

According to the interpretation we shall suggest, in I Corinthians 7:14 Paul has in view the sanctity of lawful matrimony and the purity of the resulting offspring. When he says that the unbeliever is "sanctified" by the believer, he is simply referring to the marriage covenant by which the unbeliever has been consecrated and set apart for the exclusive fellowship of the believer in the bond of marriage. He writes to reassure his Corinthian converts that this exclusive propriety, which the marriage covenant seals, is in no way abrogated by a disparity of religious commitment, great as this disparity may be. Christians, then, should never fear defilement through cohabitation with an unbelieving spouse: indeed, such defilement would imply that their children were also defiled, which they grant is not the case. In other words, he reasons from what is allowed to what is in doubt. If that relationship were unclean from which the children came, then the children would be unclean too; but everyone agrees that they are not. Rather they are "holy" in the sense that they are not contaminated with the taint of illegitimacy. Therefore, the union of which they were born is likewise above suspicion and reproach.

Samuel Miller calls this interpretation a "subterfuge than which it would be difficult to conceive one more completely preposterous."[74] And James Bannerman concludes, "The forced and unnatural interpretation put upon the passage by Antipaedobaptists cannot stand a moment's investigation."[75] But we submit that the difficulties surrounding the Paedobaptist view of this Scripture passage should teach at least a little openness to another possible view. Commending this interpretation is the fact that it is most apt at the point where the Paedobaptist interpretation is most inept. It begins where the text begins, with the unbelieving spouse who is "sanctified" by the believing spouse. And it explains the "holiness" of the unbelieving parent in the same terms as the "holiness" of the children. It also fits the context of the passage, which is the question of the sanctity of marriage, not the place of children in the church and their right to baptism.

Still, it may be objected that Paul cannot possibly be referring to the marriage covenant in the phrase "the unbelieving husband is sanctified by the wife," for the following reason: if the Corinthians questioned the sanctity of the marriage relationship when one spouse became a believer, then the apostle's affirmation of the original sanctity of that union, when both parties were unbelievers, would solve no problems. Take, for example, a case of adultery in which the innocent party seeks advice about continuing the marriage. Would we assure the man or women that he/she ought to continue because it was a valid marriage to begin with? When one must decide what to do after an act of infidelity, it is no help to assure him/her, as the innocent party, that the marriage was binding before the infidelity occurred. So it is here. If a Corinthian convert asks what he/she should do now that he/she has become a Christian who is married to a pagan, it is senseless to appeal to the validity of his/her marriage prior to the event which precipitated the crisis.

The answer to this reasoning is that the case of adultery is not truly analogous. Adultery, by definition, is a violation of the marriage vows of exclusive mutuality, whereas unbelief is not. Since the question in the minds of the Corinthian converts is whether or not a marriage contracted in unbelief

[74]*Infant Baptism*, p. 19.
[75]*The Church of Christ*, II, 99-101.

is still valid when one partner becomes a believer, Paul is not begging the question when he answers it with an appeal to the original marriage contract as still valid. Rather, as an apostle and teacher of the church, he is giving the answer to a question never before contemplated by the Christian community. At this juncture the mode of his expression should be carefully noted. He declares that the unbeliever is "sanctified" by the believer. He employs the perfect tense of the verb (ἡγίασται), thus describing an action taken in the past and standing complete at the time of speaking. Not that the act is ended, but rather it is accomplished in such a way that the result remains at the time denoted by the verb.[76]

Thus the interpretation we are suggesting is consistent with the syntax of the passage: the sanctity of the original marriage, which the Corinthians were doubting, the apostle is affirming. Therefore, "let not the believer leave the unbeliever," he says, "because the unbeliever has been and still is [Greek perfect] sanctified by the believer"; that is, he/she has been and still is set apart by the believer through the marriage covenant for his/her exclusive enjoyment in the marriage relationship. This is the only meaning that makes sense in the context.

Some Paedobaptists have objected that there is no evidence that ἁγιάζω was used concerning the sanctity of marriage at the time Paul wrote. One must remember, however, that there is no evidence of the use of ἁγιάζω in the sense Paedobaptists assign it when they construe Paul as teaching the external covenant holiness of children born of one Christian parent. Since they admit that in their understanding of this text Paul is using the verb in a "peculiar sense" which is "utterly unique" and "late Jewish,"[77] it is hardly convincing to reject an alternate interpretation for the same reason, especially if the alternate interpretation, as Markus Barth has observed, is the only one that sheds light on the "mystery" of I Corinthians 7:14.[78]

---

[76]"The perfect, although it implies the performance of the action in past time, yet states only that it stands completed at the present time." W. Goodwin, *Syntax of the Moods and Tenses of the Greek Verb*, p. 44.

[77]For example, Jeremias (among others), *Die Kindertaufe*, p. 54.

[78]See his comment in *Theologisches Literaturzeitung*, 1960, no. 1, p. 43.

Furthermore, there is clear evidence that the rabbis used the root קדשׁ (which is the Hebrew equivalent of ἁγιάζω) of espousal and marriage in keeping with its root meaning of "separation." In the *Mishna*, the treatise on betrothal and marriage uses this root no less than ten times for espousal. A man "sanctifies," that is, espouses, a wife by himself or by his messenger; a woman is "sanctified" by him or by his messenger.[79] The *Gemara* comments on this passage as follows: "The man declares that the woman, through the engagement, is forbidden to all other men and is as a sanctuary."[80]

While it is true that the rabbinical sources in which this usage is found are later than the time of Paul, this is equally true of the sources testifying to Jewish proselyte baptism. Since Paedobaptists readily appeal to the latter to support their thesis that I Corinthians 7:14 implies infant baptism, they should not rule out these other data simply because they do not serve their need. We deem it, then, highly plausible that Paul, trained as a rabbi, could have used the verb ἁγιάζω and the adjective ἅγιος in this verse in the sense of the consecration of the marriage covenant. Let not the believer, he enjoins, forsake the unbeliever. Why? Because the unbeliever has been and continues to be sanctified through the covenant of marriage by him/her who has since become a believer. Otherwise, your children would be "unclean," that is, illegitimate. But you know this is not so; rather they are "holy," that is, legitimate.

However, if the unbeliever initiates the action, the believer is not bound in such a case (v. 15); otherwise he is. Bound by what? Obviously by the obligation of the marriage covenant to continue the marriage. How else can one understand verse 14 — which is at the center of the discussion — than as it pertains to the original marriage covenant, the validity of which is being affirmed under those specific circumstances in which the Corinthians found themselves?

It is almost jejune to counter such an understanding of the text by pointing out that the New Testament nowhere

---

[79]*Kiddushim* 2:1. This fact was noted in the Baptist literature as early as John Gill, *A Body of Doctrinal and Practical Divinity*, III, 304.

[80]J. Levy, *Chaldäisches Wörterbuch über die Targumin*, p. 347.

teaches that mixed marriages are null and void, as though the Corinthians should have read their Bibles and known better than to raise such a question in the first place. Since the problem was created by pagans converting to Christianity, the Christian answer to the problem had yet to be written when the Corinthians raised the issue. In fact, the strict prohibition of mixed marriages with the heathen in the Old Testament, so far from enlightening their minds, may well have aggravated the scruples of these new Gentile Christians. Hence the urgent need for such an apostolic directive to resolve a difficult and sensitive question of conscience.

Though most Paedobaptists would rather leap over a steeple than meet with this interpretation, some have actually embraced it. In 1787 Abraham Booth cited eighteen such Paedobaptists expositors (including Melanchthon), with copious corroborating quotations from their writings. In the end, however, the issue does not turn on the interpretation of a specific passage by specific expositors; rather it turns on a whole way of thinking. Even though individual Paedobaptists have questioned the interpretation of I Corinthians 7:14 that the majority have espoused, none has ever questioned the assumption on which such an interpretation rests: that the children of Christians have the same covenant status in the New Testament church as did the children born to Abraham and his descendants in the Old Testament. Even though they do not all agree on the interpretation of a particular passage, when defending infant baptism they all read the New Testament as though it were the Old. This uncritical hermeneutical axiom is the basic error which must be seen for what it is if one is to grasp the nature of what Karl Barth has called the "burning issue" behind the argument over infant baptism in Reformation theology.

INFANT BAPTISM AND THE DEFINITION OF BAPTISM

A. INTRODUCTION

There is — and we are happy that it is so — a current in Paedobaptist theology other than the one that identifies the old and the new covenants, a current that contains a much clearer flow of biblical truth because it gives due recognition to the movement from the nationalism of Old Testament objectivity to the personalism of New Testament subjectivity. Hints of this happy inconsistency have already been given as we have reviewed the protests of Edwards within New England Congregationalism, Kierkegaard within Danish Lutheranism, and, in more recent times, Barth within the Reformed Church of Switzerland. Such protesters have risen up, in their own time and way, to challenge the imperialism of the Paedobaptist idea of objectivity which freezes the movement of redemptive history at the Old Testament level of the earthly, temporal, and typical, and casts revelation permanently in a mold that was meant to be temporary. And these challengers have done this in the name of a "conversion" experience (Edwards), an individual "subjectivity-which-is-the-truth" (Kierkegaard), an *Inpflichtsnahme*," to use Barth's term, that is, "a responsible willingness and preparedness on the part of the one being baptized to receive the promise of the grace offered him."[81]

---

[81]*Die Taufe*, p. 28.

But we need not contain the discussion within the pronouncements of individual spokesmen. The current of New Testament inwardness is not eccentric in the Paedobaptist understanding of baptism, but endemic; it is not lost in the eddies of individual opinion but dominates and structures the very meaning of baptism as defined in the classic Paedobaptist creeds and catechisms, Lutheran and Anglican as well as Reformed. These sources are remarkably subjective in their view of baptism. Baptism signifies and seals "the new birth," "purging from sins," "washing with his [Christ's] blood and Spirit from pollution of soul," "ingrafting into Christ," "regeneration from children of wrath unto children of God," "renewing of the heart," "adoption and resurrection unto everlasting life," "one's giving up of himself to God to walk in newness of life."[82] By these excellent definitions of baptism, which reflect true New Testament inwardness, Paedobaptists have permanently enriched the faith of the church.

After the surplus of disparate conviction reflected in portions of our previous discussion, it is gratifying to note this primary and fundamental agreement between Paedobaptists and their critics concerning the meaning of baptism. Those who espouse believer baptism are happy to confess with their brethren that baptism signifies and seals "ingrafting into Christ and partaking of the benefits of the covenant of grace," benefits freely offered to all who hear the gospel. As Paul says, we are "baptized into Christ Jesus" (Rom. 6:3); by baptism we have "put on Christ" (Gal. 3:27). "We were buried therefore with him by baptism into death, so that as Christ was raised from the dead by the glory of the Father, we too might walk in newness of life. For if we have been united with him in a death like his, we shall certainly be united with him in a resurrection like his" (Rom. 6:4-5).

We would not only commend Paedobaptists for the re-

---

[82]*First Helvetic Confession; Irish Articles; Thirty-Nine Articles; Heidelberg Catechism; French Confession of Faith; Westminster Confession of Faith; Westminster Shorter Catechism; Belgic Confession; Westminster Larger Catechism.*

markably lucid insights into the meaning of baptism reflected in their confessions but also give emphatic consent to the way in which these confessions proceed from a definition of baptism in general to infant baptism in particular. It is a commendable procedure, in our judgment, to subordinate the question, Shall infants be baptized? to the more basic question, What is the meaning of baptism?[83]

By so doing, however, the confessions of the Paedobaptists heighten the problem of infant baptism. For how do the excellent definitions of baptism which they contain agree with what we have read of the status of infants in the Paedobaptist scheme? Covenant children, we have been told, are not presumed to be "actually and inwardly holy persons"; one does not affirm a "regeneration of character" in those born in covenant. Yet baptism, which is the sign and seal of this most inward, most subjective grace of the new birth, should be given to these very children. Paedobaptists teach that baptism signifies "renewal in purity of life by the Holy Spirit"; yet they also teach that baptism is to be given to their children who have a "federal," "relative," "collective," "legal" holiness — but not that true inward renewal and purity of life wrought by the Holy Spirit and signified by baptism. Should anyone suppose that we are editing Paedobaptist sources to sharpen a discrepancy, we assure him that this is by no means true — nor is it necessary. The defense of infant baptism along Old Testament lines of out-

---

[83]Not all Paedobaptists have agreed to this significant sequence of thought, however. A century ago, commenting on Mark 10:14, "Suffer the little children to come unto me," Henry Alford argued: "Not only may the little infants be brought to him — but in order for us who are mature to come to him we must cast away all that wherein our maturity has caused us to differ from them and become LIKE THEM. Not only is infant baptism *justified*, but it is ... THE NORMAL PATTERN OF ALL BAPTISM: none can enter God's kingdom *except* as an infant. In adult baptism, the *exceptional case*, we strive to secure that state of simplicity and childlikeness which in the infant we have ready and undoubted to our hands" (*Greek Testament*, 7th ed., *loc. cit.*). In more recent times, the Scottish Commission renews this insistence: "... the norm of Baptism is infant baptism, as in John Knox's *Book of Common Order* (1564)" (*Baptism in the Church of Scotland*, p. 13). Such reasoning makes every baptism recorded in the New Testament an exceptional instance, a somewhat unlikely hypothesis, to say the least!

ward holiness by birth stands in stark contradiction to the meaning of baptism as enunciated in the classic Paedobaptist confessions. Let anyone climb this Paedobaptist Pisgah and view the theological landscape, and he will see that the range of arguments arising from external covenant privilege has no theological connection with the ground on which he is standing.[84]

Once the student has gained this significant insight, he is in a position critically to appreciate other arguments for infant baptism which move in the opposite direction from those we have reviewed. These arguments are oriented not toward Old Testament outwardness and solidarity but toward New Testament inwardness and individualism; they seek to give baptism more or less the same meaning for infants which it has for believers. These arguments, of course, do not occur in isolation from those we have already discussed. While some Paedobaptists argue rather consistently in terms of the holiness of "external covenant privilege," and others in terms of the "inward holiness of personal sanctification," most of them do both. Since, however, these approaches are theologically quite different in kind, it has seemed best to serve the interests of lucid analysis by treating them separately.

Therefore, having taken the measure of the argument from "external covenant privilege" after the model of the Old Testament theocracy, let us now address the task of analyzing this other sort of argument, an argument that moves in terms of New Testament inwardness and individualism. Those committed to the baptism of believers will feel a fundamental affinity with this approach, for if it can be shown that the infant children of believers partake of the same inward and

---

[84]Barth complains, justly, that an enlightened defense of infant baptism will keep in view the premises presupposed in the discussion rather than let them drop out of sight. One must honor all that he has said previously about baptism in general, even about the sacraments in general, perhaps even about the fundamental concepts considered normative for the whole general area under consideration. This, he animadverts, the Reformers just did not do (*Dogmatik*, IV, 4, pp. 189f.).

spiritual blessings that their parents enjoy, then the contention that the sign and seal of this grace should not be withheld until "riper years" takes on a new aura of plausibility.

B. LUTHERANISM AND THE PIETISTS; ANGLICANISM AND THE WESLEYANS

In an attempt to evaluate the reasoning of the Paedobaptists in this respect, it is instructive and helpful to return once more to the confessions of the Reformation as our point of departure. It should be noted at the outset that in proportion as these documents reflect a causal view of sacramental efficacy (that is, a view that closely unites the grace signified to the outward elements), it is assumed that the baptized child is truly engrafted into Christ and regenerated by the Holy Spirit in and through his baptism. This being granted, there is nothing more to be said; the sacrament of infant baptism in such a theology is as foolproof as reason can make it. It only remains to confirm the child, regenerated by baptism, before he is old enough to display any naughtiness of character that might frustrate the system. Hence the Lutheran and Anglican creeds move at this juncture with a simplicity that appears almost naive to a Baptist.

Occasionally those belonging to these communions have sensed the problem and lamented that "millions of baptized Christians grow up to adulthood with no profit from their baptism."[85] But their suggestions for remedying the situation have not been well taken by their peers. The early German Pietist Philipp Spener created a storm of controversy when he affirmed that the new birth occurs not at one's baptism as an infant but at the time of one's conscious conversion. Somewhat later, Wesley was accused of "enthusiasm" when he warned people not to lean on the broken reed of their baptism; for notwithstanding their receipt of the

---

[85]E. H. Browne, *Exposition of the Thirty-Nine Articles*, p. 620.

sacrament, they were yet children of the devil by nature, who had to be born again.[86]

Pietism and Wesleyanism, however, are theological truancies from the traditional mainstream of Lutheran and Anglican sacramentalism. In these traditions as a whole, the definition of baptism as the sign of the inward grace of renewal is harmonized with the practice of baptizing infants by the affirmation of some form of baptismal regeneration. Thus all that baptism signifies and seals is secured, without reservation, to the infant who is brought to the font. But, as we indicated at the outset of our investigation, our primary concern is not with the sacramental but rather with the evangelical defense of infant baptism. Hence we must leave the sacramentalists, whom Kierkegaard accused of minting Christians like money, and return to the Reformed tradition with its stress on baptism as the sign of the covenant promise, a promise mediated through the proclamation of the gospel and appropriated by the hearing of faith.

C. THE REFORMED TRADITION

1. Introduction

Here we face a new set of problems, for if baptism does not secure the grace of regeneration, but only signifies and seals this blessing, ought we still to give it to infants? Are we to assume that covenant children are already regenerate when they receive the covenant sign? If baptism signifies "engrafting into Christ and partaking of the benefits of the covenant of grace," benefits that include purification from sin by washing in the Savior's blood and renewing of heart, so that they who are rightly baptized are no longer to be

[86]In his *Doctrinal Tracts*, under "Baptism," Wesley affirmed that by baptism we are made children of God, being born again by the washing of regeneration. He made no effort, however, to relate this Anglican view of baptismal regeneration to his evangelical insistence on personal conversion. On the Lutheran side, cf. O. Hallesby, *Infant Baptism and Adult Conversion*. Hallesby does the same thing Wesley does, though he does at least make an effort to resolve the tension. In this effort one will admire his Christian spirit more than his theological acumen.

regarded as children of wrath but children of God, what less can we say than that children receiving this sign are assumed to be regenerate? But may we say this much of "covenant children" in the light of the stubborn fact that so many who are baptized grow up to be Christians in name only, while not a few even turn their back on Christ and "break their baptismal covenant" by rash and apostate dissent? So far as the argument for infant baptism from the covenant is concerned, this is its question of destiny. Sensing as much by a sagacious instinct, evangelical and Reformed Paedobaptists have made a noble effort to frame an answer, marshaling arguments that must receive the highest commendation if judged by the zeal and conviction with which they have been set forth.

As we turn to consider these arguments, it must be initially granted that a child *may* be regenerate from infancy. But this is quite a different matter from supposing that *all* those born to believers are to be assumed in that happy state. Yet it is precisely this latter position which Paedobaptist definitions of baptism imply. There is, as we have already remarked, a great gulf between the inwardness with which Paedobaptists define baptism as symbolizing an engrafting into Christ and their defense of infant baptism as an "external covenant privilege" after the pattern of Old Testament circumcision. When Paedobaptists argue for infant baptism from the perspective of their own definitions of the sacrament, they reason in a manner that really renders all the arguments from external covenant privilege superfluous. Here one finds a fresh start, in terms of the New Testament understanding of baptism as set forth in the Reformed confessions and catechisms.

2. The position of Calvin

A prime exhibit of such an approach is found in Calvin's *Institutes*. Although Calvin's defense of infant baptism, as we have seen, contains the leaven of Old Testament externalism, his powers of logical penetration seem at times to have driven him to the assertion that covenant children from the moment of birth are indeed the subjects of God's saving mercy and renewing grace in the full sense of New Testament inwardness. They are "cradled in the Holy Ghost," so to speak, and therefore to be carried to the baptismal font. Never has anyone in the Reformed tradition stated himself in these matters with more ebullient confidence.

> God pronounces that he adopts our infants as his children before they are born, when he promises that he will be a God to us and to our seed after us. This promise includes their salvation. Now will any dare to offer such an insult to God as to deny the sufficiency of his promise to insure its own accomplishment?[87]

Calvin does not say that when believers' children grow up to be of a pious frame, God adopts them for his own; rather, the grace of salvation is secured to them before they are born. As they are "in Adam," so they are "in Christ"; they are made partakers of him, with all his saving benefits. They are exempt from God's wrath and from the penalty of death. They are admitted into the covenant in the same sense and to the same extent as adults who exercise repentance and faith toward God. Unlike the majority of Paedobaptist expositors, Calvin does not hesitate to affirm that I Corinthians 7:14 means that believers' children are truly and inwardly holy, "sanctified by supernatural grace." Hence the antidote to their ruined condition by nature is their sanctification in Christ.[88] In his *Commentary on the Harmony of the Evangelists*, concerning the place where Jesus blesses the children, Calvin says that God washes little infants with the blood of his Son, renews them by his Spirit according to the capacity of their age; and, since they are partakers of the Spirit's gifts represented by baptism, it is unreasonable that they should be deprived of the outward sign.

No sensitive student can contemplate Calvin's position without a certain admiration. We are standing for a moment on the high ground of pure evangelical Paedobaptism, above the foggy inconsistencies that hover over most Paedobaptist abstractions and refinements. God in his infinite mercy and

---

[87]*Institutes*, IV, xv, 20.
[88]*Ibid.*, IV, xvi, 17; IV, xvi, 24; IV, xvi, 31; IV, xvi, 32.

covenant faithfulness has done for the children of the believer what he has done for the parent, and therefore they are to be baptized. And so, it appears, Calvin has bridged the gulf between the New Testament teaching of baptism and the practice of infant baptism.

But this noble vision is destined to fade as soon as we lower our eyes from heaven to earth. Though Calvin declares that God adopts believers' infants before they are born, by a promise that includes their salvation, in every age and in every place there has been manifold and melancholy evidence to the contrary. We do not deny that God may so act, and rejoice that he sometimes does; but our inability to predict at the time of one's birth the direction of one's life shows how far from adequate is Calvin's theory. The unvarnished truth is that we can be sure our children are sinners; they are indeed "in Adam." But it is not so with their position in Christ. (If, at the moment of their birth, our parental pride winks at this fact, we will be rudely disabused of our sentiments by the sheer passage of time.) For Calvin to pronounce that children of believers are "sanctified by supernatural grace" on the strength of I Corinthians 7:14 is hardly more plausible than the Roman Catholic claim that the elements in the Eucharist are literally Christ's body and blood on the strength of John 6:53. The bread and wine — for all the treatises on transubstantiation — still look, taste, feel, and smell like any other bread and wine. And baptized, covenant children, for all their "sanctification by supernatural grace," grow up talking, walking, looking, and acting like any other children in need of the grace of salvation.

3. Covenant children presumed regenerate

Most Paedobaptists have shied away from the affirmations Calvin made, seeking other answers to the problem, answers more obviously compatible with the character of life. We must commend their effort; yet we cannot but observe that the very proliferation of answers pleads the uncertainty of the case. Some of these answers are common, some not; and each apologist tends to use several of them, even though they may conflict with one another, in an effort to make his case as plausible as possible. One such approach, which has been widely taken, adjusts Calvin's pronouncements about covenant children to a degree more commensurate with sober reality. According to this position, we cannot — even as we need not — pronounce the children of believers regenerate when baptized. Some may be; some may not be. All that is necessary to their baptism is a *presumption* that they are regenerate, made on the strength of God's covenant promise to be a God to his people and to their seed after them.

Paedobaptists are quick to make the point that Baptists can do no better, since they also must *presume*, in charity, that those are regenerate members of Christ who make a credible profession of faith in him. It is not, then, an indiscriminate use of baptism that embraces the infant with the believing parent; for though some children may prove reprobate, the same possibility exists with adults baptized in the Baptist scheme of things. Not every adult who makes a profession of faith proves ultimately to be a true child of God; yet Baptists acknowledge that they have no right to withhold baptism because some who were baptized as supposed believers have proved unworthy of the Christian name. There is, then, no essential difference between believer baptism and infant baptism in this respect. Both are administered on the *presumption* that the one baptized is a member of Christ's body, to be numbered among his people and given the sign of his covenant.

B. B. Warfield amplifies this reasoning with plausible and forcible argument:

> In this state of the case it is surely impracticable to assert that there can be but one ground on which a fair presumption of inclusion in Christ's body can be erected, namely, a personal profession of faith. Assuredly a human profession is no more solid basis to build upon than a divine promise. So soon, therefore, as it is fairly apprehended that we baptize on presumption and not on knowledge, it is inevitable that we shall baptize all those for whom we may on any ground fairly cherish a good presumption that they belong to God's people — and this surely includes the infant children of believers, concerning the favor of God to whom there exist many precious prom-

ises on which pious parents, Baptists as fully as others, rest in devout faith.[89]

Baptists can only applaud Warfield's insistence that a divine promise is a more solid basis to build upon than a human profession. Speaking of God's promise as it is set forth in Ezekiel 36:26, Charles Spurgeon, a Baptist, says,

> Brethren, I will read this sentence over again, "A new heart also will I give you" and I will call your attention to the style of the language. It is *"I will"* and again *"I will"!* Jehovah's Ego is the great word. It is not, "I will if" or "I will perhaps" or "I will upon certain conditions" but — "I will give." He speaks in a godlike tone. It is royal language, the very word of him who of old said, "Light be" and light was. He who spoke the world into being speaks the new world of grace into being by the selfsame majestic voice.[90]

But the word "presumption," as Warfield uses it when he says that Baptists as well as Paedobaptists "baptize on presumption and not on knowledge," conveys that which is less than certain, that which partakes of the contingency attached to all that is human. When one says, then, that Baptists baptize on presumption, he is simply saying that they accept a human profession of faith as credible without claiming infallibly to know the heart. Hence their trust may be deceived. But unlike a human confession, a divine promise is surely above such frailty, is it not? When a Paedobaptist, therefore, argues that believers' children are only "presumptively regenerate," and appeals to the divine promise as the rationale of this presumption, does he not show himself of little faith? Is there anything more certain than that God will keep his promises? As Calvin says,

> . . . when [God] promises that he will be a God to us and our seed after us . . . this promise includes their salvation. . . . Now will any dare to offer such an insult to God as to deny the sufficiency of his promise to insure its own accomplishment?[91]

---

[89]*Polemics*, p. 390.

[90]"Covenant Blessings," a sermon preached Lord's Day Morning, April 4, 1877, *Metropolitan Tabernacle Pulpit*.

[91]*Institutes*, IV, xv, 20.

Therefore, since the promise is sure, a faith worthy of that promise should be confident that what God has spoken he is able to perform. Why, then, do the Paedobaptists have reservations about their children's enjoyment of the promise, when they have no reservations about giving them the sign of the promise? Why do they only *presume* them regenerated when brought to baptism?

Of course, it is true, as we have said, that Baptists baptize on presumption. But when they "presume" those to be truly God's people who make a credible profession of their faith, and grant them the sign of baptism, they are not "yielding the whole principle" (Warfield) of infant baptism. They are simply saying that the true church of God is made up of all those whom Christ has purchased with his blood and renewed by his Spirit; and that those who appear to the eye of judicious charity to be of this number, because of a credible profession of faith in Christ, should be regarded as members of the church. Hence baptism is lawfully administered to all who make a credible profession, even though some may prove foolish virgins at last. In the latter case we have an instance of the frailty of human judgment but not the failure of a divine promise.

4. *Covenant children given a conditional promise*

Perceiving that this is so, some Paedobaptists shift to the other foot and say that the promise as sealed in baptism is not sure after all. It is a conditional promise requiring for its fulfillment repentance and faith on the part of the child baptized, when he comes to years of discretion. Richard Baxter, for example, lists as error number five of the Baptists the contention that the covenant sealed in baptism is the absolute covenant of grace.[92] In his confutation of this error, Baxter distinguishes between the "absolute" promise of salvation and the "conditional" covenant of grace. The former, he maintains, is not sealed in baptism *and* the Lord's Supper, but in the latter only. The covenant of grace is properly called a covenant because of its mutuality, that is, because of its having a "restipulation on our parts as well as a promise

[92] *Plain Scripture Proof*, p. 223.

on God's part."[93] Baxter thus does not hesitate to say that God seals the conditional covenant to thousands who shall perish, leaving it to their own choice whether they will recognize and be faithful to the covenant. Whether there is any absolute promise of salvation at all he finds to be "very dark and doubtful and the most learned cannot agree whether there be any such thing."[94]

This is too much, even for T. F. Torrance and the other members of the Scottish Commission on Baptism. Convinced as they were, against Barth and his disciples, that infant baptism was biblical, they could not defend it along these precarious theological lines. Here their Calvinism came to the rescue.

> Under the federal theology [the commissioners complain] the whole conception of *covenant* changed into a *contract* with its mutual stipulations voluntarily undertaken as between equal partners. Although attempts were made to guard the *grace* of the new covenant, there was an inevitable stress upon man's necessary fulfillment of stipulated conditions before he could have even an interest in Christ. Against this lapse into legalism there were real protests, as from James Fraser of Brea and Thomas Boston, who insisted that the Gospel was unconditionally a message of pure grace and that the very fact that man was a sinner gave him already his "interest" in Christ, because it was precisely for sinners that Christ died. Wherever this protest came, it came as a result of the discovery that the teaching of the New Testament was contradicted by the federal theology. This is very clear in the attack by Fraser of Brea upon the teaching of Richard Baxter on baptism, which rested upon the "false and destructive principle that the covenant of grace is conditional." It was precisely this false element that made infant baptism a serious problem.[95]

[93]*Ibid.*, p. 225.
[94]*Ibid.*, p. 226.
[95]*The Interim Report*, May 1958, p. 60. The reference to "federal theology" in this paragraph appears confused. Federal theology is defined in the second edition of Webster's *New International Dictionary* as "that theological system which rests upon the conception . . . that since the Fall, man is under a *covenant of grace* wherein God of his free grace promises eternal blessedness to all who believe in Christ (the federal head of the Church)." How, then, could federal theology be the "false element" that made infant baptism a problem? As we see it, it was the false element of infant baptism that led many good federal theologians away from the covenant concept to the notion of a mutual contract. However, the point of the paragraph, that the promise of the covenant is unconditional, is well taken.

We see from such a paragraph that the promise is free, an unconditional message of pure grace, the Paedobaptists themselves being our mentors. And yet many whom God declares to be the heirs of this promise and who must be sealed with its sign are not heirs and never will partake of its blessings. How does all this fit together? According to the prophet Jeremiah (31:31-36), the new covenant, in contrast to the old, is one that *cannot be broken*. The fathers who came out of Egypt broke the first covenant the Lord made with them; but the new covenant will stand as sure as the ordinances of day and night, for it shall be engraved on the hearts of the covenantees by the omnipotent finger of him who saves by his grace. How can the heirs of this new, unbreakable covenant break that covenant? Yet Paedobaptists often speak of baptized children who grow up in unbelief as "covenant breakers" who are "unfaithful to their baptismal vows." So constant are these terms in the discussion that they have become, as it were, technical terms in the literature. Paedobaptists evidently cannot get along without them, though it is not clear how they get along with them either, if they are to remain truly Reformed.

5. Covenant children and parental faithfulness

At this point in the discussion it is conventional to censure parents whose children prove unfaithful. Allegedly, it is because they neglect to bring up their children in the fear of the Lord, according to the vows taken when their children were baptized, that the covenant promise sometimes fails of fruition. For Bushnell, with his enthusiasm for Christian nurture — an enthusiasm Baptists would do well to emulate — the very suggestion that covenant children may fail of their inheritance even when parents are faithful is almost more than can be borne. It would threaten to unhinge his whole argument. "It is my settled conviction," he declares, "that no man ever objected to infant baptism who had not at the bottom of his objection a false view of Christian education."[96] He argues that some parents fail because of defective

[96]*Christian Nurture*, p. 41.

views of the way in which children should be taught; for all their good intentions, they discourage piety in a child. Still others fail in the religious training of their children because the church counteracts their effort.

> The church makes a bad atmosphere about the house and the poison comes in at the doors and windows. It is rent by divisions, burnt up by fanaticism, frozen by the chill of a worldly spirit, petrified by a rigid and dead orthodoxy.[97]

Since the person who will not provide for his own is worse than an infidel, we must acknowledge the justice with which Bushnell excoriates parental negligence and the wisdom with which he pleads for parental faithfulness. We accept his complaint that some parents in rearing their children make mistakes which, if not cruelly intended, are yet cruelly felt. However, we are constrained to observe that the theology which implies that if parents do their part God will save the children is a theology which may be as cruel to the parents as bad nurture is to the children. Though every lawful incentive should be employed to move parents to higher resolves of consecration in the parental office, this doctrine of "you do your part and God will do his" can become a counsel of despair, a millstone about the necks of conscientious parents.

Bushnell says, "Show me the case where the whole conduct of the parent has been such as it should be to produce the best effects. . . ."[98] We venture he never was shown such and never discovered one for himself. What parent, after all, can begin to be all that he ought to be in training his children? What parent could claim that his "whole conduct has been such as it should be"? We heartily agree with our Paedobaptist brethren in their stress on parental training; but when they try to make it a scapegoat for failures in their system, failures which have much more profound theological roots, they simply drive themselves into a deeper morass of contradiction. We should never use the truth that God honors parental fealty so as to abuse the truth. When we do, we simply have one more nuance of the legalistic error of Baxter (for whom Bushnell, naturally, expresses deep appreciation), an

[97]*Ibid.*, pp. 39-40.
[98]*Ibid.*, p. 37.

error according to which the blessings of the covenant of grace are conditioned by man's faithfulness. It must be remembered that it is the very glory of that covenant that its grace overcomes not only the hardness of the human heart but the frailty of parental nurture. God does not say, "I will if you parents do your part" — what a counsel of despair! — but merely, "I will."

If anyone be unconvinced still by this "high theology of grace," let him lower his eyes to the mundane realm of everyday experience. Let him look at sacred history, written not only for our comfort but also for our learning (Rom. 15:4), and see the lessons with which its pages are filled. Abraham, whom the Lord (and all the Paedobaptists) extols as a model of parental faithfulness (Gen. 18:19), begot Ishmael, of whom it is written, "the son of the slave shall not inherit with the son of the free woman" (Gal. 4:30); Isaac, in whom the seed is called, begot Esau, a profane man (Rom. 9:7; Heb. 12:16); Samuel, the spiritual father of Israel, knew the tragedy of his wicked sons, "who did not walk in his ways, but turned aside after gain; they took bribes and perverted justice" (I Sam. 8:1-4); David, the "man after God's own heart," begot the usurper Absalom. And so it went with many of the kings of Israel; good kings came from bad fathers and bad kings from good fathers. As Spurgeon once observed, "I think the children of godly parents are like Jeremiah's figs; the good are very good, but the bad are very bad — very naughty figs such as cannot be eaten."[99]

What can be said to these things? Shall we accuse Abraham because he took a slave girl as a concubine? Shall we make Esau Rebekah's folly? Shall we indict Samuel, who fathered a nation, for neglect of his own house? Bushnell, at least, is confident of the answer. He castigates Rebekah as

> a partial mother, scorning one child, teaching the other to lie and trick his blind father and extort from a starving brother his birthright honor. . . .

> Had Israel ruled his house as he ought, had Rebekah been an honest woman, loving both her sons impartially and seeking

[99]"A Promise for Us and for Our Children," Lord's Day Morning, April 10, 1864, *The Metropolitan Tabernacle Pulpit.*

the true welfare of both — not conspiring with one to rob and cheat the other — Esau might have been a different man and Edom might have been a family in Israel.[100]

No Christian, of course, can condone the conniving of Rebekah with Jacob, but neither can one accept — unless he reads Scripture with a jaundiced eye — Bushnell's judgment against them as altogether just. While Scripture pronounces no encomiums upon Jacob and his mother in this affair, it reserves its denunciations for Esau, who "despised his birthright" for a mess of pottage (Gen. 25:34), because he was a "profane man," that is, a man whose mind was this-worldly (Heb. 12:16). Bushnell, bending every fiber of his argument to make Esau appear as Rebekah's folly, overlooks the judgment of Scripture against him.

But we hardly need pursue this matter further. It all comes out to this: the attempt on the part of some Paedobaptists to be consistent, to presume of the child who is baptized what is presumed of the parent, is as impossible as it is commendable. When the *Heidelberg Catechism* teaches children that their baptism as infants assures them that they have been spiritually washed from their sins just as really as their physical parts have been washed with water, it is a beautiful line on paper, but it is no trustworthy horoscope of life. Not baptism received in unwitting infancy but the Word of promise met "with faith in the hearers" (Heb. 4:2) is the ground of such assurance, according to an evangelical and Reformed theology.

6. *Covenant children presumed elect*

Admitting as much, some Paedobaptist symbols (and many Paedobaptist theologians) have argued that infants should be baptized not because they are regenerated, or presumed so, but because they are presumed to be elect.

The doctrine of "presumptive election" was given confessional status initially by the Reformed party of Switzerland in the *First Helvetic Confession*. In this confession baptism is defined as the "washing of *regeneration*." Given such

[100]*Christian Nurture*, pp. 37, 125.

a definition, one would have expected the authors simply to affirm the right of children to this sign as presumably *regenerate*. But — surprisingly — they do not do so. Rather, it reads: "We baptize our children in this bath because it would not be right to rob them of the fellowship of God's people" (as though the Anabaptists did this) and "because they are such as one should suppose *may be elect of God.*"[101]

Whoever takes time carefully to observe this "presumptive election" argument, as it wends its way through the literature of debate, soon becomes aware that it is curiously intertwined with another, which goes like this: It is not necessary that the inward grace of baptism and the outward sign should be coincident in time; we may baptize our children even though they do not experience inward renewal and cleansing until later in life. Like star pairs in space, these two ideas tend to gravitate around the same center. How did these two ideas come to be associated, and what do they signify?

So far as this writer has been able to judge, this dual argument is rooted historically in what may be called the existential predicament in which many of the leading Reformers found themselves. Brought to the baptismal font by parents whose minds were darkened by superstition, sponsored by godparents who shared the common ignorance of the times, and baptized by Roman Catholic priests who did not act out of any clear perception of the true meaning of the gospel, they themselves, when come to years of discretion, did not at first embrace the gospel with an enlightened faith. Later on, as mature people, having their minds illumined to understand and their wills renewed to accept the covenant promise of salvation, what were they to do? To submit to baptism as true believers in Christ would have given a fillip to the Anabaptist contention, a prospect which they could not endure to contemplate. Their only alternative was to make their necessity mother a theological invention sufficient to the situation. This they did by declaring that their baptism, as an external rite administered in infancy, was efficacious by

[101]Chs. XX and XXI (italics mine).

virtue of their *election* to salvation, even though they could not presume to have enjoyed the grace of their baptism until years later. John Knox, for example, says of his own baptism: "I confess it did not profit us; but now the Spirit of Christ Jesus, illuminating our hearts, has purged the same by faith and makes the effect of that sacrament to work in us without any iteration of the external symbol."[102]

Concerning the thesis that a presumption to election gives a right to baptism, it must be observed that Paedobaptist confessions say not a word to this effect when elaborating the doctrine of baptism; there is nothing in them about baptism as a sign and seal of blessings in prospect, blessings to which it is hoped that one is elect. Significantly, it is not until they come to infant baptism that the creeds mention election, and even then they do so with a marked reservation. This reservation is understandable, for there is no hint of such a notion to be found anywhere in the New Testament. It is for this reason that the Paedobaptists leave their learned discussions about election as the basis of baptism quite destitute of scriptural support. The authors of the *First Helvetic*, to be sure, cite Titus 3, Acts 10, Genesis 17, I Corinthians 7, and Luke 18, without delineating specific verses, in support of their thesis that infant baptism rests on presumptive election. But one has only to read these passages to feel the vague uncertainty that must necessarily mark the effort to ground this doctrine in Scripture.

In keeping with the thesis that the inward washing signified by the external rite of baptism need not be assumed when the rite is performed, it has often been affirmed that one may be truly and effectually called *after* he is baptized with no prejudice to the sacramental sign.[103] But ordinarily a medical student does not put the letters "M.D." after his name while he is still in school, on the strength of his prospects; nor does a presidential assistant affix the seal of

---

[102]*Works*, IV, 119ff., as quoted in G. W. Bromiley, *Baptism and the Anglican Reformers*, p. 74.

[103]Cf. Bromiley, p. 203, where it is argued that in point of time the personal calling of the elect may not coincide with the moment of his baptism, yet baptism remains the seal of the promised grace.

the United States government to a blank sheet of paper in the hope that the President will one day inscribe something thereon. Why, then, should children be signed and sealed in baptism regardless of whether, at the time, there is any reason to suppose that they possess what is being signed and sealed to them? On this basis, why should one be at all discriminating in administering the rite? If we need not presume that the candidate has experienced the inward grace signified in baptism, then we may always proceed to administer the external rite in the prospect and hope that what is outwardly symbolized will one day become an inward reality.

R.E.O. White's objection to this "proleptic" approach to infant baptism is well taken: it enervates the element of eschatological fulfillment indissolubly united with baptism in the New Testament. While granting the Paedobaptists' emphasis on the primacy of God's action over that of man's, and while acknowledging the corrective sought for infant baptism in the rite of confirmation, it must be affirmed that for the writers of the New Testament the new age has begun. The Christian knows that his sins are forgiven and that he has received the Spirit; in the New Testament baptism is always linked with this knowledge. Hence apostolic baptism is a sacrament of eschatological realization. He who is baptized is one who has received the good news, acknowledged Christ as Lord, and begun the Christian life. To baptize one as a sign of things hoped for (and only hoped for) is to make it a sacrament of *anticipation,* whereas in the New Testament it is always the sacrament of *fulfillment.*[104]

7. Conclusion

There are many Paedobaptists who will not say, with the Lutherans, we baptize our children because it is "necessary

[104]Speaking of election and the notion that covenant children are presumptively elect, one wonders whether the Paedobaptists' emphasis on the covenant promise vis-à-vis their own children — these children are presumed elect, even regenerate — may not appeal to many as a kind of security against the implications of the doctrine of election. Absolutely to submit oneself as a parent to a God who is sovereignly free to choose whom he will ("I will have mercy on whom I will have mercy," Rom. 9:15) is easier if we are talking about someone else's children than our own.

to their salvation" nor, with the Anglicans, that the children can thus be "made members of Christ's kingdom." But neither will they affirm with Calvin that believers' children are to be baptized because they are exempt from the curse of Adam and "sanctified by a supernatural grace." They will not venture to say that children are to be baptized because they are "presumptively regenerate" or even because they are "presumptively elect." Why then do they say children should be baptized? The answer is very simple: God has commanded believers to baptize their children. Therefore they are to be baptized, and for no other reason whatever. All attempts to explain why it should be so are futile. Our Christian duty is simply to obey the commandment, not to vindicate it.

Richard Baxter concludes many dreary pages of closely reasoned answers to Anabaptists' objections with the observation that all these cavils are

> but the spume of human reason which needs no other answer than this: God would have infants to be church members and so entered by baptism. And seeing, as I have proved, God would have it so, then all these objections are against God, and a carping at his way, and a finding out a supposed unreasonableness of inconveniency in his institutions. ... My answer is, it is God's will it shall be so; who needs none of my reasons to justify his ordinances, his own authority and will being sufficient.[105]

In other words, the final *raison d'être* of infant baptism is simply that it is the divinely instituted way of administering the covenant. In more recent times John Murray has argued in a similar way.

> When we ask the question: Why do we baptize infants, or upon what *ground* do we dispense baptism to them? it is sufficient for us to know and to answer that it is the divine institution. ... To require any further information than the divine institution, would go beyond the warrant of Scripture. ... Hence to aver that baptism is dispensed to infants on the ground of presumptive election or presumptive regeneration appears to be without warrant and also introduces perplexities into the question at issue.[106]

---

[105]*Plain Scripture Proof*, p. 124.
[106]*Christian Baptism*, p. 10.

Perhaps the finely drawn theological theories of some Paedobaptists are perplexing and without scriptural warrant, but can a Paedobaptist simply take leave of them casually and unquestioningly? Certainly the argument, "We baptize children simply because it is God's will," has no persuasive validity, inasmuch as Baptists may (and have) argued in the same way to justify believer baptism. The real fault in the argument, "We baptize infants because it is God's will," is that it assumes what is to be proved. Where is the evidence, where is the argument that will stimulate the mind to rise to a recognition of truth? More is needed than a reference to Abraham's obedience in circumcising his offspring, which turns out to be a laudation for Paedobaptists for baptizing theirs. Surely more is needed than the unadorned affirmation that infant baptism is a divine institution. Of course, a divine institution (with which we are obligated to comply) governs the administration of all sacraments. That is not disputed. The question is: Is the divine institution that governs the administration of baptism identical with that which governed circumcision? That the answer to this question is not a simple one will become evident — if it is not so already — as we turn to our next question, the question of faith and baptism.

D. THE RELATION OF FAITH TO BAPTISM AND THE PRACTICE OF INFANT BAPTISM

1. *Introduction*

Against the Anabaptists Luther argued that to require faith of those baptized would mean none could ever be sure when to give baptism, since there is no infallible proof of true faith.

> Have they now become gods to peep into people's hearts to see whether or not they believe? ... The Anabaptists are not certain that their rebaptism is correct, because they base it upon faith, of which they cannot assuredly know, and so uncertainty plagues their rebaptism. Now it is a sin and tempting to God when in divine things there is uncertainty and doubt. ... The devil can always make me doubt whether the faith in which and

upon which I was baptized was a true faith. Thus he makes me doubtful about the baptism that has been consummated. In this way I am constantly in a state of uncertainty about my salvation. . . . It is really a work of the devil on their part to talk about faith when they mean works and in the name and appearance of faith to lead poor people to trust in works. . . . We Germans are really Galatians and remain Galatians, and this is a masterstroke of the devil. He cannot stand it that the Germans have come to know Christ aright through the Gospel, namely the justification which is by faith — therefore he has sent the Anabaptists.[107]

It is not clear how Luther harmonized all this with his own insistence that justification is by faith. If we must always doubt the faith in which we were baptized, how can we be assured we have the faith that justifies? And to caricature the position of believer baptism as a work of the devil, a cryptic form of the criminal doctrine of salvation by works, is palpably unfair. Yet these charges have been echoed and re-echoed through the centuries by Paedobaptists.

Speaking of the Baptist position that "none should be baptized without serious profession," even though he be born of Christian parents, Baxter put on the mantle of a prophet and descried for his readers a dismal vision of what would happen to the church of God under such an arrangement. It would produce anarchy, for covenant children become conscious Christians by insensible degrees, and how will ministers and parents ever agree when the child understands and believes sufficiently to receive baptism? This "would be the greatest firebrand in the church that ever the church endured." But do not Paedobaptists have the same problem when it comes to admitting baptized covenant children to the Lord's table? How do ministers and parents ever agree upon when the child believes sufficiently to receive communion? Since their children become Christians by insensible degrees, how do they know when they have sufficient knowledge to discern the Lord's body and sufficient faith to feed upon Christ?

It is not without reason that Paedobaptists have shown themselves sensitive to the Baptist insistence that one who is

[107]For sources, cf. P. Althaus, *Was ist die Taufe?* pp. 28-30.

baptized must confess his faith, for the question of the relation of faith to baptism touches a nerve that vibrates to the very heart of the issue. That issue, it will be recalled, is: How can Paedobaptists justify infant baptism in the light of the definition of baptism found in their own confessions? The theories we have discussed so far concerning whether baptized infants may be presumed regenerate or elect are but the preface to the problem under investigation. The time has now come to probe more deeply into its true nature.

Briefly stated, the problem is this: *To baptize infants apart from faith threatens the theological foundations of evangelicalism.* Baptism, in an evangelical theology, is an act of confession on man's part in response to an act of renewing grace on God's part. Hence faith and baptism are but the inside and outside of the same thing. This was the stronghold from which the Reformers swept the whole ground of Roman sacramentalism with their evangelical artillery. To the *opus operatum* of Rome, the Reformers replied with *nullum sacramentum sine fide* (apart from faith there is no sacrament). "We therefore by being baptized do confess our faith," declare the authors of the *First Helvetic.*[108] Baptism, according to the *Thirty-Nine Articles,* is a "sign of profession";[109] and the *Anglican Catechism* answers the question, "What is required of persons to be baptized?" with the words, "Repentance, whereby they forsake sin, and faith, whereby they steadfastly believe the promises of God made to them in that sacrament."[110]

This clear affirmation of New Testament teaching, which was the glory of the Reformers as Reformers, was also their nemesis as Paedobaptists. On the one hand, as evangelicals they so defined baptism as to recognize faith as essential to the meaning and efficacy of the sacrament; on the other, they insisted that infants, though admittedly incapable of faith, should be baptized. This rudimentary asymmetry is even written into the very text of some of the Reformation formularies.

[108]See P. Schaff, *Creeds of Christendom,* III, *Evangelical Creeds,* p. 211.
[109]*Ibid.,* p. 504.
[110]*Ibid.,* p. 521.

The *French Confession of Faith,* for example, calls baptism a "sacrament of faith and penance," but goes on to affirm: "Nevertheless, although it is a sacrament of faith and penance, yet as God receives little children into the church with their fathers, we say upon the authority of Jesus Christ that the children of believing parents should be baptized."[111] Jesus nowhere says any such thing; and to affirm that God receives little children into the church with their fathers is to assert something that needs to be proved. But for now let the reader merely notice the words *"nevertheless, although, yet . . .* we say children should be baptized." Adversatives give color and tone to language, and as *Webster's Dictionary* points out, are "used chiefly as a connective between clauses or sentences conveying facts, ideas, or considerations which are opposed or contrary to each other. . . ." This particular creed, then, wears the contradiction between the meaning of baptism and the practice of infant baptism on its sleeve.

The *Westminster Confession* declares that baptism is a sign and seal to the party baptized "of his giving up to God through Jesus Christ to walk in newness of life. . . ," after which it gets to infant baptism with the help of a "not only." "Not only those that do actually profess faith in and obedience to Christ, but also infants of one or more believing parents, are to be baptized."[112] Baptism is further defined (*Westminster Shorter Catechism,* Q. 94) as ". . . our engagement to be the Lord's." The sequence to the next question (95) is smooth at first: "Baptism is not to be administered to any that are not of the visible church till they profess their faith in Christ and obedience to him." Then comes the inevitable adversative conjunction: *"But* the infants of such as are members of the visible church are to be baptized."[113]

And so it goes. Paedobaptists confess their faith in baptism, yet give it to infants without their making such a confession; they engage in baptism to be the Lord's, yet administer it to those who engage nothing; they confess baptism to be the sacrament of faith and penitence, yet grant it to those who

[111]*Ibid.,* p. 379.
[112]*Ibid.,* pp. 661, 662.
[113]*Ibid.,* pp. 696, 697 (italics mine).

evidence neither the one nor the other; they acknowledge that repentance and faith are required of those baptized, yet baptize those who cannot meet these requirements; they call baptism a sign of profession, yet baptize those who make no profession. And they hold these contradictions together with a hoop of but's, nevertheless's, although's, and not only's.

It is, of course, too much to say that the Paedobaptists have conjoined faith with baptism out of a fraternal deference to Baptist conviction. The reason they have done so is rather that the New Testament positively compels it. The doctrine of the Trinity itself is not more explicit in the New Testament than the teaching that faith is the prerequisite of baptism. (This datum, more than anything else, seems to have shaken the confidence of Barth, as a Paedobaptist, and resulted in his about-face.) Those convinced of believer baptism, however, must commend their Paedobaptist brethren for their fidelity to Scripture in this regard, even though it inconveniences their practice of baptizing infants. For this reason, though they question infant baptism, Baptists accept with alacrity the doctrine of baptism common to evangelical Paedobaptists and hope that the cleavage over infant baptism is not so radical as the Paedobaptists, in their traditional condemnation of Anabaptism, have led the world to suppose.

Though adequate discussion of the New Testament data on the relationship of faith to baptism belongs to the doctrine of baptism as such, we must dwell upon it here because of its importance for the special question before us, which is the propriety of baptizing infants. Every serious student of the Bible knows that according to the New Testament, one receives the kerygma, the heralding of the good news of salvation in Christ, by faith. It is this act of embracing the apostolic proclamation that makes one a member of the fellowship of the faithful. Baptism, then, like preaching, involves the act of confessing one's faith, and seals to the baptized one participation in the saving event, namely, the death and resurrection of Jesus.[114] Johannes Schneider observes:

> The apostolic history shows beyond all peradventure of doubt the place which baptism assumed in the order of salvation. At

[114]See R. Bultmann, *Theologie des Neuen Testaments*, I, 88, 308.

the beginning of the book of Acts, in chapter 2, we have in this regard a typical report. First comes the Spirit-filled preaching of Peter. The *Heilsbotschaft*, the message of salvation, is heard. It pricks the heart and leads to the interrogation, "What shall we do?" The answer is, "Turn about and get yourselves baptized." To those who shall be baptized the Holy Spirit is promised. The order of sequence is thus: preaching, believing acceptance of the message, repentance, baptism, reception of the Holy Spirit.[115]

Schneider goes on to make the point that this structuring of the New Testament data proves that the appeal of scholars like Jeremias and Cullmann to Jewish proselyte baptism as the model of Christian baptism is too facile. Even if the historical problem be overlooked,[116] the formal similarities between Christian and proselyte baptism are more than offset by the central place given to personal faith in the former, which makes for an inner, essential difference. The emphasis on repentance in Acts, beginning with Peter's sermon, indicates that the primitive church, in its practice of baptism, was oriented in terms of *John's* baptism, not *proselyte* baptism. Repentance followed by a baptism "unto the remission of sins" is a Johannine pattern. Schneider insists that it is, then, only when one denies to faith the status given it in the New Testament that he can justify infant baptism, for it is beyond all cavil that faith is the threshold over which one must step into the Christian life. Only one who believes has a right to baptism.

2. *The Paedobaptist view of infant faith (fides infantilis)*

Paedobaptists have wrestled with this problem of infant baptism and faith since the early days of the Reformation. As a priest, Luther accepted the theory of the Roman Catholics that the faith of the church validates the baptism of the child. But when his life was revolutionized by the insight that one is justified by personal faith, this position no longer

---

[115]*Die Taufe im Neuen Testament*, pp. 33ff.

[116]*Ibid.*, p. 41. Schneider thinks proselyte baptism "probably" is pre-Christian (p. 20), but see his p. 21, n. 5.

satisfied him.[117] Later, however, the Zwickau prophets and
other enthusiastic demagogues threatened to turn the Reformation into a revolution in which all would be lost. As a
result, Luther's mind became so set against all Anabaptists
that he could not tolerate their insistence on personal faith as
a prerequisite to baptism. Thus he found himself caught in
the middle and, as far as our question is concerned, talked
both ways. While regarding faith as important to justification, he refused to lay any great stress on the question of
whether the one baptized believes or not. All hangs, he declared, on God's Word and commandment.

He concludes the chapter on baptism in his *Larger
Catechism* with a protracted harangue on infant baptism, full
of rant and fiddle-faddle. The devil, he says, has muddled the
world over the question of whether children can believe and
be rightly baptized: "He who is simple, let him thrust the
question from him and refer it to the scholars." But, he
continues, if one wants an answer, let him note that infant
baptism must be pleasing to Christ, since there are so many
who have received it who in later years give evidence of
having the Holy Spirit by their lives and doctrine. If God did
not accept infant baptism, he would not give so much as a
lick of the Holy Spirit to such folk, with the result that in
time past and up to the present there would not be a Christian
on the face of the earth.[118] Luther then refers to his favorites

---

[117]Nonetheless, it is still used in Lutheran circles. Cf. Dietrich
Bonhoeffer, *Sanctorum Communio*, p. 180: "Evangelical baptism, like
Catholic baptism, is infant baptism. Since, however, the child does not
himself receive faith, not even as *fides directa*, though the sacrament requires faith, there remains as subject perceiving the sacrament in faith, only
the objective spirit of the congregation. The latter receives into its bosom
the child through baptism in faith; since however, where a member of the
congregation is, there the entire congregation is, the entire congregation
believes in and through the child." The present writer is incredulous in the
face of this argument.

[118]On this whole line of reasoning in Luther, Barth asks: "But is this
argument altogether honest? Could one not thus justify as *usus* the papacy,
the Roman mass, the late Scholastic doctrine of justification and everything
else against which Luther stood as *abusus?* . . . Poor church should the Holy
Spirit refrain from using her services and making them fruitful because of
her transgressions!" (*Dogmatik*, IV, 4, *Fragment*, p. 209).

— Bernard, Gerson, and Huss — and pronounces, "This is almost the best and strongest proof for the simple and unlearned."[119]

There is another Luther, however, who did not talk this way — a Luther who sought to answer the problem by insisting that infants must indeed have faith in order rightly to receive baptism. As early as his *Commentary on Galatians* (1519) he broached the thesis that the little child hears and believes the gospel, being made susceptible of the words pronounced over him by the baptizing priest through the work of the Holy Spirit. In fact, it is easier for the word to penetrate a child's mind than an adult's because his is naturally more receptive. If the child does not hear rationally, yet he hears spiritually. In his sermon for the third Sunday after Epiphany (Matt. 8:1ff.) he says:

> The sophists in the universities and the papal gang have fabricated the story that young children are baptized without personal faith, namely on the faith of the church which the sponsors confess at his baptism; . . . but if one asked them as to the ground of such an answer and where it stands in Scripture, then one finds them in a dark smoke-hole; or they point to their clerical cap and say: 'We are the most learned doctors and say it is so; therefore it is right and you are not permitted to inquire further. . . .' [But] baptism helps no one, is also to be given to no one, except he believes for himself, and without personal faith no one is to be baptized. As St. Augustine himself says: '*Non sacramentum justifica, sed fides sacramenti*' [the sacrament does not justify, but the faith of the sacrament]. . . . Were we not able to prove that the young children themselves believe and have personal faith, it is my sincere counsel and judgment that one straightway desist and the sooner the better, and never more baptize any child so that we no more mock and blas-

[119]For the context of the above quotations see Luther's "Von der Taufe, von der Kindertaufe," *Der Grosse Katechism* in *Katachetische Schriften*, IV, *Sämmtliche Werke*. Interestingly enough, in this same place Luther declares: "Sinking under the water and rising up out of the water are the two essential parts of the form of baptism as signifying the death of the old Adam and the rising of the new man." This was safe, since the early Anabaptists were not immersionists like the later English Baptists. If they had been, he would no doubt have drowned them with proofs that immersion was also of the devil.

pheme the most blessed majesty of God with such baseless tomfoolery and jugglery.[120]

When Christ says that the kingdom belongs to children, we must, declares Luther, take it for granted that they believe, since the kingdom belongs only to believers. If one objects that children give no evidence of faith, "then were we also not Christians while we are asleep." He challenges the Zwickau prophets to prove that children do not believe.

Prominent Lutheran theologians like Johann Gerhard, following the reasoning of Luther, have held to the doctrine of infant faith; and, among the Reformed, the position has occasionally been espoused that covenant infants have a kind of inchoate faith germinating like a seed in the soul.[121] Yet few have found the courage to rest the weight of their case on so tenuous a foundation. Like Calvin's theory that covenant children are inwardly sanctified by a supernatural grace, Luther's notion that there is an infant faith is highly suitable to Paedobaptist practice but incompatible with Scripture and common sense.

However, some Paedobaptists are reluctant to abandon the idea of infant faith completely. They have felt that the Anabaptists, in their strictures upon this notion, were cryptically guilty of "rationalizing" faith:

> As they [the Anabaptists] saw it, faith is possible only where there is self-awareness. It is impossible in the case of infants. But this kind of impossibility is only the rational impossibility which provokes Mary and Nicodemus to ask how these things can be. It can be argued only when it is forgotten that faith is the work of the Holy Spirit who can fill the infant John no less than the adult Cornelius. It stands in flat contradiction to the call of the gospel which is not that we should become adults but children. It is not the real impossibility, namely, that sinners should understand the things of God without the enlightenment of the Holy Ghost. And it robs those who die in infancy of any hope of salvation unless the full logic of

---

[120]As quoted by Johannes Warns, *Die Taufe: Gedanken über die urchristliche Taufe, ihre Geschichte und ihre Bedeutung für die Gegenwart*, pp. 69, 71. This significant work by a leader of the so-called Fellowship Movements in Germany has been translated under the title *Baptism: Studies in the Original Christian Baptism.*

[121]See Calvin, *Institutes*, IV, xvi, 20.

Pelagianism is accepted and they are regarded as innocent in themselves and able to be pleasing to God without faith.[122]

This paragraph is worthy of pause. The thesis that faith can occur only where there is self-awareness is, we are told, a piece of rationalization. Only when one is unmindful that faith is the work of the Spirit, who filled the infant John, will one succumb to such rationalism. This rationalizing view of faith contradicts the call of the gospel; it substitutes a false impossibility for the true biblical impossibility; and, if consistently carried through, it leads either to infant damnation or Pelagianism.

We do not feel that this line of reasoning can be defended. The Bible always speaks of repentance and faith — those Siamese twins of grace — in terms of a change of mind, an enlightening of the understanding, a renewal of the will, which comes by hearing the Word and issues in a conscious commitment to Christ. Hence every Paedobaptist definition of faith ever written assumes self-awareness in the one who has faith. Faith is a "certain knowledge" and a "hearty trust," as the *Heidelberg Catechism* says (Q. 21); it is that act whereby "we appropriate to our use the promises of life"; by it "we receive and rest upon Christ alone for salvation."[123] How can an infant "know" and "appropriate" the promise of the gospel, and "receive and rest" upon Christ, without being *aware* that he is "knowing" and "appropriating" and "receiving" and "resting"? It is hardly convincing to answer that although reason cannot penetrate the mystery, nothing is impossible with God the Holy Spirit. Roman Catholic dogmaticians ever since Aquinas have given the same sort of answer to the question of transubstantiation. Indeed, it would seem that if there can be faith without self-awareness, there can be body and blood without attributes.

As for the thought that the Holy Spirit, who works faith, also filled the infant John, this would seem to be an observation more true than relevant inasmuch as Scripture neither says nor implies that John as an infant had faith. That he may

---

[122]G.W. Bromiley, *Sacramental Teaching and Practice in the Reformation Churches*, pp. 53, 54.

[123]*French Confession*, XX; *Westminster Shorter Catechism*, Q. 86.

have been regenerate we do not dispute, but regeneration is not faith any more than an acorn is an oak. To slide over such distinctions is simply to confuse the issue. The *Anglican Catechism* asks the child, "Why are infants baptized when by reason of their tender age they cannot perform repentance and faith?" The very putting of such a question presupposes that infants are incapable of faith; yet no one would accuse the *Anglican Catechism* of Anabaptist rationalizing.

As for the charge that the insistence on self-conscious faith as a prerequisite to baptism stands in "flat contradiction to the call of the gospel" that we become children, whoever can argue thus will surely never be at a loss. The infant in his sponsor's arms, sleeping, weeping, but in any case blissfully ignorant — is this what we are called to be in the gospel?[124]

> The truth [says Kierkegaard] is, one cannot become a Christian as a child. . . . Becoming a Christian presupposes (according to the New Testament) a personal consciousness of sin and of oneself as a sinner. So one readily sees that this whole thing about becoming a Christian as a child, yea, about childhood being above all other ages the season for becoming a Christian, is neither more nor less than puerility. . . .[125]

And the same may be said of the tragic theological choice between infant damnation and Pelagianism which has been set before those who side with the Anabaptists on the question of infant baptism.

> If it [baptism] be denied to infants, then logically that means either that infants have no sin that needs to be remitted, or that their sin is not remitted. The Anabaptists could not avoid this dilemma and the majority quickly revealed themselves to be frankly Pelagian in their conception of original sin and freedom.[126]

This reasoning would be convincing were one shut up to a sacramentalist view of baptismal efficacy. But unless one wishes to affirm that infants dying in infancy will be deprived of the beatific vision for lack of baptism, it is hardly apparent

---

[124]Keble sings plaintively of the "slumbering features" of the child in baptism. See his *Christian Year*, "Holy Baptism."

[125]"The Formula of 'Christendom,' " p. 213.

[126]Bromiley, *Baptism and the Anglican Reformers*, p. 111.

that the Pelagian tendencies which some Anabaptists may have entertained were entailed in their refusal to baptize infants. A quotation from Menno Simons, leader of the largest party of Anabaptists, may further clarify the issue of Pelagianism and Anabaptism: "We also believe and confess that we are all born of unclean seed, that we through the first and earthly Adam became wholly depraved and children of death and hell."[127] This is hardly Pelagian ground.

Speaking of Pelagianism, some interesting bits of theology can be gleaned in this regard from Paedobaptists themselves. Consider, for example, the following from a defense of infant baptism by a Methodist, Raymond H. Huse. This author observes that for many weary generations, in New England especially, sensitive childhood was obliged to drag around the millstone of inherited sin. The practical result of this unethical notion was that children were always counted as outside the fold of Christ, there to await renewing grace miraculously given that should bring them in. Huse disdains Watts' lines,

> Soon as we draw infant breath,
> The seed of sin springs up to death,

as the old Calvinistic theory. All this, he assures us, is theological fiction. "A newborn babe in his mother's arms, a little child playing in the sunlight, cannot be classified as a sinner." Therefore, reasons Huse, he should be given a preparatory membership in the church by baptism.[128]

---

[127] *The Complete Writings of Menno Simons*, p. 130. Statements like this can be easily multiplied.

[128] *The Soul of the Child*, pp. 33, 147. The Paedobaptist mind is versatile: we are told that Anabaptists must (logically) become Pelagian *in order not* to take away all hope from unbaptized infants. Richard Baxter charged that Anabaptists were Pelagian *because* they do not take away all hope from the unbaptized infant:

> Most of the Anabaptists that I hear of, do hold that all the infants in the world are pardoned by Christ, and shall be saved if they die in infancy, and run in the downright Pelagian road. . . . Now the Gospel nowhere gives out pardon to every infant in the world; nay it frequently and plainly makes a difference. The parents' will doth accept the offer and choose for them that cannot choose for themselves; for others, whatever God will do with them, doubtless they have no promise of mercy." (Proposition One, *Confirmation and Restauration*, p. 165)

3. Infants made an exception to the New Testament "faith-baptism" sequence

Customarily, Paedobaptists have not challenged the advocates of believer baptism to prove that infants do not have faith, nor have they accused them of being cryptic rationalists. Rather they have candidly confessed that the New Testament does indeed regard faith as a personal, self-conscious act that is ordinarily required of those who are baptized. But inasmuch as infants cannot believe, they must be regarded as an exception to this rule. Of the many passages in the New Testament that might be selected to introduce one to the nature of Paedobaptist reasoning in this respect, none is more instructive than the so-called Great Commission of Jesus in Matthew 28:19-20:

> Go therefore and make disciples of all the nations, baptizing them in the name of the Father and of the Son and of the Holy Spirit, teaching them to observe all that I have commanded you. . . .

As God's chosen people in Old Testament times were to be circumcised as a mark of their separation from the nations, so, according to this text, those who belong to Christ are to be baptized and thereby distinguished from the world as his disciples. There is, of course, the obvious difference that Christ's disciples come from all nations; in Jesus' commission Old Testament nationalism gives place to New Testament universalism.

For our discussion, however, the most significant difference is the absence of all allusion in Matthew 28 to circumstances determined by birth. When circumcision was instituted as the covenant sign (Gen. 12), Abraham was instructed to circumcise all born in his house or bought with his money. But when Jesus commissioned his apostles to baptize, only those who were made disciples through the preaching of the gospel were to receive the sign. Accordingly, in the book of Acts, as the apostles went forth, those who responded to their preaching by repentance toward God and faith in Jesus Christ (Acts 20:21) received baptism and thus became Christ's disciples.

It is true that the syntactical structure of Matthew 28:19-20, as it stands, does not absolutely require voluntary discipleship as the prerequisite of baptism. The Greek does not say, "having gone and having made disciples, *then* baptize them," but rather, "having gone, make disciples, baptizing them" (πορευθέντες ... μαθητεύσατε ... βαπτίζοντες ...). Hence it is grammatically possible to construe the text — as did Francis Xavier in his fabulous Asian mission — as follows: "Having gone, make disciples *by means of* baptizing." As far as infants are concerned, this is what all Paedobaptists do, even those who are evangelicals. Some of them, like Dean Henry Alford, who feel that infant baptism is normal and believer baptism exceptional, argue that Jesus for this very reason expressed himself as he did in his commission to baptize.

> It will be observed that in our Lord's words, as in the Church, the process of ordinary discipleship is *from baptism to instruction* — i.e., *admission in infancy to the covenant,* and growing up into τηρεῖν πάντα κ.τ.λ. — the *exception* being, what circumstances rendered so frequent in the early church, *instruction before baptism in the case of adults.*[129]

In other words, we are to interpret the Lord's commission to his disciples (Matt. 28:19-20) in terms of what happens in Paedobaptist churches like the Church of England, in which Alford served, rather than in terms of what happened in the apostolic church. If we wish to know what Jesus really had in mind when he commissioned his apostles, let us not look at what the original apostles did, as recorded in the book of Acts — that was exceptional. Rather let us consult the Paedobaptist directories for the administration of baptism to infants!

[129]*Greek Testament,* Matthew 28:9 (italics his). The most elaborate contemporary attempt to turn the faith-baptism sequence of the Great Commission and the whole New Testament into a baptism-faith sequence, in order to justify infant baptism, is found in Cullmann's *Tauflehre,* written to refute Karl Barth. Faith, according to Cullmann, is not a prior condition necessary to make baptism an act of God, nor is it the guarantee of the future integrity of the candidate. It is only a sign *(Zeichen),* a criterion for the church in selecting those adults to be baptized. In the case of an infant, the same sign is found in that he is born into a Christian family. Both of these are merely divine pointers *(Hinweise)* to the later, postbaptismal faith which is decisive.

Most Paedobaptists, however, are not that confident. That one should begin his discipleship with baptism is so inimical to the meaning of discipleship in the spirit and teaching of the New Testament that the majority have frankly admitted that what Jesus meant when he commissioned the apostles is what happened in the book of Acts, where Christian discipleship begins with faith, not with baptism. Even the indomitable Paedobaptist convictions of Richard Baxter are held in abeyance as he declaims on this point:

> Go disciple me all nations, baptizing them. As for those who say they disciple *by* baptizing and not *before* baptizing, they speak not the sense of the text; nor that which is true and rational — else why should one be baptized more than another? . . . I profess my conscience is fully satisfied from this text that it is one kind of faith, even saving faith, that must go before baptism; and the profession whereof the minister must expect.[130]

But if the commission of Jesus, as carried out in apostolic times, implies the order of (1) discipling, (2) baptizing, and (3) teaching, what shall we say to infant baptism, which involves the order of (1) baptizing, (2) teaching, and (3) discipling? When the baptized child, being fully catechized, is finally confirmed as a Christian in his own right, he has arrived at the end point in the Paedobaptist scheme, which is the starting point in the Great Commission. Is not infant baptism, then, an instance of putting the cart before the horse? Or can we justify an arrangement that begins where the Lord commissioned the church to end? Calvin argues as follows (and he has been quoted a thousand times, even to his illustration):

> Is there even a single syllable in this whole discourse [Matt. 28] respecting infants? What kind of argumentation, then, is that with which they assail us? Persons of *adult* age are to be instructed in order that they may believe before they are to be baptized; *therefore* it is unlawful to administer baptism to infants. . . . But to render their fallacies still more palpable, I will show the absurdity of them by a very plain similitude. The

---

[130]*Plain Scripture Proof*, p. 399 (italics mine).

apostle says, "that if any would not work neither should he eat" (II Thess. 3:10). Now if any man would pretend from this that infants ought to be deprived of food, would he not deserve universal contempt? Why so? Because it will be a perverse application to all men indiscriminately of what was spoken of men of a certain class and of a certain age. Now is there any greater propriety in their reasoning in the present case? For what everyone sees to belong exclusively to persons of adult age, they apply to infants in order to make them subject to a rule which was prescribed only for persons of riper years.[131]

As a formal piece of logic this argument is invincible; and as an hermeneutical principle it is indispensable. Little wonder, then, that it has been applied broadly by the Paedobaptists to cover all the passages of the New Testament which teach that faith is the presupposition of baptism. Those passages are speaking of *adults,* and therefore they have no bearing (we are told) on the question of *infant* baptism. But logically possible as this argument may be, is it plausible? Is it likely that, when Jesus commissioned his apostles to disciple and then baptize adults, he simply assumed that they would understand that they were also to baptize and then disciple infants? Is it likely that the Holy Spirit inspired the author of Acts to preserve for us instances of believer baptism while leaving infant baptism to a tacit inference?

The opponents of infant baptism must admit that such is indeed a possibility; but if the Paedobaptists are really comfortable with this possibility, it is curious that they should so easily reverse themselves in the matter of believer communion. They keep back "covenant children" from the covenant meal because I Corinthians 11:28 says, "Let a man examine himself and so let him eat of the bread and drink of the cup." But why should not "examine and eat" admit of the same exception as "believe and be baptized"? The answer to this

---

[131]*Institutes,* IV, xvi, 28 and 29. This statement, it will be noted, takes the opposite line of reasoning from Dean Alford's mentioned above. Alford argues for infant baptism *because* Christ contemplated infant baptism when he gave the commission to baptize. Calvin argues for infant baptism because Christ did *not* contemplate infant baptism when he gave the commission to baptize. When one grasps the argument for infant baptism by the horns, he may find he has it by the tail!

question is as obvious as the pyramids. The Paedobaptists tailor the text to their theology rather than their theology to the text; they explain Scripture to fit their practice rather than judge their practice by the Scripture. Their exegesis is made to order. Since they do baptize infants who are incapable of faith, the plain New Testament requirement that one should confess his faith before he gets baptized does not apply to infants. Since they do not communicate infants, the plain New Testament requirement that one should examine himself before he takes communion does apply to them.

4. The Paedobaptist view of vicarious faith (fides vicaria)

a. Introduction

The uneasy conscience behind the defense of Paedobaptism reveals itself at this juncture. Many Paedobaptists have been reluctant to affirm that the New Testament order of faith, then baptism, is simply to be set aside in the case of infants. To help the mind over this problem, they have suggested the notion of faith by proxy (fides vicaria). This idea antedates the Reformation by many centuries and was simply appropriated by Protestants, especially Lutherans and Anglicans; its origins are in the same historical development that made infant baptism the common practice of the church.

It will be recalled that the first descriptions of baptismal procedure, preserved for us from antiquity, are couched in language suitable only to those who are able personally to confess their faith. After the pattern of the New Testament, the candidate renounced the world, the flesh, and the devil, and embraced Jesus Christ as Lord. Soon thereafter the evidence appears for infant baptism as the usage of the church, especially in Gaul and North Africa, and baptismal liturgies mentioning children make their debut. The most ancient of these is the so-called *Apostolic Tradition* of Hippolytus (ca. A.D. 215), reflecting the Roman usage. This formulary reads simply: "And they shall baptize the little children first, and if they can answer for themselves, let them answer, but if they cannot, let their parents answer or someone from the family."[132]

Here we have the seed of vicarious faith, a seed for which time proved a fertile soil. Apparently the apostolic and New Testament usage, wherein faith was always required of those baptized, left such an indelible impression that the early church formally maintained the faith-baptism sequence even in the case of infant baptism. If the child were too young to confess his faith, then someone had to confess it for him, since, in any case, where baptism is administered faith must be confessed.

This novel idea that the mute ignorance of infancy can find a compensation in the confession of a stand-in, though it developed unchecked, did not go unchallenged. As late as the fifth century, Boniface, bishop of Rome, troubled by those who could not see the reasonableness of sponsorship in baptism, wrote the great Augustine a letter in which his own skepticism is thinly veiled.

> Suppose [says he] I set before you an infant and ask you whether when he grows up he will be a chaste man or a thief. Your answer doubtless will be, "I cannot tell." And whether he in that infant age has any good or evil thoughts? You will say, "I do not know." Since you therefore dare not say anything either concerning his future behavior or his present thought, what is the meaning that when they are brought to baptism their parents as sponsors for them may answer and say they do that of which their infant age is not able to think? ... For we ask those by whom they are presented and say: "Does *he* believe in God?" (which question concerns that age which is ignorant whether there be a God). They reply, "He does believe." ... I entreat you to give me a short answer to these questions in such a manner as that you do not urge to me the prescription or the customariness of the thing but give me the *reason* of the thing.

Augustine replied:

> As the sacrament of Christ's body is after a certain fashion Christ's body and the sacrament of Christ's blood is his blood, so the sacrament of faith is faith, and to believe is nothing else

[132]*Apostolic Tradition,* ch. xxi, p. 45.

but to have faith, and so when an infant that has not yet the faculty of faith is said to believe, he is said to have faith because of the sacrament of faith and to turn to God because of the sacrament of conversion, for that answer belongs to the celebration of the sacrament. . . . An infant though he be not yet constituted a believer by that faith which consists in the will of believers, yet he is a believer by the sacrament of that faith. For as he is said to believe, so he is called a believer, not from his having the thing itself in his mind but from his receiving the sacrament of it. And when a person begins to have a sense of things he does not repeat that sacrament, but he understands the force of it and by consent of will squares himself to the true meaning of it. . . . I have given such an answer to your question as, I suppose, is to ignorant and contentious persons not enough, but to understanding and quiet people more than enough.[133]

This is a most curious piece of theological reasoning on the part of the great bishop of Hippo. Boniface asks the question, On what ground can the sponsor affirm that the child has faith? Augustine answers, On the ground that the child has received the sacrament of faith. But how can this be, when in all the liturgies the question regarding the child's faith is put, and the answer that he has faith is given, *before* the baptism is administered? How can it be true both that the child is to be baptized because it is affirmed that he has faith, and that it is to be affirmed that he has faith because he has been baptized? Is this more of the "rational impossibility, which is the possibility of faith"?

As for the sponsors, it appears that originally they were the ones responsible for preparing catechumens for baptism by instructing them in the principles of the Christian faith. But when the practice of infant baptism became generally established, the role of the sponsors shifted and they became the spiritual mentors of the child, responsible for his doctrinal and moral training after his baptism. In keeping with this usage, the thought developed that the natural parents (who in Boniface's day sponsored their own children) had, by their act of bringing him to baptism, transferred the child to

[133]For both sides of this correspondence, see "Epistola ad Bonifacium," Letter 98, *The Nicene and Post-Nicene Fathers*, I, 410 (italics mine).

those who were qualified to train him in things divine. These sponsors, then, became his spiritual parents, his godfather and godmother.[134]

As time went on, sponsorship evolved into a tangled web of inanities. The theory of spiritual affinity (*cognatio spiritualis*), for example, led to rules in the Middle Ages forbidding parents to sponsor their own children.[135] It was also ruled that men should sponsor girls, and women boys. The Council of York (A.D. 1195) restricted the number of sponsors to two men and a woman for a boy, two women and a man for a girl. Eventually the spiritual relationship between the godparents and the child, and even between the godparents themselves, was believed to bring them within the prohibited degrees of consanguinity, so that a godfather could not marry his goddaughter or her godmother.[136] Endorsed by the Council of Trent (1545-1563), sponsorship in this full-blown sense has become a permanent part of Roman Catholic doctrine.

b. The Lutheran and Anglican churches

At the time of the Reformation, Lutherans and Anglicans retained the institution of sponsorship essentially in its Roman form, though rejecting its medieval elaboration. The Puritans in England, on the other hand, contended that sponsorship should be limited to the parents who presented the child for baptism. Amid all the discussion, a number of questions were brought forward: What is the faith the infant engages to confess when he is baptized? Is it the faith of the sponsor who speaks for him, or the faith of the church that embraces him into the fellowship of the congregation? Is the

---

[134]Reflecting this arrangement, the parents who bring the child to baptism are sometimes called the "sponsors" in distinction from the "godfathers" and "godmothers," who are spiritually responsible for the child after he has received baptism. See D. S. Bailey, *Sponsors at Baptism and Confirmation.*

[135]This because as parents they were tainted by coitus, which is never free of sin. Thus they were rendered unworthy of so godly an affinity with the child born of their carnal union.

[136]This because it was supposed that the sacrament of baptism creates a metaphysical relationship between the several godparents and the baptized one, comparable to that created by the sacrament of marriage.

sponsor confessing his own faith? or the faith of the child? or simply guaranteeing a future faith in the child, of which his own is the surety?

As we noted above, Luther believed that the infant had faith and was therefore not averse to addressing the questions in baptism directly to the child, who (supposedly) confessed his own faith on the lips of his sponsor. Others, both in Germany and England, who saw problems in vicarious confession, felt the questions should be directed to the sponsors rather than to the child, assuming that the former confessed their own faith as a pledge of the future faith of the child. When some English Puritans tried to do away with such an arrangement altogether, they were reminded that if infants can sin vicariously in Adam, they can repent and believe vicariously in their godparents. Besides, it was further argued, inasmuch as faith must be confessed at baptism, abolishing sponsorship would concede the point to that plague of all theology, Anabaptism, since then no one would be left to confess his faith but the one baptized. This was enough to charm the most obstreperous complaints and secure immortality for the institution of sponsorship in the English Church.[137] As a result, the "Office of Public Baptism of Infants" in the *Book of Common Prayer* has retained godfathers and godmothers (the *American Episcopal Prayer Book* reads "sponsors").

This usage is not incidental to the structure of the rite of infant baptism. To perceive how important sponsors are in the baptism of infants, one has only to remark that the *Apostolic Tradition* dispensed with the baptism of children in thirty-one words (out of about 3,300), while the Anglican liturgy dedicates approximately 5,000 words to the baptism of infants, followed by the "Office for the Public Baptism of Such as are of Riper Years," modestly set forth in about 2,500 words. In other words, more than 99 percent of the baptismal rubric in the *Apostolic Tradition* is devoted to believer baptism and scarcely 1 percent to infant baptism. (The earliest handbook of Christian baptism, the *Didache*, is entirely concerned with believer baptism.) The Anglican baptismal liturgy, by contrast, devotes about 33 percent of its

---

[137]See Bromiley, *Baptism and the Anglican Reformers,* pp. 126ff.

instruction to believer baptism and 66 percent to infant baptism.

Now since the infant is totally passive, this liturgy would be a grand waste of words were it not for the sponsors. Their presence is indispensable to the whole colloquy, for when the minister is not speaking to them about the child, he is speaking to the child while he looks at them and the child answers by them. The sponsors having confessed their faith — or rather having confessed the child's faith for him — the minister then asks, "Wilt thou be baptized in this faith?" And the child, speaking through his sponsors, answers, "That is my desire." The minister then asks, "Wilt thou then obediently keep God's holy will and commandments and walk in the same all the days of thy life?" And again the child answers by his sponsors, "I will." Following this confession and a prayer, the minister baptizes not the persons who answered but him for whom they answered. This is an interesting turn, for if the child can renounce his sin, confess his faith, and promise to obey God vicariously, why can he not be baptized vicariously? If it is unthinkable that the sponsors should kneel and have the waters of sacred baptism into the triune Name applied to their heads in the infant's stead, how may we be sure that it is God's will that they make to him the most solemn promises ever to move mortal lips in the infant's stead? The Lutherans and Anglicans have not elaborated this point, *et pour cause*.[138]

c. The Presbyterian and Reformed churches

Leaving the Anglican and Lutheran tradition, we shall examine in some detail the approach to this problem in the Reformed tradition. As a whole, the Presbyterian and Reformed communions have hardly been more satisfied with a vicarious confession than with Luther's notion that the child exercises faith for himself somewhere in the limbo of the subconscious. Calvin, as we have seen, denied out of hand that the New Testament order of "believe and be baptized"

---

[138]One wonders why Anglicans could not circumvent any problems of sponsorship by asserting that the child answers for himself the questions asked, even though no sound is heard. After all, if the infant can have faith without self-awareness, may he not give answers without sound waves?

was ever intended for infants. The Reformed and Presbyterian liturgies, therefore, have no rubric under which the infant's faith is confessed for him. The only sponsors are the parents themselves, who confess no other faith than their own, promising for the child only that they will so instruct him that it may be hoped that he will confess Christ for himself when he shall have come to years of discretion. At first blush this might appear to be a more sane and sensible procedure than one in which an infant confesses his faith by proxy.

However, the view that a child is baptized apart from confessing his faith is, in a very profound sense, further removed from the teaching of the New Testament than is the theory of vicarious faith. It does indeed appear incongruous for a minister to ask a newborn infant, "Wilt *thou* be baptized into this faith?" and for several adults to answer in the singular, "That is *my* desire," when they, having already been baptized, desire no such thing. Yet beneath this implausible liturgy lies the truth that baptism is the sacrament of faith; and where faith is not expressed, the sacrament cannot mean all that it is defined to mean by the Paedobaptists themselves. When the Anglican catechism teaches children that at baptism they met the qualifications of repentance and faith in their sureties, though this may seem absurd, it is at least consistently so.

But where is the evidence, prior to Calvin (and perhaps Zwingli), that anyone was ever baptized without meeting the qualification of renouncing his sins and professing faith in Christ? Either children did it for themselves — fancy a three-year-old renouncing the devil, as in Gregory's day — or sponsors did it for them if the children were still in infancy. Vicarious faith may be incompatible with the spirit of the New Testament, but it is hardly more so than Calvin's notion that the faith-baptism sequence, uniformly reflected in the New Testament, does not apply to infants. As far as we can judge, Calvin's thesis was more of a novelty in the sixteenth century than anything the Anabaptists ever said about baptism. While his view did not require proxies, it opened up what may be even graver theological questions; for if faith is not confessed when baptism is administered, is it the same sacrament when applied to infants as it is when applied to believers? Before Paedobaptists in the Reformed tradition commend their sobriety in rejecting vicarious faith, they should reflect on this question.

Some, like William Cunningham, have cautiously conceded that it may be correct to say that adult baptism is "that from which mainly and principally we should form our conceptions of what baptism is and means and was intended to accomplish," and that adult baptism affords "the proper fundamental type of the ordinance." But when Cunningham goes on to say that "it is adult baptism alone which embodies and brings out the full idea of the ordinance," or when James Bannerman declares, "It is an error . . . to make baptism applicable in the same sense and to the same extent to infants and to adults," some demur with the observation that "there does not appear to be good warrant for such discrimination."[139]

A Paedobaptist has reason not to like this statement of the case, for it really implies that infant baptism is a third sacrament, or at least a defective and incomplete form of the sacrament of baptism. But Cunningham, Bannerman, and other Paedobaptists in the Reformed tradition have reason to state the case as they do, for, after all, infant baptism does *not* fully satisfy the meaning of baptism as it is defined in the New Testament and in the classic confessions of the Presbyterian and Reformed churches.

According to that tradition, the sacraments "solemnly *engage us* in the service of God"; they are instituted to "strengthen and increase *our faith";* they "seal and apply Christ and his benefits *to believers";* by baptism the party baptized "enters into an open and professed *engagement* to be wholly and only the Lord's"; baptism signifies and seals one's *"giving up unto God* through Christ, to *walk* in newness of life."[140] Now when an infant — who is not a believer, has no faith to be increased, and engages nothing — is baptized,

---

[139]John Murray, *Christian Baptism*, p. 40, n. 25.
[140]*Westminster Confession*, ch. xxvii, sec. 1; xxviii, sec. 1; *Westminster Larger Catechism*, Q. 162; *Westminster Shorter Catechism*, Q. 92; *W.L.C.*, Q. 165; *W.C.*, ch. xxviii, sec. 1 (all italics mine).

we submit that some distinction between believer baptism and infant baptism is unavoidable.

John Murray, to be sure, insists that baptism

> has one import and it bears this same import whether it is dispensed to adults or to infants. It signifies union with Christ, purifying from the pollution of sin by the regeneration of the Spirit, and purifying from the guilt of sin by the blood of Christ. It can have no other import for infants than this.[141]

But this is simply to mention the graces of baptism, listed in the confessions, which infants may possess, while omitting all references to those graces, likewise listed in the confessions, which they obviously cannot possess. One cannot affirm that baptism signifies and seals to the infant his "engagement to be the Lord's," his "giving up unto God through Jesus Christ to walk in newness of life," for the infant makes no such engagement. Either one must allow that the engagement is made by proxy, or that infant baptism does not embody and bring out the full idea of the ordinance as defined in the standards of the Presbyterian and Reformed churches.

We may sum up this whole issue of faith and baptism by observing that the Paedobaptist has many an arrow in his quiver when infant baptism is at stake. He can argue that an infant has faith, though this contravenes all the evidence of experience and common sense. He can believe that a sponsor may have faith for the infant, though this is wholly without warrant in the Scripture and repugnant to the fundamental truth that no one can receive and rest upon Christ for salvation by proxy. He can believe that baptism signifies something less for infants than for believers. If he is Reformed, he will baptize the infant as though the latter were a Christian; if Lutheran or Anglican, he will go so far as to make him talk like a Christian. But whether he makes infants an exception to the requirement of Scripture that faith precede baptism, or holds to faith by proxy, or admits that infant baptism is an incomplete form of the sacrament, he is espousing notions alien to the New Testament. Here we see the glory and

---

[141]*Christian Baptism*, p. 41.

misery of the Paedobaptist. He argues these things in order to be true to Scripture; for this he is to be commended. But these very arguments, dictated by the necessity of his system, drive him to conclusions that are without warrant in Scripture.

> The one great *dogmatic* problem [says Barth] with every theory of infant baptism . . . is that of the relationship between the *event of baptism*, on the one hand, and the *faith* of the one baptized on the other. . . . There is no getting around the fact, in every attempt, unavoidable as it may be, to think through the relationship between *baptism* and *faith* for a given doctrine of infant baptism, that one shall run into the most unhappy dead end street, since in this question, one obscurity and perplexity conjures up others; one follows another and that of necessity.[142]

E. CONFIRMATION: THE COMPLETION OF INFANT BAPTISM

1. The Lutheran and Anglican traditions

The Reformers minced no words in depriving confirmation of the sacramental status to which Rome had elevated it. Luther once referred to it as foolery and lying prattle, devised to adorn the office of the bishops that they might have at least something to do in the church,[143] while Calvin spoke of that preposterous mimicry by which men seek salvation in oil.[144] Yet for all their blistering polemic, the Reformers found confirmation to be indispensable, at least in some form or other.

The reason this was true is not far to seek. One may resolve the question of infant baptism and faith by reckoning that the infant has faith, active but unexpressed (Luther), or a primordial seed of faith slumbering in its bosom until the dawn of personality (Calvin). One may appeal to the faith of the church or regard the faith of the parent or sponsor as a

---

[142]*Dogmatik*, IV, 4, "Fragment," pp. 204, 208 (his italics).

[143]In the "Babylonian Captivity" he expresses amazement that the theologians should ever have thought of making a sacrament out of the laying on of hands. See *Three Treatises*, p. 218.

[144]*Institutes*, IV, xix, 8.

vicarious faith. Yet when all is said and done, the baptism of an infant involves no personal confession, no *request* for baptism on the part of the one baptized. Therefore, as Barth has observed, it would constitute a *Gewaltakt* (imposition) upon a child to baptize him — similar to the forced baptisms of Charlemagne — unless some provision were made for his subsequent, voluntary, and personal confession of faith.[145] Schleiermacher said: "Child baptism is a complete baptism only when one regards the confession of faith, which follows upon a finished period of instruction, as belonging to such baptism as its final act."[146] For this reason confirmation, in some form or other, survived the broom of the Reformation in all the major Protestant communions. Infant baptism lifted up its voice with an eloquent plea for completion.[147]

In 1539, Bucer reintroduced confirmation among Hessian Lutherans (although Luther had repudiated it) in an effort to curtail the influence of the Anabaptists of Hesse and Strasbourg. From this modest beginning, confirmation spread to all parts of the Lutheran communion. In 1548, Melanchthon acquiesced when the *Augsburg Interim* went so far as to style it a "sacrament necessary to salvation." To this concession Flaccus vigorously protested, while others sought to eradicate such "superstition" by emphasizing the value of the instruction which confirmation afforded. Even the seventeenth-century Pietists, with their emphasis on a personal conversion experience, did not challenge confirmation in principle, but rather sought, following Spener's example, to revitalize the usage (where it had fallen into disuse) as a means of bringing those who were baptized in infancy to a subsequent decision of faith in puberty. Though they were not strikingly successful in this worthy effort,

---

[145]*Die Taufe*, p. 34. In this place Barth alleges that it was this problem that led the "clever Calvin" to stress the *subsequent* faith of the child rather than the *seed* faith in the infant. We might add that it also led the consistent Cullmann in our day to stress the *subsequent* faith of the adult rather than the *prior* faith of the convert. See his *Die Tauflehre*, pp. 43f. See above, p. 173, n. 129.

[146]*Die Christliche Glaube*, p. 138, as quoted in K. Barth, *Dogmatik*, IV, 4, p. 34.

[147]Reflecting the Protestant point of view, which denies confirmation full sacramental status while retaining its sacramental significance, Webster's dictionary defines confirmation as "a rite supplemental to baptism."

Spener's influence did help to confirm confirmation as a permanent feature of Lutheranism to the present day. In Lutheranism, confirmation is the rite through which the baptized child "confirms his baptism," "renews his baptismal vows," "makes a personal confession," and is received into the full membership of the church.

As for Anglicanism, although adults who are baptized are also confirmed, the service of confirmation in the *Book of Common Prayer* is obviously written from the standpoint of children who were baptized as infants. In the preface the minister declares that none shall be confirmed but such as can say the creed, the Lord's Prayer, the Ten Commandments, and answer the questions in the catechism, which is proper,

> to the end that children being now come to years of discretion and having learned what their godfathers and godmothers promised for them in baptism, they may themselves with their own mouths and consent openly before the church ratify and confirm the same and also promise that by the grace of God they will evermore endeavor themselves faithfully to observe such things as they by their own confession have assented unto.

The bishop then puts the question to the candidates as follows:

> Do you here in the presence of God and of this congregation renew the solemn promise and vow that was made in your name at baptism; ratifying and confirming the same in your own persons and acknowledging yourselves bound to believe and to do all those things which your godfathers and godmothers then undertook for you?[148]

Here we have the lodestar of the Prayer Book Office. The child *confirms* what his sponsors did for him in baptism. This, of course, does not give confirmation much theological status. Though it is made a separate office, it is but an appendix to infant baptism. As Flaccus complained of Bucer's service in the German Lutheran church, confirmation is essentially the same as a service of adult baptism,

---

[148] *The Book of Common Prayer*, "The Order of Confirmation."

"only the water is wanting to make it a rebaptism."[149]

Varied and sometimes ingenious attempts have been made to relieve this negative emphasis and give confirmation a positive image, that it may — without becoming a third sacrament — have theological significance in its own right. The most plausible of these efforts construes confirmation as the rite signifying the impartation of the Holy Spirit through the laying on of apostolic (i.e. episcopal) hands. Appeal is made to several passages in the New Testament, especially in the book of Acts, to justify this view. In the instance of the disciples at Samaria (Acts 8:14-17), Peter and John did indeed lay hands on them, after their baptism, and they received the gift of the Spirit. But in itself this is hardly a paradigm for the rite of confirmation as we know it today, a rite that is given in puberty to those baptized in infancy. Furthermore, the sequence reflected in Acts 8 and 19:6 — baptism, laying on of hands, reception of the Spirit — is not uniform even in the book of Acts itself, not to mention in the New Testament as a whole. Ananias, for example, laid hands on Paul before the latter's baptism (Acts 9:17); and in some instances in Acts baptism seems to have been given altogether apart from such an exercise. As for the rest of the New Testament, Paul says nothing about such a practice in connection with baptism in any of his epistles, nor does any of the other New Testament writers.[150]

In the Anglican communion, debate over confirmation has tended to accent the cleavage between the Anglo-Catholics and the Evangelicals. For the former, the Holy Spirit is the agent who regenerates in baptism and the gift who is received inwardly in confirmation. Confirmation, then, admits one to the church and Holy Communion. For the latter, the Holy Spirit is active in baptism in a way that

---

[149]See Warns, *Die Taufe*, p. 271.

[150]Virtually all communions practice the laying on of hands at ordination (I Tim. 4:14); and in those churches where the charismatic gifts are stressed, the baptism of the Spirit is often associated with this custom. Interestingly, the English Baptist service book, *Orders and Prayers for Church Worship* by Payne and Winward, recommends the laying on of hands as part of the baptismal rite, or soon afterwards, thus renewing a seventeenth-century practice widespread among Baptists in England and in the American colonies. See Beasley-Murray, *Baptism*, p. 125.

makes one a member of the body of Christ. Confirmation simply ratifies and completes what is done in baptism. It is, then, a kind of lay ordination symbolizing one's incorporation into active church life.[151]

2. The Reformed tradition

In the Reformed tradition confirmation has had an ambivalent history. Without it, infant baptism is deprived of a denouement; with it, the propriety of infant baptism is compromised as an incomplete sacrament. This antinomy is written large in Calvin, who prefaces his declamations against Roman confirmation with a plea that the "ancient custom" be restored, whereby those baptized in infancy, having come to adolescence, gave account of their faith and were dismissed by the bishop with a laying on of hands and a solemn benediction.[152] That Calvin should renounce all claim to Scripture and rest his case solely on "ancient custom" is itself instructive; even more striking is the fact that he does not cite any relevant evidence, even from the Fathers. As Gregory Dix has said, when Reformers like Bucer, Melanchthon, and Calvin declared that confirmation in the primitive church was a catechizing of baptized children who had reached maturity for the public ratification of their faith, followed by a solemn blessing, "they were talking historical nonsense." But they reached this "astonishing fantasy" quite simply and innocently by reading back into antiquity the medieval usage wherein the child, baptized in infancy, was subsequently instructed by the parish priest.[153]

In other words, what the Reformers did was purge the medieval usage of abuse. The child is no longer taught to say his Hail Mary's and name the seven sacraments; he is now taught to say the *Heidelberg* or *Westminster Catechism* — and what an improvement! But a purged medieval usage is a medieval usage still. The improvement does not alter the fact (a

[151]For a careful review of the details of the ongoing debate over baptism and confirmation in the Church of England from the days of William Temple to the present, see Moody, *Baptism*, pp. 162ff.
[152]*Institutes*, IV, xix, 4.
[153]*Confirmation Today*, pp. 21ff.

Paedobaptist himself being our witness) that baptism in infancy, followed by confirmation in puberty, is a medieval custom, not an ancient one, much less an apostolic one.

Thus are those in the Reformed tradition caught between Scylla and Charybdis. They can hardly embrace a usage that is medieval in its pedigree, but neither can they abandon it. For if they choose the latter course, baptism as administered to infants remains incomplete in the case of those coming to years of discretion. Baptized children, therefore, must be taught to confess their faith; for without a confession of faith there is no sacrament. As A. A. Hodge once conceded, "As far as we misunderstand or ignore this beautiful ordinance of confirmation, we abandon to the mercies of our Baptist brethren the whole rational ground of infant baptism."[154]

As a postscript to our discussion of confirmation in the Reformed communion, we must say a word about conversion. We have already noted that a high view of sacramental grace can hardly find room for the thought of a subsequent "conversion experience" on the part of those baptized in infancy. But this problem is not unique to a sacramental theology. Even with an evangelical view of baptismal efficacy, an infant baptism-confirmation system tends to be a closed system. It has little place for the experience of conversion, so essential to evangelicalism. To insist that conversion is necessary to evangelicalism is not to say that every Christian must have a dramatic conversion experience; there is the "nurture of grace" which often brings one to the "grace of conversion" gradually rather than suddenly. But whether one becomes a Christian gradually or suddenly, imperceptibly or dramatically, a Christian is one who has been converted, that is, has made a radical decision against evil (repentance) and for Christ (faith). Confirmation tends to banish this element of *existenz* from Christianity. Though there are happy exceptions, the arrangement that begins with infant baptism and ends with confirmation produces what Dix (referring to the Church of England) has aptly called an "amorphous mass of

[154]*Popular Lectures on Theological Themes*, p. 389.

Pelagian good will, which muffles the whole impact of the Gospel and the witness of the church today."[155] The saving antidote to this impasse is to substitute for man-made confirmation New Testament confirmation, *which is baptism* — the sacrament wherein God confirms to the penitent sinner the covenant blessing of a new heart, and the sinner on his part engages to be the Lord's.[156]

[155] *The Theology of Confirmation in Relation to Baptism*, p. 18.

[156] Interestingly, Robert S. Paul, a Congregationalist and Paedobaptist, actually urges a step in this direction. He suggests that all Christians submit to a rite of immersion at the time they come to their first communion as an act of public confession. If they have been baptized in infancy, this rite would be their confirmation; if not, it would be their baptism! This suggestion seems to have received too little attention, considering its potential for bringing together evangelicals who have been so long segregated in worship for want of agreement on infant baptism. See *The Atonement and the Sacraments*, pp. 340f.

III

INFANT BAPTISM
AND BELIEVER
COMMUNION

A. INTRODUCTION

We have had occasion to note the asymmetry between Paedobaptist definitions of baptism as the sacrament of faith and the practice of giving it to infants, who cannot profess faith. When infants come to years of discretion and are able to "confirm" the vows taken for them by their sponsors, then they confess their faith; but in no case should their baptism be postponed until this time. "Although" baptism is a sacrament of faith, "nevertheless" it is to be given "not only" to believers "but" to their children also.

When we turn to the sacrament of the Lord's Supper, the Paedobaptist confessions are happily free of such antinomies. Gone are the nevertheless's, the although's, the but's, and the not only's. The great evangelical confessions are masterpieces of symmetrical wholeness at this point. In the bread and wine faith's eye seizes the pledge that the body of Christ is our meat and his blood our drink.[157] The *Belgic Confession* expresses it beautifully: "When we eat the sacrament with our mouths we also do as certainly receive by faith (which is the hand and mouth of our soul) the true body and blood of Christ, our only Saviour, in our souls for the support of our spiritual lives" (Article 35). The *Westminster Confession* says: "Worthy receivers outwardly partaking of

---

[157] *The French Confession,* ch. xxxviii.

the visible elements in this sacrament do then also inwardly by faith really and indeed, yet not carnally and corporeally, but spiritually, receive and feed upon Christ crucified . . ." (ch. XXIX, 7). In other words, when we repair in a worthy manner to the Lord's table, his body and blood are given, taken, and eaten after a heavenly and spiritual manner; they are received and eaten *by faith*.[158] Therefore, only those who have the faith thus to receive and feed upon Christ should come to the Lord's table; and the ignorant, the profane, and the hypocritical are duly warned that in coming they eat and drink judgment to themselves.

But what of covenant children? They surely are not to be numbered with the profane and the hypocritical. Why then do they not partake? On this matter the confessions observe a sphinx-like silence. If one disturbs this silence, the Paedobaptist answers that nothing is said of infant communion because infants obviously have not the knowledge to discern the Lord's body nor the faith to feed on him, which are presupposed in the worthy receiving of the Lord's Supper.

Now this all makes excellent sense as far as it goes. It would indeed offend right reason to say that in the Eucharist we eat and drink Christ unto our souls by faith, and then to insist that infants may do this apart from faith. But to reason thus constitutes a reversal of the argument that infants may be *baptized* apart from faith. How, then, do Paedobaptists defend believer communion without standing where the Baptists stand vis-à-vis baptism? The time has come to look at the way in which they answer this question.

B. PAEDOBAPTISTS CONTRAST THE SACRAMENTS

Apologizing for the "accumulation of reveries" which the Anabaptists have forced upon his readers, Calvin devotes a paragraph to answering the objection that there is no more reason why infants should be admitted to baptism than to the

[158]Cf. also *Irish Articles*.

Lord's Supper. Granting that infant communion was practiced in the ancient church, now "it has very properly been discontinued," he observes.[159] In the development of his argument Calvin makes several points that have been frequently elaborated by later Paedobaptist writers down to the present time. He assures his readers that baptism is a rite of initiation, that it is nonrepeatable, and finally, that it is a "passive" sacrament. Since in all these respects baptism differs from the Lord's Supper, it is proper that the church should grant baptism to infants while reserving the bread and wine for those who have attained to years of discretion and understanding.

Let us look at these arguments more closely. First of all, what of the notion that baptism differs from communion in that it is the rite of initiation into the church, whereas the Supper is appointed for those of riper years? Ursinus presses this point in his *Commentary on the Heidelberg Catechism.* To the objection that infants ought to be admitted to the Lord's Supper if they are to be baptized, he answers, Not so, because communion is different from baptism.

> Baptism is the sacrament of initiation and reception into the church, so that none are to be admitted to the Lord's Supper unless they be first baptized. But the Lord's Supper is the sacrament of our abiding in the church; or it is the confirmation of our reception: for God has instituted it that he might declare and seal unto us this truth, that having once received us into the church, that he will forever preserve us, so that we shall not fall away from it; and that he will also continue the benefit once bestowed upon us and will feed and nourish us upon the body and blood of Christ unto eternal life. Adults who are beset with various temptations and trials need this support.[160]

Either this argument is so profound that it eludes the present

---

[159]For a brief survey of the rise and usage of child communion in the Christian church, see J.J. Herzog, "Kinderkommunion," *Realencyclopaedie*, X, 289-291. Calvin's claim that it was discontinued for proper reasons is, perhaps, too facile, inasmuch as infant communion has never been discontinued in the Eastern Orthodox Churches; and in the Roman Catholic Church it appears to have been dropped because of the theory of transubstantiation, the fear being that infants and small children might crumble the host or slaver the blood.

[160]*Commentary on the Heidelberg Catechism*, pp. 370-371.

writer, or it is merely beside the point. What does the *order* of the sacraments have to do with the question, Shall infants receive them? Infants should be baptized, we are told, because baptism is the sacrament of initiation into the church; but they ought not to partake of the Lord's Supper because it is the sacrament which confirms their reception into the church. Infants need the initial pledge that their sins are washed away, but they do not need the pledge that this benefit shall be continued to them. John Murray, speaking to this same question, says that baptism

> signifies and seals what lies at the basis and inception of a state of salvation. . . . The Lord's Supper, on the other hand, signifies something which is consequent unto the state of salvation. It presupposes that which is sealed by baptism.[161]

But who would deny this? All it implies is that one should not come to communion who has not been baptized; and if he does so, he violates the divinely appointed sacramental order. On this point all parties heartily concur, yet Paedobaptists continue to elaborate the argument.

And what is to be concluded from the fact that baptism, unlike communion, is given but once in the course of one's Christian life? Cullmann, in his answer to Barth, makes the point that it belongs to the essence of the Lord's Supper that it be repeated; whereas baptism, by contrast, cannot be repeated, as far as the individual is concerned. Furthermore, in the Lord's Supper, it is the gathered congregation (*Gemeinde*) as such to which the death and resurrection of Christ is related, whereas in baptism it is the individual within the church.

> For this reason Karl Barth's objection that in granting infants access to baptism, consistently their access to the Lord's Supper must also be granted, does not hold water. In reality the *repeated* appropriation of the death and resurrection of Christ by the *believing fellowship* in the supper has its meaning alongside baptism, which is once for all, precisely in this, that here (at the Lord's table) are now really those who have already *believed* (to the exclusion of the unbelieving and those who are not capable of faith) who, from time to time in the eucharistic event, confirm anew their salvation as a fellowship.

[161]*Christian Baptism*, p. 30.

> Contrariwise, in baptism the individual is for the first time
> and once for all placed in the locale of redemption where the
> death and resurrection of Christ, the forgiveness of sins and the
> Holy Spirit, for the present — that is, between the resurrection
> and the return of Christ — according to God's will, shall be
> effectual for him. *This once for all act of being initiated into this
> definite place*, that is, into the church of Christ, is what distin-
> guishes baptism from the Lord's Supper; participation in the
> death of Christ is what binds them together.[162]

Even with the help of italics these arguments appear more
innocuous than telling so far as Barth's point is concerned.
We can find in them no indictment of the Baptists and no
comfort for the Paedobaptists. What difference do such considerations make so far as infant participation in the sacraments is concerned?

Finally we must ask the question, What of the notion
that baptism is appropriate to infants as the "passive" sacrament, in contrast to the Lord's Supper, which is an "active"
sacrament? Calvin states: ". . . as far as it relates to baptism,
the Lord makes no distinction of age, whereas he does not
present the Supper to all alike, but only to those who are
capable of discerning the body and blood of the Lord. . . ."
Ursinus echoes the master here also. Baptism, he tells us,
merely requires the Holy Spirit and

> faith, whether actual or potential. . . . Regeneration and an
> inclination to faith are sufficient for baptism; but in the Lord's
> Supper there are conditions added and requirements which
> exclude infants from its use. It is required of those that observe
> it that they show the Lord's death and examine themselves as
> to whether they have repentance and faith.[163]

Ergo, infants are to be excluded from communion but not
from baptism. This argument might be called the classic
Paedobaptist defense, not because it exhibits a high degree of
excellence but because it is never omitted from the discussion. Every time the question comes up, Paedobaptists insist
that in baptism the subject is passive, whereas in the Lord's
Supper he is active. A. A. Hodge, for example, simply states

---

[162]*Die Tauflehre*, pp. 24-25 (italics his).
[163]*Commentary*, p. 371.

this with catechetical finality.[164] And Oscar Cullmann plays this string to the point of tenuity. In baptism, he tells us,

> *God engrafts; he does not simply communicate that he engrafts;* and in this *moment*, therefore, the reception of this act by the one baptized consists in nothing else than that he is the passive object of this divine action; that he *is engrafted* by God, he "is added" (Acts 2:41), an unequivocal passive. ... In the Lord's Supper the body of Christ is not enlarged through new members who "are added" (Acts 2:41), but the existing community as the body of Christ is each time newly strengthened in this its highest end. In the baptismal act, on the other hand, something else happens to the body of Christ: it is quantitatively enlarged through this "addition" of those who "are baptized into the body of Christ."[165]

Whether or not baptism simply assures the one baptized that he is engrafted into Christ's body or actually effects this engrafting, in either case the "unequivocal passive" in Acts 2:41 about which Cullmann is so insistent — "were added" (προσετέθησαν) — is preceded by a deponent middle verb (ἀποδεξάμενοι). As many as "received his word" (ἀποδεξάμενοι τὸν λόγον αὐτοῦ) were baptized and were added; or this can be rendered literally, "As many as gave his word access to themselves, these were baptized and these were added. . . ." Why does Cullmann stress the passive verb and say nothing about the middle verb? Is it not because he is a Paedobaptist, writing to defend infant baptism? Since infants do not "receive the word" but are simply "added" to the church by baptism without "giving the word access to themselves," therefore he suppresses the active, cognitive portion of the text in order that the passive element may stand in sharper relief.

The truth remains that each experience of "receiving the word" or "putting on Christ" or "believing" or "repenting" — terms that are invariably associated with baptism in the New Testament — involves just as high a degree of activity by those baptized as does "showing forth the Lord's death," "discerning the Lord's body," or eating "in remembrance

---

[164]See *Outlines of Theology*, p. 624.
[165]*Die Tauflehre*, pp. 26-27 (italics his).

of him" by those who partake of the Lord's Supper. When those first anxious inquirers asked Peter, What must we do? he did not answer that they should be passive and do nothing. He told them very plainly to *act*, with the imperative, "Repent and be baptized" (Acts 2:38).[166]

The whole effort to make one sacrament active and the other passive is a cul-de-sac, one more impassioned Paedobaptist impasse.[167] How can Calvin be so confident as to ask, concerning the Eucharist, "What remembrance shall we require from infants of that event of which they have never attained any knowledge?" What if we were to answer him, "All that is required of them is an inclination, a propensity to remember"? What if we were to suggest that, should he dissect the "seed of faith" which he suggests covenant children have lodged in them by the Holy Spirit when baptized, he would find that it also contains the "seed of remembrance"? And if he should protest that this germinal remembrance is inadequate to satisfy the requirement "this do in remembrance of me" (I Cor. 11:25), we might reassure him by pointing out that I Corinthians 11 says nothing concerning infants. It is unreasonable, therefore, to suppose that just because adults are to examine themselves regarding their faith to discern the Lord's body, children, who obviously have no such discernment, should be brought under the restrictions of this text. When the apostle says, "If anyone will not work, neither shall he eat" (II Thess. 3:10), would it not be "perverse" to apply this doctrine to infants? Why, then,

---

[166]See A. Gilmore, ed., *Christian Baptism*, pp. 126-127, 137ff. See also above, the discussion of *fides vicaria*, pp. 176ff.

[167]*The Westminster Larger Catechism* (Q. 167) asks: "How is our baptism to be improved by us?" to which a large answer is given, including the following: "By a serious and thankful consideration of the nature of it . . . and our solemn vow made therein; by being humbled for our sinful defilement . . .; by growing up to assurance of pardon of sin . . .; by endeavoring to live by faith . . . and to walk in brotherly love." If the infant is passive in the reception of his baptism, he surely is not in the improvement of it! Of course, the fact that even Paedobaptists require faith of adults who are baptized deprives this talk about baptism as the *passive* sacrament of its force. It is simply a convenient theory to accommodate the prior fact that infants are passive when baptized. The sacrament becomes very *active* as soon as the candidate is old enough to act intelligently and responsibly.

should we exclude them from communion by citing Scripture which obviously does not apply to them?

Whether they admit it or not, by insisting on a personal profession of faith as necessary to a worthy receiving of the Lord's Supper, the Paedobaptists take the very position they have condemned as "subjectivism" when critiquing the Baptist view of baptism. By Baptist subjectivism Paedobaptists mean that to require a personal confession of faith of all those baptized is to find the true work of baptism not in the "objective," reconciling work of Christ but in the baptized person's own inner, "subjective" movement of repentance and faith. This inner, subjective experience becomes the real dying and rising of baptism to which the sacrament bears witness. That we are dead and risen again *in Christ* becomes a mere background truth, as it was in the Middle Ages. What counts is that *we* died and rose again, that *we* repent and believe, or at least profess so to do; and of course this emphasis is all out of proportion.[168] However, when speaking of the Lord's Supper, Paedobaptists forget all their complaints about subjectivism. They insist that there must be a confession of faith on the part of all who partake; that Christ is received only by those who come to the table in faith; and that this simple but deep requirement must be kept in the very forefront when the sacrament is administered. Otherwise it will fail of its true purpose and effect.[169]

Surely there is a basic asymmetry between the parts of such reasoning. Do Paedobaptists accuse those who require faith of all who are baptized of a subjectivism that robs baptism of its true significance as a sacrament of the gospel? How then can they insist that a "personal confession of faith" is "essential" to the receiving of the Lord's Supper? When Baptists say faith is a prerequisite in all who are baptized, presumably they have reduced the "baptism of the Lord" to "believers' baptism."[170] But the Paedobaptists can without flinching affirm, "The main point is that profession must

[168]See Bromiley, *Sacramental Teaching*, p. 52.
[169]*Ibid.*, pp. 74, 75, 81.
[170]On the distinction between "believer baptism" and "believers' baptism," see below, p. 226, n. 14.

precede communion," presumably without reducing the communion of the Lord to believers' communion. We must not insist that faith precede baptism; we *must* insist that it precede communion. As for baptism, "far more basic than the response is the work which evokes it; and since it is this proper work which baptism proclaims, and of which it is the means, its administration need not be restricted to those in whom we think to see a response or whom we judge capable of it." But we need only rub our dialectical lamp to discover that the Lord's Supper "will necessarily fail of its true purpose and effect unless it is received with penitence and faith, and thus confirms and strengthens the response of the recipient."[171] Between these two series of propositions there is a theological hiatus; the chain of reasoning is missing a link and therefore simply lacks sufficient cogency to move the critical mind to assent.

C. THE BASIC SIMILARITY BETWEEN PASSOVER AND EUCHARIST

To proceed further, having assured us that infants cannot meet the scriptural requirements of communion, Calvin concludes that the same was true of the Old Testament Passover. "Circumcision . . . was destined for infants. The Passover, which has now been succeeded by the sacred supper, did not admit guests of all descriptions promiscuously, but was rightly eaten only by those who were of sufficient age to be able to inquire into its signification."[172] As for this point, all would readily grant that the Passover was not a promiscuous meal. Yet there were not the same restrictions for admission to the Passover in the Old Testament as Paedobaptists impose for partaking of the Lord's Supper. Calvin, by his phrasing of the matter, rather evades than relieves this problem.

[171]All quoted material in this paragraph is from Bromiley, *Sacramental Teaching*, pp. 55, 56, 75, 81.
[172]*Institutes*, IV, xvi, 30.

In order to appreciate the issue that confronts the Paedobaptist here, we must remember that the argument from infant circumcision to infant baptism, so pivotal in the whole debate, is but a detailed application of the more basic theological principle of continuity in redemptive revelation. Paedobaptists, then, should not appeal to a parallel between circumcision and baptism which they refuse to acknowledge between the Passover and the Lord's Supper. In fact, as far as the evidence of Scripture is concerned, the parallelism between the covenant meals of Passover and Eucharist is even more overt than that between the initiatory rites of circumcision and baptism. The Passover which Jesus celebrated with his disciples on the night of his betrayal has much to do in every way with the character of the Supper which he himself instituted. The fulfillment of the promise commemorated in the Passover ("when I see the blood, I will pass over you") gives meaning to the solemn proclamation by the Lord at the institution of the Eucharist: "This cup is the new covenant in my blood, which is poured out for you" (Luke 22:20). Markus Barth is very instructive in his observation that the Synoptists would hardly have made such a point of the details surrounding this meal — that it was at night; that it occurred in Jerusalem; that the disciples reclined at table, which was different from the ordinary custom; that they drank wine, which was not commonly done; and that at the close of the meal they sang a hymn — had they meant by all this simply to fix the time of Jesus' death. More was involved than chronology. They wanted to show that the Lord's Supper was intimately related to the Passover meal. The question of whether or not the final supper which Jesus celebrated was the Passover meal is not simply a historical issue; it is also, and more importantly, a theological one.[173]

For our discussion this means that if we can infer infant baptism from infant circumcision, much more can we infer infant communion from the Old Testament practice of giving the Passover to little children. At this juncture the Paedobaptist points out that infants could hardly have masticated the flesh of the paschal lamb. Though circumcised the eighth

[173]*Theologische Studien*, Heft 18, October, 1945.

day, infants obviously could not have eaten the Passover at such an early age. But no one supposes the Passover was eaten in "early infancy"; in order to eat the Passover, naturally children had to be sufficiently grown to eat something.[174]

Actually, for our discussion, the physical limitations of children in eating the solid food of the Passover meal have no more relevance for communion than the postponement of circumcision until eight days after birth has for baptism. There is no more *theological* significance in the one than in the other, as Paedobaptists know just as well as others. The issue is spiritual, not physical: it is not a question of the child's degree of physical development at the time he received circumcision and Passover, respectively, but whether faith was required in the reception of the one and not of the other. The Paedobaptists have made much of the fact that the children of the Israelites in Old Testament times were circumcised apart from personal faith. However, it is also true that these same children partook of the Passover in Old Testament times apart from personal faith. But the children of Western Christendom may *not* eat the Eucharist apart from personal faith. In the light of such disparity, it is more of an artifice than an argument to stress the commonplace that infants who had no teeth were incapable of chewing a piece of lamb.

A related aspect of the Passover feast was the insistence that it be celebrated according to households, as is evident in the text of the institution:

> Tell all the congregation of Israel that on the tenth day of this month they shall take every man a lamb according to their fathers' houses, a lamb for a household; and if the household is too small for a lamb, then a man and his neighbor next to his house shall take according to the number of persons; according to what each can eat you shall make your count for the lamb. (Exod. 12:3-4)

[174]According to rabbinical authority, "All members of the 'haburah' [Passover company] are to be in a state to eat at least a 'kezayit' [the equivalent of an olive]." Emil G. Hirsch, professor of rabbinical literature and philosophy at the University of Chicago, writing for the *Jewish Encyclopedia*, IX, "Passover."

It is not simply, as with baptism in the book of Acts, that in certain instances the Passover was celebrated by a whole household; the institution as such *required* a household celebration. The Passover was not to be celebrated by individuals but only in households. And while it is no doubt true that the devout Jew brought to the Passover a devout faith, there is not a word in the Old Testament to imply that such was *required* of all who partook, including the children. Of course, the phrase "according to what each can eat" excludes sucklings, yet by the same token it implies that sufficient maturity to eat solid food was the only prerequisite a Jewish child had to bring to the Passover meal. It was a national feast, even as circumcision was a national sign; and birth into the Jewish nation gave a right to the one as well as to the other. It was "according to what each can *eat*" that the count was to be made, not according to what each *believed*.

Some have thought to void this conclusion by appealing to Exodus 12:26-27: "And when your children say to you, 'What do you mean by this service?' you shall say, 'It is the sacrifice of the Lord's passover, for he passed over the houses of the people of Israel in Egypt, when he slew the Egyptians but spared our houses.' " Paedobaptists have seen in this text a correspondence to their own practice. "Infants," we are told, "were never admitted to the Passover until they were capable of comprehending the nature of the sign."[175]

The trouble with this reasoning is that Paedobaptists do not make the ability to understand the meaning of the Lord's Supper the ground of admission to the sacrament. To do so would be to approve of Solomon Stoddard's doctrine that Holy Communion should be viewed as a converting ordinance.[176] The standard Protestant doctrine — Paedobaptist as well as Baptist — is not that the child who can ask the question, What means this feast? is qualified to partake, but he who can answer it with a faith that feeds on Christ for salvation. Furthermore, there is no evidence that the Old Testament meant to teach that the questioning of the child was the occasion for his admission to the Passover. The law

---

[175]A. A. Hodge, *Outlines*, p. 624.
[176]See above, "The Halfway Covenant," pp. 116-118.

of institution admitted him as soon as he could eat, whether he asked any questions or not. The child's questions were rather the occasion for his instruction in the meaning of the feast.

When one takes the measure of Paedobaptist reasoning, then, in relation to the incongruity of infant baptism and believer communion, he can only conclude that it is more willing to live with the problem than able to relieve it. Having embraced their children in the covenant by giving them baptism, Paedobaptists exclude them from that same covenant by refusing them participation in the covenant meal. Having reasoned from inclusive circumcision to inclusive baptism, they turn about and go from an inclusive Passover to an exclusive Eucharist. But to do this is to grip the sword of circumcision — with which they have sought to vanquish the threat of believer baptism — by the point. For if Paedobaptists make the table of the Lord more selective than the Passover feast, if they keep back their own children from that sign and seal of the covenant which is the crowning symbol of Christian fellowship, then what becomes of their orotund protestations that Baptists define the privileges of the new covenant more narrowly than the old and exclude children from long-enjoyed, precious covenant privileges? When it becomes clear to the critical mind that the same could be said, sentence for sentence and period for period, of believer communion, such protestations lose their poignancy. In fact, a child will feel more "left out" when forbidden a part in communion than he ever will if not baptized; for in the former instance all are participating, in the latter all save the one being baptized are observers like himself. Thus Baptists work no greater hardship on their children when they keep them from baptism until such time as they confess faith in Christ than do Paedobaptists, who keep their children from the Lord's table for the same reason.

One can only register amazement, therefore, at the manner in which Paedobaptists continue to press this point of covenant privilege. Is the new covenant less generous than the old? asks John Murray. Are infants in the new dispensation less susceptible to the grace of God? To exclude infants from baptism would imply a complete reversal of a two-thousand-year practice. "We cannot believe that the New Testament economy is less beneficent than the Old." We can, then, expect no retraction but only expansion and extension. This consideration, he says, raises problems for the Baptist "which cannot be suppressed or evaded and which cannot be pressed with too much emphasis."[177]

What the Paedobaptist means is that this argument is so weighty it cannot be pressed with too much emphasis *when speaking of baptism*. But such selectivity is hardly fair. If we are going to press this argument, let us press it; if we are going to emphasize it, let us emphasize it — when speaking of communion as well as baptism. Surely infants are not less susceptible to the grace of God sealed in the Holy Supper than they are to the grace sealed in the waters of baptism. What sort of expansion is it which moves from an inclusive Passover to an exclusive Eucharist?

A few courageous Paedobaptists have repented of their inconsistency and advocated the restoration of infant communion, but they have for the most part cast their seed on stony ground. William Wall, in his classic *History of Infant Baptism,* wavered to the extent of saying, "It is a question . . . whether giving the communion to infants be an error or a duty"; and Bishop Jeremy Taylor declared himself openly for infant communion.[178] Several other Paedobaptist divines have made similar appeals. But such efforts are only truancies from the broad road of Paedobaptist consent. The most entrenched proponents of infant baptism have turned a deaf ear to these pleas and proven themselves both sterile in thought and chary of words when it comes to discussing the matter. Many pamphlets defending infant baptism do not so much as mention this inconsistency — perhaps in some

[177]*Christian Baptism*, pp. 4-6.
[178]See his *Worthy Communicant*, ch. 3, sec. 2, where he complains that it was the doctrine of transubstantiation that deprived infants of communion, "upon the pretense, lest that [the infant], puking up the holy symbols, the sacrament should be dishonored."

instances because the author never even thought of it.[179]

But in the final analysis, this silence can hardly be due to ignorance. Rather, it would seem, such an antinomy in the Paedobaptists' position is one on which they cannot gaze with equanimity. The argument from the covenant for infant baptism, when managed with adroitness, has about it an aura of plausibility; but the more convincingly it is pressed, the more embarrassed is the defense of believer communion. In this regard, it is interesting to note how Paedobaptist scholars have exhumed everything the Fathers of the church ever said in favor of infant baptism. On the other hand, one of the last thorough studies of the history of infant communion — so far as this writer has been able to discover — appeared in 1736. Written by Peter Zorn, it has remained veiled behind its original Latin to the present day.[180] If Baptists did not know enough *to* translate it, could it be that Paedobaptists knew enough *not* to?

[179]While the communication of infants has rarely been advocated, in some churches in the Reformed tradition the communication of small children is now allowed. In the United Presbyterian Church in the U.S.A., to cite a well-known case, when parents deem it appropriate and sessions authorize it, baptized children who have made no personal confession of faith may receive the elements. See *The Book of Order, Directory for Worship,* the section on the sacrament of the Lord's Supper. As of this writing, an overture advocating a similar usage is before the Presbyterian Church of the U.S. See *The Presbyterian Journal,* XXXV, 39 (June 30, 1976), 4f. See also "The Age of Admission to the Lord's Supper," *Westminster Journal,* XXXVIII, no. 2 (Winter 1975).

[180]*Historia Eucharistiae Infantum.*

IV

ADDENDUM: STRICTURES UPON CERTAIN ASPECTS OF THE PAEDOBAPTIST ARGUMENT

Having come to the end of our basic analysis of the argument from the covenant for infant baptism, we shall make a few final remarks on certain aspects of the discussion with which we have been only indirectly concerned up to this point. The reader may have noted how often in the course of the general discussion Paedobaptists have been quoted not only in the framing, but also in the refuting, of a particular point in the overall argument. Of course, one should not expect or demand a rigid uniformity in all they say, but Paedobaptists hardly agree on anything, it seems, save the conclusion that infants are to be baptized. Their argument (we are thinking here particularly of the Reformed tradition) is a trumpet which gives an uncertain sound; their practice is a practice in search of a theology.

When the Baptist theologian Augustus Strong used the lack of consensus among the protagonists of infant baptism to argue against the practice, B.B. Warfield rejoined:

> Let us confess that we do not all argue alike or aright, but is this not the proof rather of the firm establishment in our hearts of the practice? We all practice alike and it is the propriety of our practice, not the propriety of our defense of it, that is, after all, at stake.[181]

In other words, the Paedobaptists' hearts are fixed; they have the will to believe they should baptize their children, though

[181]*Polemics*, p. 406.

they cannot agree as to why they should do so. But the question is not how firmly Paedobaptists are convinced in their hearts, but whether that conviction is according to truth. And the latter is determined not by the uniformity of their practice but by the lucidity, penetration, and biblical character of the arguments with which they defend the practice. The sum of a series of unconvincing arguments is as unconvincing as its parts. A critical mind will rather suspect than succumb to the massive machinery by which the theologians have sought to erect the house of Paedobaptism.

We do not, we cannot, doubt that Zwingli, and especially Calvin — the Reformers who principally fathered the argument from circumcision for infant baptism — possessed profound dialectical powers; but at this point they simply followed the usage of a thousand years and placed their confidence in a bad argument. No doubt the excess and intransigence which some Anabaptists showed, the heresies which some of them championed, and the radicalism by which some of them abused the principle of liberty drove the Reformers to a conservative and churchly zeal in defending the doctrine and usage of infant baptism. But these pressuring circumstances, provided by the times in which the Reformers lived, do not apply to our own times. There no longer remains, therefore, any reason for their followers to repeat the same arguments over and over, until their minds are fixed in a kind of paralogism. While in most matters Paedobaptists have been stimulating and penetrating thinkers, on the question of infant baptism they have become the victims of a theological paralysis which makes them incapable of fresh thoughts. They seem curiously unaware of how much wood, hay, and stubble, how many unexamined affirmations, stock responses, and shibboleths are mixed in with the more challenging and worthy elements of their argument.

Furthermore, Paedobaptists tend to be illiterate when it comes to any serious consideration of the case for believer baptism. This is seen in the reaction of continental and British Paedobaptists to Karl Barth's attack — as though he had said something new, profound, and earthshaking. Cullmann, for example, calls it the most serious challenge to infant baptism ever attempted, greater than anything achieved by the great Anglo-Saxon Baptist churches.[182] The truth of the matter is that while Barth's courage was most commendable, much of what he said had been said many times by Baptists.

Speaking of courage, it is discouraging to see how even candid Paedobaptist researchers are yet tyrannized by their own tradition. Even Barth is very careful to make it plain he is no Baptist.

> There can be no question about an objective destroying of the essence of baptism, an objective destroying of its power, an objective hindering of its work and thus of an objective ineffectiveness of baptism on the basis of a bad administration and a bad reception of the sacrament. ... Baptism without the responsible willingness and readiness on the part of him who is baptized is true, real, and effective, but it is not *correct*, not performed in obedience, not performed according to proper order and therefore necessarily an obscure form of baptism.[183]

As Schneider has observed, this is a critical point in Barth's doctrine of baptism.[184] One cannot say a real "no" to infant baptism and at the same time affirm that it is objectively and essentially valid. As King Agrippa was almost persuaded to be a Christian, Barth is almost persuaded to be a Baptist. He has the courage to follow his theology until it brings him to the brink of *existenz*, of decision, of action; but maybe action is too much to expect. One should be thankful for what he has had the courage to say and not show oneself ungrateful for what he has not had the courage to do.

At its unworthiest (and disencumbered of its polysyllabicisms) the Paedobaptist apology sometimes degenerates into mere sentiment. Although the Anabaptists have been the ones to suffer and die for their convictions, Paedobaptists sometimes assume the posture of martyrs, as though they were standing for the truth against the world.

[182]*Die Tauflehre*, "Vorwort."

[183]*Die Taufe*, pp. 15, 28. To the same effect, F.S. Leenhardt, *Le Baptême Chrétien*, pp. 70-73. However, this initial statement of Barth (1943) should be weighed against his final, unequivocal rejection of infant baptism in *Dogmatik*, IV, 4, *Fragment*, which appeared in 1967.

[184]*Die Taufe*, p. 10.

> It [infant baptism] is the divine institution, not indeed commended by human wisdom and not palatable to those who are influenced by the dictates of human wisdom, yet commended by the wisdom of God.[185]

We submit that infant baptism is in every way palatable to human wisdom. People who accept nothing else in Christianity will have their children baptized — will even be urgent about it. Parents have an April heart when it comes to their offspring, and Paedobaptists know it. Therefore, they have not only indulged rhapsodies of emotion as a substitute for substantial argument, but have reprobated the Baptists as without natural affection.

> The close and endearing connection between parents and child affords a strong argument in favor of the church membership of the infant seed of believers. The voice of nature is lifted up and pleads most powerfully in behalf of our cause. The thought of severing parents from their offspring in regard to the most endearing relations in which it has pleased God in his adorable providence to place them, is equally repugnant to Christian feeling and natural law. Can it be, my friends, that when the stem is in the church, the branch is out of it? Can it be that when the parent is within the visible kingdom of the Redeemer, his offspring, bone of his bone and flesh of his flesh, should have no connection with it?[186]

When one ponders it, the plea that our children should be baptized because they are "bone of our bone and flesh of our flesh" is as curious as it is common on Paedobaptist lips. This phrase is used in Scripture of the relationship between man and wife, yet the Paedobaptists do not argue that the spouse of a believer should be baptized because of the faith of the believer. Now we submit that if the parent-child relationship is an eloquent argument for infant membership in the church, and if Paedobaptist Christian feeling is revolted at the thought that in God's "adorable providence" children shall not share with their parents in this "endearing relationship" of "visible" church membership, how much more revolting is the thought that one's spouse, one's own flesh, shall not share in this blessing until he or she professes faith.

[185]Murray, *Christian Baptism*, p. 24.
[186]Samuel Miller, *Infant Baptism*, p. 54.

If the Paedobaptists cannot stand to have the stem in and the branch out, how they can stand to have half the stem in and half out! Is this not to swallow the camel and strain at the gnat? And, as we have said before, to slander the Baptist view for "severing the parent from the offspring," as though the Baptist child must wait in the parking lot while the parent goes to church, reflects an ignorance that refuses to be enlightened.

The Methodist Raymond Huse, whose sentiments on original sin have already been noted, tells us that as a young theological student he had prejudices against infant baptism because he felt the emphasis should be on the ethical, volitional character of our decision for Christ. But then he had a "saintly" teacher "of blessed memory," Samuel F. Upham, who frequently told his classes as young Huse "listened eagerly": "I shall never forget how when I was a naughty boy my mother would take me into her arms and say to me, 'You must not be bad; you are God's little boy. I gave you to him in holy baptism.' And it has followed me all my life."[187] Huse continues:

> Dr. Upham was well up toward threescore years and ten when he uttered those words. His brow was crowned with snow, but his voice choked and tears ran down his cheeks unrestrained — and a hush filled his classroom. Somehow with the memory of that hush in his soul a budding young preacher would find it hard to be an Anabaptist.[188]

With a similar gush of sentiment, Donald Baillie stresses the truth that "a baby must have love" by repeating Father John Barrister Tabb's lines:

> The baby has no skies
>   But Mother's eyes,
> Nor any God above
>   But Mother's love.
> His angel sees the Father's face,
> But he the Mother's full of grace;
> And yet the heavenly kingdom is
> Of such as this.

[187]The reader is reminded that the New Testament never speaks thus: it never admonishes children to their duty by appealing to their baptism.

[188]*The Soul of the Child*, pp. 154-155.

And then he triumphs: "This is no sentimentalism, nor is it magic, but sacramental doctrine."[189] Of course it is no sentimentalism to say that a baby needs a mother's love. But when the sacrament of infant baptism is dragged by the heels into this emotionally surcharged atmosphere, we protest that the argument does then indeed descend into sentimentalism. As though a Baptist mother could not love her child as well as a Paedobaptist one! To go from the maternal touch— "epidermis against epidermis" — to the sacramental touch — "water against epidermis" — is to smite logic with apoplexy. But enough of the taffeta and lace of Paedobaptist pleading.

The Paedobaptist apology is burdened not only with rhapsodic flights of emotion but also with sheer complexity. The whole case for infant baptism needs a close shave with Occam's razor. We have rehearsed the details in the preceding analysis and need not reiterate them at this point. But in sum, Paedobaptists have defended a double church membership, noncommunicant and communicant; a double holiness, one that is outward, legal, and federal as against one that is vital, inward, and spiritual; a double aspect of the new covenant as administered in Christ, external and internal; and a double sacrament, or at least an incomplete sacrament looking to confirmation for its fulfillment. The law of parsimony would seem to favor the position of believer baptism. An explanation that does justice to the teaching of Scripture with a minimal number of subtle refinements, elaborate distinctions, and complicated assumptions is, all things being equal, the approach to be preferred. Why should one, for instance, advocate a Ptolemaic explanation of the universe, with its spheres within spheres, when Copernicus and Newton did better without them? It is our thesis that the position that limits baptism to those who confess their faith in Christ better meets the demands of the fundamental law of simplicity and economy.

Furthermore, as the position of believer baptism is superior in its theoretical simplicity, so it is at least not inferior in its practical application. That is to say, a baptized child has no practical advantage over a Baptist child. If the

[189] *The Theology of the Sacraments*, pp. 86-87.

latter has been enriched with the Paedobaptist jewels of good catechetical instruction, he has entered into his Christian inheritance. Only a sacramentalist would question the child's safety in the event of death; and if he live, being instructed in the nurture and admonition of the Lord by parents and teachers, there is no apparent reason why he should not wait to be baptized until he makes a credible confession, just as the baptized child must wait until he discerns the Lord's body before partaking of the Lord's Supper.

In the place of answers to this reasoning, Paedobaptists substitute touching reflections on the benefits of infant baptism to the *parents* and other witnesses. We grant that beaming parents and grandparents may be deeply moved by the baptism of a child or grandchild, but what of the child himself? Shall their distended delight compensate for his innocent ignorance? What a pity to be baptized without even knowing it! Let anyone compare young Charles Spurgeon's baptismal experience with that of an infant in arms and then ask himself which is the more spiritually rewarding to the recipient.

I left my relations and became what I am today, a Baptist, so-called, but I hope a great deal more a Christian than a Baptist. . . . I therefore cast about to find a Baptist minister and I failed to discover one nearer than Islehan in the Fen country, where resided a certain Mr. W. W. Cantlow. My parents wished me to follow my convictions and Mr. Cantlow arranged to baptize me. My employer gave me a day's holiday for the purpose. I can never forget the third of May, 1850. It was my mother's birthday and I myself was within a few weeks of being sixteen years of age. I was up early to have a couple of hours of quiet prayer and dedication to God. Then I had some eight miles to walk to reach the spot where I was to be immersed into the Triune Name according to the sacred command. What a walk it was! What thoughts and prayers thronged my soul during that morning's journey! It was by no means a warm day, and therefore all the better for the two or three hours of quiet foot travel which I enjoyed. The sight of Mr. Cantlow's smiling face was a full reward for that country tramp. I think I see the good man now and the white ashes of the fire by which we stood and talked together about the solemn exercise which lay before us.[190]

[190]*Autobiography*, I, pp. 147ff.

Part Three:
BELIEVER BAPTISM DEFENDED AND EXPOUNDED IN TERMS OF COVENANT THEOLOGY

OBJECTIONS TO
BELIEVER BAPTISM

A. BIBLICAL AND UNBIBLICAL INDIVIDUALISM

In reacting, as Kierkegaard did, against the collectivism of mass Christianity and external covenant privilege, there is indeed the danger that one may fall into the opposite error of an unbiblical individualism. Paedobaptist warning in this regard must not go unheeded. Donald Baillie, for example, in defending the thesis that baptism comes to the child in response to the parents' faith, comments: "And that is just as it ought to be, and in keeping with the whole outlook of the New Testament, which has none of our false individualism."[1] The *Interim Report* of the Church of Scotland even goes so far as to declare the idea of believer baptism "... entirely modern, bound up with the Renaissance idea of human individualism and autonomy, and representing a radical divergence from the Biblical teaching of the nature of man."[2] Let us pause, then, to consider this Paedobaptist polemic against individualism.

In his famous essay entitled "The Out-Populating Power of the Christian Stock," a mélange of the sublime and the ridiculous, Bushnell says some excellent things in an excellent way — things which contemporary Christians (especially Baptists) need to hear and heed.[3] His fear is the

---

[1]*The Theology of the Sacraments*, p. 83.
[2]As quoted in Beasley-Murray, *Baptism*, p. 314.
[3]*Christian Nurture*, pp. 165ff.

loss of our own children by an "atomizing scheme of piety" and by a "trivial, unnatural, weak and at the same time violent . . . overdone scheme of individualism which knows the race only as mere units of will and personal action [and] dissolves even families into monads . . . and expects the world to be finally subdued by adult conversions. . . ." But in refuting the errors into which those advocating believer baptism admittedly could fall, Bushnell is driven by his notion of covenantal solidarity, oriented in terms of an Old Testament externalism, into a kind of redemptive Malthusianism. Paedobaptists will conquer the world for Christ by the cradle. "The Abrahamic order and covenant," we are told, "stood upon this footing formally proposed and promising to make the father of the faithful a blessing to mankind by and through the multitude of his offspring."[4] Just as Abraham's seed in Egypt

> overpopulated the great kingdom of the Pharaohs until the land was filled with them and the jealousy of the throne awakened, just as Palestine under Jewish hegemony boasted a great and populous empire, so Christianity, by its own superior laws of population, will finally live down Mohammedanism and completely expurgate the world of it. The campaigning centuries of European chivalry pressing it with crusade after crusade could not bring it under; but the majestic populating force of Christian faith and nurture can even push it out of the world as in a silence of a dew fall.[5]

How disrespectfully time has treated this gyrating Paedobaptist vision! But one who is theologically astute need not make time his augur. To apply the facts of Old Testament externalism and nationalism — the Jews flooding Egypt and Palestine with a "holy" issue — to the New Testament church in such a unilateral way is bad theology, bound to be in error in its conclusions because it is in error in its presuppositions. It does not take into account, as we have observed many times, the movement of redemptive history.

Bushnell goes on to assure us that his millennial hope will have nothing of a jubilee of the gathering of adult souls only into the kingdom, "while the poor unripe sinners of

[4]*Ibid.*, p. 168.
[5]*Ibid.*, p. 17.

childhood . . . are in no sense in it, but are waiting their conversion time on the outside!"[6] This well-known complaint that those who advocate believer baptism are such as leave their own offspring to the devil and treat them as isolated little units of individual rebellion deserves no other refutation than a cool smile. Granting that the Paedobaptists have a commendable zeal for the nurture of their children which all should emulate, we still affirm that each individual — with God's help — must acknowledge the covenant for himself, and that no one, *not even father or mother*, can ever do this for him. It is beyond cavil that the family has been ordained by God as the primary means of the child's nurture in the things of God while he is still an individual in embryo, that when he shall have come to riper years he may commit himself as "the individual" (Kierkegaard) to the God of his fathers and by faith embrace the blessings of the covenant. But until that commitment is made, we have no right from Scripture — unless we revert to the external blessings granted to Abraham's literal seed in Old Testament times — to assume that the natural ties which bind our children to the human family also bind them to the covenantal family of the redeemed.

We thus reject Bushnell's affirmation that, biblically speaking, ". . . grace shall travel by the same conveyance with sin; the organic unity which I have spoken of chiefly as an instrument of corruption is to be occupied and sanctified by Christ and become an instrument also of mercy and life."[7] According to the Bible, matters are not that simple. Grace does not travel by the same conveyance as does sin, for we are sinners when born; we are saints only when born again. Whatever such a distinction may entail chronologically (note our remarks on infant regeneration above), theologically speaking it entails an absolute, qualitative difference which cannot be ignored with impunity.

The ancient case against Baptistic individualism (for Richard Baxter it spelled anarchy; for Cotton Mather, a spiritual "cold death"; for Horace Bushnell, a Faustian

---

[6]*Ibid.*, p. 170.
[7]*Ibid.*, p. 94.

committal of our children to the devil) has been given a more sober and trenchant statement in modern times by James Daane. According to Professor Daane, individualism of the Baptist variety impugns the divine image. In a stimulating series of devotional studies concerned with the doctrine of the Trinity, he has put his case in a few brief but pithy lines:

> God is not an individual; he is one in three and three in one. Man was created in the image of this kind of triune God. This should spell the end of all definitions of human nature in terms of mere individualism. Man's nature consists in male and female. Together they become one flesh, and thereby multiply and become three. (March 9)

> This means that the image of God in man among other things consists of this structure of human nature suggested by the father, mother, and child. (March 10)

> God dealt with all men through Adam. Through Adam's sin the many were made sinners. In redemption, too, God deals with all men through the One; God now deals with all men in and through Jesus Christ. In perfect harmony with this method, God deals *within* the church with children in terms of their parents. Here lies the ground of infant baptism and the meaning of the covenant. (March 15)

> We Americans have been brought up on the tradition of individualism. In business, in politics, in morals, even in religion, we have been taught that it is "every man for himself." ... The largest part of the American church has been invaded by the spirit of individualism. ... This unbiblical individualism has led to a denial of infant baptism, to the belief that a child cannot be a member of the church by birth, but only by individual choice. ... Individualism loses all appreciation for the Biblical idea of the one for the many. (March 14)[8]

Such a statement of the case against individualism cannot be lightly set aside as of trifling significance, for God is indeed a God-in-fellowship; and like him we are made in and for fellowship.[9] As a basic expression of that fellowship, the family is doubtless a primary means used by God to convey

---

[8] *The Back to God Hour Family Altar*, March 1952.

[9] Unlike Professor Daane, I do not see that Scripture links the image of God to the familial structure of father, mother, and child. Rather, it is as male and female that God created man in his image (Gen. 1:28). For a larger discussion, see my *Man as Male and Female*, pp. 33ff.

the blessings of salvation. It is also true that redemptive revelation is structured covenantally, and any Baptist who denies these truths demeans his own heritage. But to advocate believer baptism is not to say that membership in the church rests solely on the choice of the individual, as though the covenant of grace were simply a form of Rousseau's social contract. A Pelagian or synergist might be thus inclined to construe the covenant as a sort of contract whose ultimate validity depends on the will and choice of the individual. But there is nothing in the position of believer baptism, however Pelagian and synergistic some Baptists may — unfortunately — be, that requires one to embrace such unbiblical views.

Those who advocate believer baptism do indeed deny that a child can be "a member of the church by birth," but not because of an "unbiblical individualism." Rather, they do so because of a biblical evangelicalism. When the church was the nation of Israel and the nation of Israel the church, a person could be "born into the church" because it was an outward, theocratic institution. But in the New Testament, the only way to become a member of the church is not by natural birth but by a new birth: ". . . unless one is born *anew*, he cannot see the kingdom of God" (John 3:3). And this most inward, spiritual renewal, which is the *prius* of the individual's choice, is the gracious work of the Spirit, who, like the wind, moves where he will (John 3:8). To be "born of the flesh," even of regenerate flesh, is to be flesh still (John 3:6); "and those who are in the flesh cannot please God" (Rom. 8:8). Therefore, to choose Christ is to be chosen by Christ; the choice is individual because individuals are chosen. God has made every man's face unique and has called each of us by name.[10] It is God's electing grace, therefore, working in and through the free choice of the individual, that gives one covenantal status as the covenant is newly administered in Christ.

[10]To say that we receive this name in our baptism is to substitute sacramental doctrine for the evangelical doctrine of effectual calling. In Reformed and evangelical liturgies of baptism, therefore, although the minister calls the candidate by name, he does not *give* him his name. See above, p. 76, n. 2.

This is individualism, but not individualism in the bad sense of one who will not have the Lord God reign over him because he says, "I am the master of my fate, I am the captain of my soul." Rather, it is individualism in the biblical sense of one who has heard God say, "I have called you by your name, you are mine"; and who confesses his faith in the exquisitely beautiful lines with which the *Heidelberg Catechism* begins, lines in which a form of the individual, personal pronoun occurs no less than eleven times:

> What is your only comfort in life and in death?
>
> That I, with body and soul, both in life and in death, am not my own, but belong to my faithful Savior, Jesus Christ, who with his precious blood has fully satisfied for all my sins, and redeemed me from all the power of the devil; and so preserves me that without the will of the Father in heaven not a hair can fall from my head; yea, that all things must work together for my salvation. Wherefore, by his Holy Spirit he also assures me of eternal life, and makes me heartily willing and ready henceforth to live unto him.

Therefore, when one makes a personal, individual commitment to Christ, the prerequisite for receiving the covenant sign of baptism, he is simply spelling out the implications of an individualism which the Paedobaptists themselves have taught him. He is taking seriously what the *Canons of Dort* proclaim when they ground the assurance of one's election not in one's birth, nor in the status of one's parents as believers, but in those "infallible fruits" vouchsafed to the individual as indwelt by the Spirit.[11] Those who espouse believer baptism also recognize the elect individual not by his pedigree but by the "true faith in Christ" which he affirms when he stands, to use Kierkegaard's phrase, at the "crossroads of time and eternity," when he says yes to the divine yes.

Speaking of Kierkegaard, the melancholy Dane had some things to say about "the individual" which, understandably, are not music to Paedobaptists' ears, yet might well be taken as medicine for their souls.

[11]See especially Article XII.

For a "crowd" is the untruth. In a godly sense it is true eternally, Christianly, as St. Paul says, that "only one attains the prize" — which is not meant in a comparative sense, for comparison takes others into account. It means that every man can be that one, God helping him therein — but only one attains the prize.

If this thing of "the individual" were a trifle to me I could let it drop; indeed I should be delighted to do so and should be ashamed if I were not willing to do it with the most obliging alacrity. But such is far from being the case. For me — not personally but as a thinker — this thing of the individual is the most decisive thing. . . .

If I were to desire an inscription for my tombstone I should desire none other than "That Individual." With the category of "the individual" is bound up any ethical importance I may have. "The individual" — that is the decisive Christian category and it will be decisive also for the future of Christianity.

Kierkegaard affirms that the prime condition of religiousness is to be a single individual.

"The individual" is the category through which, in a religious aspect, this age, all history, the human race as a whole, must pass; and he who stood at Thermopylae was not so secure in his position as I who have stood in defense of this narrow defile, "the individual," with the intent, at least, of making people take notice of it.[12]

Though it is true, even at the human level, that there can be no "I" without a "thou" — as Kierkegaard's own disciples have helped us to see (Ferdinand Ebner, Martin Buber)[13] — yet in order to have a true church of Christ, there must be a fellowship of *saints (communio sanctorum)*, not an "amorphous mass of Pelagian good will." It was against this error of a surplus of solidarity which turns the Christian church into "Christendom" that Kierkegaard launched his attack as the champion of individualism. While he may appear to have

[12]*The Point of View*, pp. 111ff.; see n. 2 on "The Individual."
[13]On the contribution of Ferdinand Ebner to our understanding of the fellowship in and through which the Kierkegaardian individual exists as an individual, a contribution which Karl Heim called a "Copernican act," see the comments on the dimension of the personal in my *Emil Brunner's Concept of Revelation*, pp. 63f.

overstated the case for "the individual," he appears so only as long as we forget the opposite error against which he protested, that solidarity of external holiness which membership in the visible church, secured through infant baptism, confirms and guarantees.

Those who plead for believer baptism, then, need not be intimidated by the charge of individualism so long as that individualism is biblically oriented — that is, so long as it is held in terms of God's electing love and mediated to "the individual" by the effectual preaching of the cross and the response of faith, a faith that makes one truly a member of Christ's body the church. In other words, the biblical individual is not a puny edition of Nietzsche's Superman, but a person in fellowship with God and with the people of God. He is alone, but "alone with God," as Kierkegaard put it, in order that he might not be alone. "For the gate is narrow," says the Lord, "and the way is hard, that leads to life, and those who find it are few" (Matt. 7:14). Happily, families may pass through this narrow gate — but only in single file. Therefore, every Christian, like Bunyan's Pilgrim, must begin the journey that leads to the heavenly city by passing through the Wicket Gate as an *individual*.

B. BIBLICAL AND UNBIBLICAL SUBJECTIVISM

Closely akin to the charge of individualism is the complaint, sometimes brought against those who advocate the baptism of believers only, that their position leads to a false, unbiblical "subjectivization."[14] It is true that Baptists administer baptism only on a credible profession of faith as

[14] See Bromiley, *Sacramental Teaching*, pp. 55-56, where it is intimated that Baptist subjectivism "emerges with peculiar distinctiveness when baptism is made a sign of our work rather than that of the Trinity on our behalf, and even nominally it becomes 'believers' baptism' rather than the baptism of the Lord." Some have returned this compliment by styling infant baptism "unbelievers' baptism." The term "believers' baptism" has always stood in contrast, not to "the baptism of the Lord," but to "infant baptism." Strictly, it should be written "believer baptism," without an "s'," since it refers to baptism administered to believers, just as "infant baptism" refers to baptism administered to infants. Hence the use of "believer baptism" rather than "believers' baptism" in this study.

evidence of the new birth, which involves an inward, subjective experience. If this leads to "subjectivization," then to subjectivization one must go. Though the word itself may intimidate some because of its ponderous size, to those whose eyes have been enlightened, the danger that believer baptism will betray the church into "subjectivization" is more chimerical than substantial. Anyone who appreciates the movement of redemptive history from Old Testament nationalism to New Testament individualism will appreciate the correlative movement from Old Testament objectivity to New Testament subjectivity.

This movement is in evidence even in the prophets of the Old Testament, who anticipated the doom of Israel both as a political fact and as a divine judgment. The remnant of the pious who survive this catastrophe are indeed Israelites, heirs of Abraham; but in the vision of the prophets the accident of physical birth recedes into the background and the factor of individual, inward renewal comes to the fore. R. E. O. White, speaking of the implications of the theology of the remnant for the biblical doctrine of initiation, observes that

> the remnant is to be qualified for its task in ways that have to do, not with its racial origin and lineage, but with its repentant mood, its experience of God's Spirit, its knowledge and understanding of God's ways and will, its purification and forgiveness, and its responsiveness to the gracious initiative of God in deliverance from oppression and restoration to His favor.[15]

Once this truth is perceived, the difference between the "old" and the "new" covenants can be appreciated for what it really is, a difference in the degree of inwardness and subjectivity enjoyed by the covenantees.

> "Behold, the days are coming, says the Lord, when I will make a *new* covenant with the house of Israel and the house of Judah, not like the covenant which I made with their fathers when I took them by the hand to bring them out of the land of Egypt. . . . But this is the covenant which I will make with the house of Israel after those days, says the Lord: I will put my law *within them,* and I will *write it upon their hearts;* and I will be

---

[15]*Biblical Doctrine of Initiation,* pp. 39ff., with relevant citations from other writers.

their God, and they shall be my people."[16]

Of course, the sign of this new covenant belongs to the covenantees. But who are they? Those who can say, "We have a Christian for our father," just as the Jews said to Jesus, "We have Abraham for our father" (John 8:33f.)? Not so. The covenantees are not those who are *born* into the covenant, those whose father and mother have the law "written upon their hearts," but those who *themselves* have had this experience, having been born again by the Spirit of God. This subjective, inward, existential, experiential, spiritual change is the hallmark of the new covenant. It is not, then, a false, unbiblical subjectivism, but a true, biblical one which reserves baptism for those who will both confess Jesus Christ with their mouths and also believe in their hearts that God has raised him from the dead (Rom. 10:9).

C. ON THE RESTRICTING OF COVENANT PRIVILEGE

Paedobaptists tend to be insensitive to the movement of revelation from the broader dimension of Old Testament externalism to the deeper dimension of New Testament inwardness. Thus they feel that the rejection of infant baptism intolerably narrows the definition of covenant privilege. Can it be, they ask, that the gospel in its nobler, more complete, and more generous display of grace should not embrace children in the church, when even in the Old Testament they were not denied this privilege of being a part of it? The fallacy in this type of argument is that it urges a quantitative solution to a qualitative problem; it pleads for Old Testament breadth at the expense of New Testament depth of covenant privilege. The difficulty becomes apparent as soon as the question is put: Precisely what are those "covenant privileges," enjoyed by Old Testament Jewish and New Testament (Paedobaptist) children, which are denied to those

[16]Jeremiah 31:31-33 (italics mine).

children whose Christian parents fail to present them for baptism at birth? Such (Baptist) parents pray for their children, instruct them in the fear of the Lord, and are happy to call them God's children whenever they give evidence that they are such by making a personal confession of faith. If appeal to a personal confession sounds unbearably subjective to Paedobaptist ears, it may be answered that the promise of God, according to the New Covenant, is to write his law in the minds and hearts of the covenantees. Therefore, as soon as God himself claims them as his by fulfilling in them this promise of his grace, their parents are happy to number their children with the children of God.

Some Paedobaptists are confident that the "retrograde change" which such a position supposedly entails would have evoked, at the inception of the Christian church, an outcry from Jewish Christian parents because they were accustomed to circumcising their children. Since the New Testament shows no evidence of such — since there is no protest about "leaving children out" — we must conclude, it is reasoned, that as Christians they baptized their children just as they had from time immemorial circumcised them.

It should be observed, however, that such an argument from silence would have weight only if Jewish Christians were forbidden, as Christians, to circumcise their children. But this was not the case. Even after their conversion Jews continued to circumcise their children, as can be seen from Luke's account of Paul's last meeting with James and the Jerusalem elders (Acts 21:17-21). James told Paul on that occasion that myriad Jews who were believers held him in timorous, if not suspicious, regard because they thought he was teaching the Jews of the Diaspora not to circumcise their children or walk according to Jewish customs. That both James and Paul regarded this charge as false seems incontrovertible from the sequel of the Acts narrative, according to which James urged Paul to demonstrate his zeal for the Jewish way of life by assuming a Nazarite vow with four other men — which Paul engaged to do. We can only conclude, then, that Paul did not teach the Jews to give up the circumcision of their children;[17] and surely James did not. Why, then, should the Christian Jews have protested the neglect of their children because they were not baptized?

It is quite true that Paul repudiated circumcision as the symbol of Pharisaic legalism. It is also true that he believed that baptism signified and sealed the same spiritual benefits that Abraham's circumcision did, thus demonstrating that circumcision no longer had *theological* significance for Christians ("For neither circumcision counts for anything nor uncircumcision, but keeping the commandments of God," I Cor. 7:19). But it is an oversimplification of the evidence to suppose that the early Jewish Christians as a whole grasped the implications of all this with anything like the clarity of thought Paul attained in his epistles. For them, undoubtedly, circumcision remained "something," and they gave it to their children as their forebears had done for centuries, even as they continued to keep the Passover and observe the Sabbath day.[18]

This zeal for circumcision, when taken together with a lack of concern on the part of Jewish Christians for any apparent slighting of their children, may indeed imply the Baptist position rather than the Paedobaptist. Some Paedobaptists have admitted as much. Lambert, for example, writes:

> No doubt, to the first Christians the full truth of the relation between the old and the new was not yet manifest. It was not until the shadows of doom had fallen upon Jerusalem and the temple, that it began to dawn on the minds of Jewish Christendom that the old dispensation was forever and utterly done away. Previous to that time they continued to circumcise their children and to observe all the ordinances of the law of Israel (cf. Acts 21:21). And even Paul, with all his wonderful liberality to those of Gentile birth, maintained the advantage for the Jew of circumcision, and clung personally to the religious customs of his fathers (Rom. 3:1f., 9:3f.; Acts 27:17). All this may help to explain to us how it was that infant baptism was

[17]Of course, Paul did not teach *Gentile* Christians to adopt the custom of circumcision. Indeed, if they did so out of any legalistic motivation, as did some of the Galatians, he rigorously opposed them.

[18]Concerning the early Jewish Christians and their observance of the Sabbath day, see my *The Lord's Day*, pp. 43f.

not practiced at the beginning. When it is said that Jewish Christians, accustomed as they had been to see their children circumcised, would have claimed baptism as a natural right, it is perhaps forgotten that *the first Jewish Christians may not have thought of claiming the new ordinance for their children precisely because they still practiced the old one.* They still regarded circumcision as a definite sign and seal of the divine covenant set upon their male children.[19]

This view of the matter, with its concession that "infant baptism was not practiced at the beginning," is the only adequate way to account for the further fact that in all the debate over retaining circumcision, never is infant baptism mentioned. At no point, perhaps, does the disquietude with which B.B. Warfield defends infant baptism come more to the surface than when he argues that the Jerusalem Council (Acts 15) turned about the question of whether baptism succeeded circumcision, with Paul and the apostles unanimously in the affirmative; while the Baptists, by denying this substitution, consort with the "fanatical, pharisaical church-party!" He concludes, "Let us take our places, along with Paul and all the Apostles."[20]

This is a classic case of special pleading. There is not a word about baptism in the whole circumcision debate recorded in Acts 15. Something is certainly awry with the system when it compels one to such a reconstruction of the evidence. And what is awry seems quite clear: it is the false identity which Paedobaptists, especially in the Reformed tradition, have postulated between Old Testament circumcision and New Testament baptism, an identity which they must maintain at all costs lest they lose the argument for infant baptism. For this reason they make every effort to prove that Paul taught his Gentile converts to baptize their children as the Christian equivalent of Old Testament circumcision. Indeed, it would have been natural for the apostle to alleviate the scruples of his Jewish Christian brothers and sisters by assuring them that he always did this. But the fact that we have no evidence that he ever reasoned in this manner with

[19]*Sacraments in the New Testament*, p. 214 (italics mine).
[20]*Polemics*, pp. 404-405.

them indicates that he did not regard the parallelism between baptism and circumcision to be as precise as Paedobaptists have made it.[21]

---

[21]For more on this matter, see Jeremias' discussion, *Die Kindertaufe*, pp. 51-57.

II

COVENANT THEOLOGY
IMPLIES BELIEVER
BAPTISM

A. INTRODUCTION

We have maintained that the old economy had a forward
look: rather than being an end in itself, it prepared for the age
to come. "Now Moses was faithful in all God's house as a
servant, to testify to the things that were to be spoken later
. . ." (Heb. 3:5). Faith, then, descries in the history of ancient
Israel more than mere history. In the bondage in Egypt; in
the Exodus under Moses; in the wilderness wandering, with
its manna from heaven and water from the rock, its fiery
cloud and pillar of smoke, its tabernacle, priests, and sac-
rifices; in the crossing of Jordan; and in the inheritance of
Canaan there is bodied forth, in the form of solid and substantial events, the history of the true Israel after the Spirit, in
all her varied experience from redemption initiated to redemption consummated. Christ is that prophet like Moses
(Acts 3:22), yet counted worthy of more honor than Moses
(Heb. 3:3), who delivers his people from the Egypt of their
sins (Matt. 1:21) into the liberty of the glory of the children of
God (Rom. 8:21). He is that bread come down from heaven
(John 6:33); if someone eats of it, he will never hunger, till he
shall come at last to that better land, that city which has
foundations, whose builder and maker is God (Heb. 11:10).

In keeping with the forward movement of revelation, the
spiritual and inward significance of circumcision was increasingly stressed (even in the Old Testament); and this

progression is in harmony with our thesis that the shadowy age of types looked to the fuller revelation of New Testament realities. In fact, when we come to the New Testament, there is nothing left to circumcision but its ethical and spiritual meaning. It no longer has any significance at all for the New Testament saint as an external rite. With the passing of the typical age of the covenant and the inauguration of the age of semi-eschatological fulfillment, only the spiritual grace of a righteous life marks one as a citizen of the kingdom of God.

In other words, from the standpoint of the New Testament, one who has outward circumcision without inward circumcision has no circumcision at all. Hence Paul can say that if a man transgresses the law, even though he be a Jew, his circumcision has become uncircumcision. Circumcision which is merely outward in the flesh is just not circumcision (Rom. 2:25ff.). For one who has become a new creation in Christ, such merely outward circumcision is uncircumcision (Col. 3:11). In fact, merely outward circumcision not only has no more value than uncircumcision; it is really, Paul suggests in a moment of fierce rhetorical zeal against the Judaizers (Gal. 5:12), a mutilation, an act of self-destruction. Those who are truly circumcised are all those who worship God in the Spirit, boasting in Christ Jesus and having no confidence in the flesh (Phil. 3:2-4).

The Paedobaptist position that believers' children have a right to baptism as members of the church by birth is on a collision course with this movement of Paul's thought. Since there are no longer covenant blessings in an external sense, there is no justification for giving the covenant sign to those who are our children in an external sense, that is, our children according to the flesh.[22] Baptism corresponds to circumcision rather in its ethical and spiritual meaning. In

---

[22]Of course, there are blessings in the Christian life that are very outward and tangible. Christians are not so heavenly minded that they cannot pray for daily bread, nor so ungrateful that they do not thank God for providing it. Nor should they be so spiritual that they do not give a cup of cold water in Christ's name to those who thirst. But to say as much is quite a different matter from speaking of a "chosen" people in the "promised" land in the Old Testament meaning of these terms. The latter (theocratic) way of thinking leads — to use contemporary terms — to American civil religion; the former, to a humble acceptance of God's providential care. Between these two there is a great gulf.

keeping with this truth, the New Testament unfailingly expounds the meaning of baptism in terms of spiritual and inward blessings exclusively. In other words, while circumcision belonged both to Isaac, in whom the seed was called (Rom. 9:7), and to Ishmael, in whom the seed was not called (Gal. 4:30), baptism belongs to "every one whom the Lord our God calls to him" (Acts 2:38-39), and to those only. One who has not known the call of God has no claim to the rite which seals the promise given in that call.

Paedobaptists, however, would have us believe that baptism, like circumcision, belongs both to those who are born of Christian parents and to those who are born of the Spirit of God. Whereas Paul says that those who are children after the flesh are not the children of God (Rom. 9:7-8), Paedobaptists say that they are, since God reckons our children after the flesh to be his children too. (Lutherans and Anglicans say he makes them his children by means of baptism.) Therefore, as Abraham circumcised all his children after the flesh, we should baptize all our children after the flesh. As there was an Israel after the flesh (I Cor. 10:18), so also there are now Christians after the flesh. The *Directory for the Public Worship of God*, prepared by the Westminster Assembly, declares: "The seed of the faithful are Christians."[23]

Such a position, as we have tried to show, is encumbered with theological problems. It leads to a theological impasse that would seem to call for a fundamentally new start. And yet — we are happy to say — it is not a *fundamentally* new start that is required, since one need not abandon covenant theology to embrace believer baptism. Rather, one needs only to construe aright the insight from biblical theology that revelation is historical, as we shall now seek to show.

B. THEOLOGICAL STATEMENT OF THE POSITION

The nub of our criticism of "the argument from the covenant" for infant baptism has been that it stresses the covenant idea as the unifying concept of redemptive history

---

[23] See "Of the Sacrament of Baptism," *The Confessions of Faith, Together with the Sum of Saving Knowledge*, p. 294.

to the point of suppressing the *movement* of redemptive history, a movement from the age of anticipation and promise to the age of realization and fulfillment. One cannot but applaud the Paedobaptist affirmation of the centrality and perpetuity of the covenant concept as a fundamental category of biblical revelation. To understand this affirmation aright, however, one must always use it in such a way that he reckons with the truth that the old covenant made with the Jewish people has now become the new covenant in Jesus Christ. At the risk of being accused of having but one idea, we must return to this point because of its significance. If we are correct in blaming the miscarriage of Paedobaptist reasoning on a failure to see the implication of the historical movement in revelation, then we may hope that the recognition of this movement and what it implies will provide the clue we need to make progress toward a solution.

It is our conviction, to be specific, that the troubled waters of Paedobaptism can be rendered a clear and flowing stream if one recognizes that the promise of the seed made to Abraham had a twofold reference. In the age of type and anticipation, it embraced not only those who shared Abraham's faith but also the whole nation of Israel, which descended from his loins according to the flesh. In the age of fulfillment the promise embraces the true seed according to the Spirit, typified by the literal seed according to the flesh. This true seed of Abraham is "born, not of blood nor of the will of the flesh nor of the will of man, but of God" (John 1:13). If in the typical age of the Old Testament all the literal seed of Abraham are to be circumcised, then in the age of fulfillment all those who answer to the type as the true seed of Abraham are to be baptized. And who are they? The New Testament gives an unequivocal answer: those who are of faith are the sons of Abraham (Gal. 3:7). Therefore, those who are of faith are to be baptized — *which is precisely believer baptism.* Here, then, is the Thesean thread that will lead us out of the labyrinth of the theological debate in which we have been involved, while preserving the rich treasures of biblical thought stored in the perspective of "covenant theology."

This argument is anything but new. Some of the original Anabaptists seem to have used it, and even Calvin was forced to admit that it contains a grain of truth.[24] Abraham Booth, in his *Paedobaptism Examined*, explicitly reasons his way through to the conclusion that circumcision is analogous to, not identical with, baptism.

> The different state of things under the old and new economies, and the apostle's distinction between the carnal and the spiritual seed of Abraham, being duly considered, the argument from analogy will run thus: As, under the old covenant, circumcision belonged to all the *natural* male descendants of Abraham; so, under the new covenant, baptism belongs to all the *spiritual* seed of Abraham, who are known to be such by a credible profession of repentance and faith.[25]

In a sermon on the meaning of Abraham's circumcision, Spurgeon makes a similar statement:

> It is often said that the ordinance of baptism is analogous to the ordinance of circumcision. I will not controvert that point, although the statement may be questioned, but supposing it be, let me urge upon every believer here to see to it that in his own soul he realize the spiritual meaning both of circumcision and baptism, and then consider the outward rites; for the thing specified is vastly more important than the sign. . . .
>
> "Well," says one, "a difficulty suggests itself as to your views, for an argument is often drawn from this fact, that inasmuch as Abraham must circumcise all his seed, we ought to baptize all our children." Now observe the type, and interpret it not according to prejudice, but according to Scripture. In the type the seed of Abraham is circumcised; you draw the inference that all typified by the seed of Abraham ought to be baptized, and I do not cavil at the conclusion; but I ask you, who are the true seed of Abraham? Paul answers in Rom. 9:8, "They who are the children of the flesh, these are not the children of God, but the children of the promise are counted for the seed." As many as believe in the Lord Jesus Christ, whether they be Jews or Gentiles, are Abraham's seed. Whether eight days old in grace, or more or less, every one of Abraham's seed has a right to

[24]*Institutes,* IV, xvi, 12. Calvin charges, however, that the Anabaptists taught that the Old Testament was *merely* outward, national, and typical, which would be a serious theological error. But we take such generalizations about the Anabaptists *cum grano salis.*

[25]*Paedobaptism Examined,* II, 265.

baptism. But I deny that the unregenerate, whether children or adults, are of the spiritual seed of Abraham. The Lord will, we trust, call many of them by his grace, but as yet they are "heirs of wrath even as others." At such times as the Spirit of God shall sow the good seed in their hearts they are of Abraham's believing seed; but they are not so while they live in ungodliness and unbelief or are yet incapable of faith and repentance. The answering person in type to the seed of Abraham is, by the confession of everybody, the believer, and the believer ought, seeing he is buried with Christ spiritually, to avow that fact by his public baptism in water, according to the Savior's own precept and example.[26]

C. CONSIDERATIONS COMMENDING THE POSITION

The concept of the covenant is perhaps the most pregnant single category in Scripture used to express the meaning of salvation history.[27] In the position advocated above, this central biblical concept is used in such a way as to preserve the continuity of redemptive history while doing justice to its movement. In other words, it allows for continuity without requiring identity.

In order to have continuity it is not necessary to have *identity*, but only *analogy*, in the signs of the covenant. Of course, a true analogy must rest on an element of basic identity; we cannot say one thing is like another if there is no point of identity whatsoever. But if one takes the position we have outlined, there is a point of identity between circumcision and baptism in that both are sacraments of grace on God's part initiating the recipient into the fellowship of God's covenant people. A true analogy must also display dissimilar features in the things compared. In this case, circumcision is *unlike* baptism in that it had an outward reference in keeping with the old administration of the covenant; it was the sign of citizenship in the nation of Israel.

[26]"Consecration to God, illustrated by Abraham's Circumcision," Lord's Day morning, Dec. 13, 1868, *The Metropolitan Tabernacle Pulpit.*

[27]Note Eichrodt's choice of the covenant concept as the unifying theme of his monumental *Theologie des Alten Testaments.*

Were one to use diagrams such as are found in introductory textbooks on formal logic to help inchoate thought achieve sharper definition, one could represent possible relationships between circumcision and baptism in several different ways.

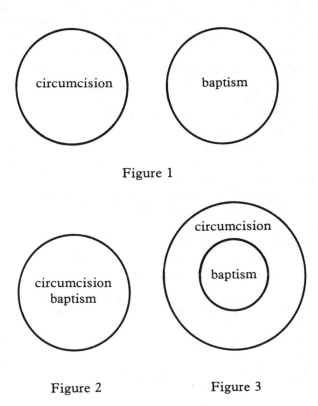

Figure 1

Figure 2   Figure 3

Figure 1 represents the disjunction of which Calvin accused the Anabaptists: the view that circumcision has nothing to do with baptism, but is simply an Old Testament rite done away in Christ. Indeed, many Baptists (and others) do make such a disjunction; some even go so far as to say, "The

New Testament is our creed."[28] They affirm the diversity in holy history in such an absolute way as to impugn its unity. Figure 2 represents the view accepted by those who argue from infant circumcision to infant baptism. They affirm the unity of holy history in such an absolute way as to impugn its diversity.[29] Figure 3, in our opinion, avoids both extremes. It represents a position in which circumcision is neither unlike baptism nor identical with it. Given such a position, one can maintain the continuity of redemptive history, which is the strength of covenant theology, without suppressing its diversity, which is the weakness of the argument from the covenant for infant baptism. Here is an approach consonant with the truth that revelation is historical.

Once we have applied this fundamental corrective, several other persistent problems in the Paedobaptist approach resolve themselves. First of all, it eliminates the antinomy between the definition of baptism as the sacrament of repentance and faith and the giving of that sacrament to infants who are capable of neither. One has only to review the endless burden of arguments about the status of children in the covenant, the nature of their subjective condition, the difficulties inherent in proxy faith, and the like, to perceive how much simpler and less encumbered is the position that grants

[28]We acknowledge that such a statement is often made uncritically. The very people who are most emphatic in their insistence that the New Testament is their creed sometimes reinforce their point by waving a Bible containing the Old Testament. Often this Bible is a Scofield Reference Bible. Being popular among many Baptists in America, undoubtedly "Dispensationalism" — as Scofield's view is called — has contributed to a tendency to press the diversity between the Old and New Testaments to extremes. But the error is not confined to America, as is evident from the following comment by a prominent spokesman for Baptists in Britain: "Baptism differs from circumcision as the new aeon differs from the old; the two rites belong to different worlds" (Beasley-Murray, *Baptism*, p. 342). We prefer Augustine's more balanced dictum, "The Old is in the New revealed; the New is in the Old concealed."

[29]Of course, neither Baptists nor Paedobaptists will press these matters consistently. Happily, the former recognize the relevance of the Old Testament, and the latter the newness of the New Testament in basic theological issues. It is only when polarized by the debate over infant baptism that such extremes are taken. Only heretics (in this case, the Marcionites on the one hand and the Judaizers on the other) make fundamentally wrong assumptions and follow them out consistently. This very consistency is why they are heretics.

baptism not when one is born but when one confesses faith.

In the second place — and closely related to the previous point — is the consideration that the position outlined above eliminates the problems associated with confirmation. At best, such a distinct rite makes baptism a sacrament in two parts, of which division the New Testament knows nothing; and it always poses the possibility of a third sacrament in need of adequate theological justification.

In the third place, this position solves the nagging problem of so-called apostate covenant children. This writer has heard the argument that one cannot define the meaning of the covenant from the negative instance of the apostate child. Christ is the Savior of the world, even though all are not saved. However, it might just as well be said that Christ is *not* the Savior of the world, even though all are *not* lost. This is why the proposition "The covenant is made with Abraham and his seed" cannot be defined from the negative instance of the unbelieving seed. While it is true that the covenant is made with Abraham and his seed, it is also true that the covenant is *not* made with Abraham and his seed: ". . . not all are children of Abraham because they are his descendants" (Rom. 9:7); "and do not presume to say to yourselves, 'We have Abraham for our father'; for I tell you, God is able from these stones to raise up children to Abraham" (Matt. 3:9). What is needed at this juncture is more precise definition. When we say that the covenant cannot be defined from the negative instance of the apostate child, what does this mean? It means that we must define the covenant positively in terms of those who confess Christ as Lord, which is precisely what those advocating believer baptism do. We grant that unbelieving children are a sorrow to their parents and a disappointment to their teachers, whatever view of baptism one may adopt. But they are a theological surd only when one baptizes them on the basis of their birth to Christian parents.

One will reach the same result when he thinks through the argument that in the Baptist scheme there are apostate adults who allegedly are just the same as apostate covenant children on the Paedobaptist scheme. The trouble with this argument is obvious. According to the Baptist, the apostate

adult does not have the indispensable attribute of a covenantee, which is faith in Christ. But according to the
Paedobaptist, the child *does*, since he is born of believing
parents. If it be answered, No, the child must appropriate the
covenant in his own person by faith to be truly a covenantee,
is not this to say that believers are the true covenant children,
which is the position we have advocated?

In the fourth place, our position makes for symmetry in
one's baptismal and eucharistic practice. Since the Passover,
like circumcision, had an earthly reference — namely, Israel's
deliverance as a people from Egypt — all Israel ate the Passover. But because this deliverance typified the redemption
of the true Israel from the bondage of sin into the liberty of
the children of God, therefore in the age of fulfillment all
members of the true Israel (believers) partake of the Christian Passover, which is the Eucharist. This understanding
corresponds to the Paedobaptist practice of believer communion and is consistent with the practice of believer baptism.
Calvin insisted that there is no objection to infant baptism
that is not also an objection to infant circumcision. It would
be more theologically significant to say that there is no objection to believer baptism that is not also an objection to
believer communion.

No doubt many Paedobaptists would rather practice infant communion than believer baptism. We can commend
those who would for their consistency. However, unless one
begins with correct premises, "progressing" from inconsistency to consistency is really regress rather than progress. To
go from an inclusive baptism to an inclusive Eucharist would
only aid the transformation of the church into an "amorphous mass of Pelagian good will." If the Paedobaptists ever
break down the one restraint on nominal, external, hereditary
Christianity that they have left, that is, the requirement that
the baptized infant shall confess his faith before he partakes
of communion, then all significant differences between the
church and the world will be threatened. This is not to say
that the position of believer baptism is foolproof; but it tends
to inculcate in everyone baptized that without which New
Testament Christianity cannot survive, namely, an "I-Thou"

encounter with the living God in the form of a personal commitment to Jesus Christ as Lord and Savior.

Kierkegaard once asked this question: How is it that "Christendom" is from generation to generation a society of non-Christians? His answer should be pondered:

> The Christianity of "Christendom" sees that everything depends upon establishing the maxim that one becomes a Christian as a child, that if one is rightly to become a Christian, one must be such from *infancy. This is the basic falsehood. If this is put through, then good night to the Christianity of the New Testament!*[30]

[30]*The Instant*, No. 7, "The Formula of 'Christendom,'" *Attack Upon Christendom*, p. 212 (italics mine).

BIBLIOGRAPHY

BOOKS AND ARTICLES CONTRIBUTING TO THE DISCUSSION

Aland, Kurt. *Die Säuglingstaufe im Neuen Testament und in der Alten Kirche.* Munich: Kaiser-Verlag, 1961.

Alford, D.H. *Greek Testament,* II, 7th ed. Cambridge: Deighton, Bell, & Co., 1877.

Althaus, P. *Was ist die Taufe?* Göttingen: Vandenhoeck, 1950.

"Asterius." *RGG,* I, Dritte Auflage. Tübingen: Mohr, 1956.

Backus, Isaac. *Works,* I. Boston: Edward Draper, 1777.

Bailey, D.S. *Sponsors at Baptism and Confirmation.* London: S.P.C.K., 1952.

_____. *The Theology of the Sacraments.* New York: Charles Scribner's Sons, 1957.

Baillie, J., McNeill, J.T., and VanDusen, H.P., eds. *Library of Christian Classics,* XXIV. Trans. by G.W. Bromiley. Philadelphia: Westminster Press, 1953.

Bannerman, James. *The Church of Christ,* II. Edinburgh: T&T Clark, 1868.

Barker, Thomas. *Duty and Benefits of Baptism.* London: John Brownely, 1771.

Barth, Karl. *Die Kirchliche Lehre von der Taufe,* Dritte Auflage, Theologische Studien, Heft 14. Zürich/Zollikon: Evangelischer Verlag, 1947.

_____. *Kirchliche Dogmatik,* IV, 4. Zürich: TVZ Verlag, 1967.

Barth, Markus. *Die Taufe, ein Sacrament?* Zürich: Evangelischer Verlag, 1951.

Bauer, W. *Greek-English Lexicon.* Trans. by W.F. Arndt and F.W. Gingrich. Chicago: The University of Chicago Press, 1957.

Baxter, Richard. *Plain Scripture Proof on Infant Church-Membership and Baptism.* London: Robert White, 1651.

Beasley-Murray, G. *Baptism in the New Testament*. London: L. Wayland, 1787.

Bender, H.S., ed. *The Complete Writings of Menno Simons*. Trans. by L. Verduin. Scottdale: Herald Press, 1956.

Bonhoeffer, D. *Sanctorum Communio*. München: Kaiser-Verlag, 1960.

Booth, Abraham. *Paedobaptism Examined*, II. London: L. Wayland, 1787.

Bratcher, R.G. "Church of Scotland Report on Baptism," *Review and Expositor* (Apr. 1957), p. 206.

Bromiley, G.W. *Baptism and the Anglican Reformers*. London: Lutterworth Press, 1953.

——————. *Sacramental Teaching and Practice in the Reformation Churches*. Grand Rapids: Eerdmans, 1957.

Browne, E.H. *Exposition of the Thirty-Nine Articles*, 10th ed. London: Longman, 1874.

Brunner, Emil. *Offenbarung und Vernunft*. Zürich: Zwingli-Verlag, 1941. [*Revelation and Reason*. Trans. by O. Wyon. Philadelphia: Westminster Press, 1946.]

——————. *Wahrheit als Begegnung*. Zürich: Zwingli-Verlag, 1938. [*Truth As Encounter*. Trans. by W. Loos and David Cairns. Philadelphia: Westminster Press, 1964.]

Bucher, G.W. Willard, tr. *Commentary of Ursinus*. 3rd American ed. Grand Rapids: Eerdmans, 1956.

Bultmann, Rudolf. *Theologie des Neuen Testaments*, I. Tübingen: Mohr, 1948.

Bushnell, H. *Christian Nurture*. New York: Charles Scribner's Sons, 1890.

Buttrick, G.A., et al. *The Interpreter's Bible*, 12 vols. Nashville/New York: Abingdon, 1957.

Calvin, John. *Commentary on Acts*, II. Grand Rapids: Eerdmans, 1966.

——————. *Commentary on Genesis*, I. Trans. by J. King. Grand Rapids: Eerdmans, 1948.

——————. *Institutes of the Christian Religion*. Trans. by John Allen. Philadelphia: Presbyterian Board of Education, 1936.

Church of Scotland Report on Baptism. *The Biblical Doctrine of Baptism*. Edinburgh: St. Andrew's Press, 1960.

The Confessions of Faith, Together with the Sum of Saving Knowledge. Belfast: Graham and Heslip, 1933.

Cullmann, O. *Die Tauflehre des Neuen Testaments*. Zürich: Zwingli-Verlag, 1948.

——————. "Les traces d'une Formule Baptismale dans le Nouveau Testament," *Revue d'Histoire et Philosophie Religieuses* (1937), 424ff.

Daane, James. *The Back to God Hour Family Altar* (Mar., 1952). Grand Rapids: Christian Reformed Publishing House.

Dinkler, Erich. "Taufe," *RGG*, VI, Sec. 2:1. Dritte Auflage. Tübingen: Mohr, 1959.

Dix, Gregory. *Confirmation Today*. Westminster: Dacre Press, 1946.

_____. *The Theology of Confirmation in Relation to Baptism*. Westminster: Dacre Press, 1953.

_____. *The Shape of the Liturgy*. Westminster: Dacre Press, 1946.

Easton, B.W. *The Apostolic Tradition of Hippolytus*. Hamden: Archon Books, 1962.

Edwards, J. *Works*, Vol. III. New York: 1844.

Eichrodt, Walter. *Theologie des Alten Testaments*. Leipzig: Hinrichs Verlag, 1939. [*Theology of the Old Testament*. Two volumes. Trans. by J.A. Baker. Philadelphia: Westminster Press, 1961.]

Flemington, W.F. *The New Testament Doctrine of Baptism*. London: S.P.C.K., 1948.

Gill, John. *A Body of Doctrinal and Practical Divinity*, III. London: 1795.

Gilmore, A., ed. *Christian Baptism*. London: Lutterworth, 1959.

Goodwin, W.W. *Syntax of the Moods and Tenses of the Greek Verb*. London: Macmillan; New York: St. Martin's Press, 1965.

Hall, Robert. *Miscellaneous Writings*. London: Ward, Lock & Co. Ltd., 1815.

Hallesby, O. *Infant Baptism and Adult Conversion*. Trans. by C. Carlsen. Minneapolis: The Lutheran Free Church Publishing Co., 1924.

Harnack, Adolf von. *Die Mission und Ausbreitung des Christentums in den ersten drei Jahrhunderten*. Leipzig: J.C. Hinrichs, 1924.

Henry, Matthew. *Treatise on Baptism. The Complete Works of Rev. Matthew Henry*, I. New York: Fullerton & Co., n.d.

Herzog, J.J., ed. "Kinderkommunion," *Realencyclopädie*, X. Leipzig: J.C. Hinrichs, 1901.

Hirsch, Emil G. "Passover," *Jewish Encyclopedia*, IX. New York: Funk and Wagnalls, 1905.

Hodge, A.A. *Outlines of Theology*. Grand Rapids: Eerdmans, 1949.

_____. *Popular Lectures on Theological Themes*. Philadelphia: Presbyterian Board of Publication, 1887.

Hodge, Charles. "The Church Membership of Infants," *Princeton Review*, XXX (1958), 353f.

Huse, E. *The Soul of the Child*.

Jeremias, Joachim. *Die Kindertaufe in den ersten vier Jahrhunderten*. Göttingen: Vandenhoeck & Ruprecht, 1958.

_____. *Hat die Urkirche die Kindertaufe geübt?* Göttingen: Vandenhoeck & Ruprecht, 1949.

_____. *Nochmals: Die Anfange der Kindertaufe*. München: Kaiser-Verlag, 1962.

Jewett, Paul K. *Emil Brunner's Concept of Revelation*. London: James Clarke, 1954.

——————.*The Lord's Day*. Grand Rapids: Eerdmans, 1971.

——————.*Man as Male and Female*. Grand Rapids: Eerdmans, 1975.

Keble, J. *Christian Year*. London/New York: Frederick Warne & Co., 1889.

Kierkegaard, S. *Attack Upon "Christendom."* Trans. by Walter Lowrie. Princeton: University Press, 1946.

——————. *The Point of View*. Trans. by Walter Lowrie. London: Oxford University Press, 1950.

Kittel, G. *TWNT*. Stuttgart: Kohlhammer, 1954.

Lambert, J.C. *Sacraments in the New Testament*. Edinburgh: T. & T. Clark, 1903.

Leenhardt, F.J. *Le Baptême Chrétien*. Neuchâtel: Delachaux & Niestlé, 1944.

Levy, J. *Chäldaisches Wörterbuch Über die Targumin*. Leipzig: Sweiter Band, 1867.

Lightfoot, John. *Horae Hebraicae et Talmudicae. Opera omnia*. London: Oxford University Press, 1686.

Luther, Martin. *The Babylonian Captivity. Three Treatises*. Trans. by T.M. Jacobs. Philadelphia: Muhlenberg Press, 1947.

——————. "Von der Taufe, von der Kindertaufe," *Der Grosse Katechism. Katachetische Schriften*, IV. *Sämmtliche Werke*. Zehnter Band. St. Louis: Concordia Publishing House, 1885.

Marcel, P. *The Biblical Doctrine of Infant Baptism*. London: James Clarke & Co., 1953.

Miller, Samuel. *Infant Baptism, Scriptural and Reasonable*. Philadelphia: Presbyterian Board of Education, 1876.

Moody, Dale. *Baptism: Foundation for Christian Unity*. Philadelphia: Westminster Press, 1967.

Murray, J. *Christian Baptism*. Philadelphia: Orthodox Presbyterian Church, 1952.

——————. "Christian Baptism," *Westminster Theological Journal* (Nov. 1951), 22.

Neander, A. *General History of the Christian Religion and Church*, I. Trans. by J. Torrey. Boston: Houghton Mifflin, 1871.

Paul, R.S. *The Atonement and the Sacraments*. New York: Abingdon, 1960.

Payne and Windward, eds. *Orders and Prayers for Church Worship*. London: Carey, Kingsgates Press, 1960.

Pusey, Edward B. *Scriptural Views of Holy Baptism*. London: J. Parker, 1867.

Roberts, Alexander, and Donaldson, James, eds. *Ante-Nicene Christian Library*. Edinburgh: T & T Clark, 1858.

——————. *The Ante-Nicene Fathers*. Ten vols. Revised by A. Cleveland Coxe. Grand Rapids: Eerdmans, 1956.

Roddy, Clarence. Unpublished doctoral thesis, *Roger Williams, Apostle of Liberty*. New York: School of Education, New York University, 1948.

Rowley, H.H. "The Origin and Meaning of Baptism," *Baptism Quarterly*, XI (1945), 310ff.

Schaff, P., ed. *Evangelical Creeds. Creeds of Christendom*, III. Grand Rapids: Baker, 1966.

_____. *Nicene and Post-Nicene Fathers*, 1st ser., 14 vols. Grand Rapids: Eerdmans, 1956.

_____, and Wace, H., eds. *Nicene and Post-Nicene Fathers*, 2nd ser., 14 vols. New York: Christian Literature Co., 1894.

Schlink, E. *Die Lehre von der Taufe*. Dritte Auflage. Theologische Studien, Heft 14. Zürich/Zollikon: Evangelischer Verlag, 1947.

Schneider, J. *Die Taufe im Neuen Testament*. Stuttgart: W. Kohlhammer Verlag, 1952.

Spurgeon, C. *Autobiography*, I. London: Passmore and Alabaster, 1899-1900.

_____. *Metropolitan Tabernacle Pulpit*. London: Passmore and Alabaster, 1856-1908.

Stauffer, E. *Die Theologie des Neuen Testaments*. Stuttgart: Kohlhammer, 1948.

Strack-Billerbeck. *Kommentar zum Neuen Testament aus Talmud und Midrasch*. München: Beck, 1922.

Surkau, H.W. "Katechetic." *RGG*, II, Dritte Auflage. Tübingen: Mohr, 1959.

Taylor, Jeremy. *Worthy Communicant*. London: W. Pickering, 1853.

United Presbyterian Church in the U.S.A. *The Book of Order, Directory for Worship*. Philadelphia: The Office of the General Assembly of the United Presbyterian Church in the U.S.A., 1971-1972.

Verduin, Leonard. "Karl Barth's Rejection of Infant Baptism," *The Reformed Journal* (Feb. 1960), 13-17.

Wall, William. *The History of Infant Baptism*, I. London: Griffith, 1705.

_____. *The History of Infant Baptism*, I. Ed. by H. Cotton. Oxford: J. Downing for R. Sympson & H. Bonwick, 1862.

Warfield, B.B. *Studies in Theology*. New York: Oxford University Press, 1932.

Warns, Johannes. *Baptism: Studies in the Original Christian Baptism*. London: Paternoster, 1957.

_____. *Die Taufe: Gedanken über die urchristliche Taufe, ihre Geschichte und ihre Bedeutung für die Gegenwart*. Hamburg: Bad, 1913.

Weston, David. *The Baptism Movement of a Hundred Years Ago and its Vindication*. A discourse delivered at the 112th anniversary of the First Baptist Church, Middleborough, Massachusetts, January 16, 1868.

Westminster Assembly. *The Confessions of Faith, Together with the Sum of Saving Knowledge.* Belfast: Graham and Heslip, 1933.

White, R.E.O. *The Biblical Doctrine of Initiation.* Grand Rapids: Eerdmans, 1960.

Windisch, H. "Zum Problem der Kindertaufe in Urchristentum," *ZNW* (1929), 142.

Zorn, Peter. *Historia Eucharistiae Infantum.* Berlin: Schmidt, 1936.

Zwingli, Huldreich. *De Baptismo. Library of Christian Classics,* XXIV. Trans. by G.W. Bromiley. Philadelphia: Westminster, 1953.

INDEX